The Meaning of Yalta

"In appraising possibilities of this nature, the outstanding fact to be noted is the recent phenomenal development of the heretofore latent Russian military and economic strength—a development which seems certain to prove epochal in its bearing on future politico-military international relationships, and which has yet to reach the full scope attainable with Russian resources. In contrast, as regards Britain several developments have combined to lessen her relative military and economic strength and gravely to impair, if not preclude, her ability to offer effective military opposition to Russia on the continent except possibly in defensive operations in the Atlantic coastal areas. . . .

"It is apparent that the United States should, now and in the future, exert its utmost efforts and utilize all its influence . . . to promote a spirit of mutual cooperation between Britain, Russia and ourselves. So long as Britain and Russia cooperate and collaborate in the interests of peace, there can be no great war in the foreseeable future."

—Fleet Admiral William D. Leahy, *Personal Chief of Staff to the President, in a top-secret letter to Secretary of State Cordell Hull, May 16, 1944.*

The Meaning of Yalta

Big Three Diplomacy and the New Balance of Power

JOHN L. SNELL, *Editor*
FORREST C. POGUE
CHARLES F. DELZELL
GEORGE A. LENSEN

With a Foreword by Paul H. Clyde

LOUISIANA STATE UNIVERSITY PRESS
Baton Rouge

Copyright 1956
by
LOUISIANA STATE UNIVERSITY PRESS

Library of Congress Catalog Card Number: 56:7960

Second printing: 1959
Third printing: 1965
First paperback edition: 1966

Manufactured in the United States of America by
Edwards Brothers, Inc.

TO OUR WIVES
Christine, Bobbie, Gena, and Maxine

Foreword

A GREAT American, Elihu Root, who at one time was Secretary of State, once observed that when foreign affairs are ruled by autocracies or oligarchies the danger of war lies in sinister purpose. He went on to say that when foreign affairs are directed by democracies the danger of war lies in mistaken beliefs. Of the two forms of control in foreign affairs, Root preferred the democratic because, as he said, while there is no human way to prevent the autocrat from having a bad heart, there is a human way to prevent people from having erroneous opinions. "That way," said Root, "is to furnish the whole people, as a part of their ordinary education, with correct information about their relations to other peoples, about the limitations upon their own rights, about their duties to respect the rights of others, about what has happened and is happening in international affairs, and about the effects upon national life of the things that are done or refused as between nations; so that the people themselves will have the means to test misinformation and appeals to prejudice and passion based upon error."[1]

The study which follows within the covers of this small book is an able and a devoted effort by four young American historians to apply this philosophy of foreign affairs so ably expressed by Root and, in particular, to direct its application to the processes by which men seek to create peace out of war.

The problems of peacemaking are neither new nor static. Ten years after Napoleon was exiled to St. Helena, the peace settlement of 1814–15 was already undermined by the forces of nationalism and liberalism. Ten years after the end of World War I, the treaties of peace had already been revised

[1] Elihu Root, "A Requisite for the Success of Popular Diplomacy," *Foreign Affairs,* I (September, 1922), 5.

measurably. More than ten years have now passed since the end of World War II; yet peace is hardly a reality. Many of the crusading efforts and arrangements of 1945 have been undone in both Europe and the Far East.

So far there has been no single, formal conference to make the peace following World War II. Indeed, such peace as has been achieved is a product of continuous and labored effort. Some parts of this structure of peace were thrown together hastily, and they bear the earmarks of shoddy workmanship. Other parts have been fabricated with the infinite care of master craftsmen. The timekeeper's book records the stages of construction: Casablanca, Quebec, Moscow, Teheran, Quebec again, Yalta, Potsdam, Paris—then to Panmunjon, Berlin, and Geneva. But the edifice is not yet finished.

Of all these stages of construction, the workmanship at Yalta has been subjected to the most serious questioning. Yalta may be described as the "summit" in the personal diplomacy of Roosevelt, Churchill, and Stalin. It was the most important of the Big Three meetings in wartime, for it cemented the military victory and shaped the broad outlines of the future. Yalta was also drama. It was the most vital and tragic of the Big Three meetings. Fifty-seven hundred miles east of Washington, in a former palace of the czars, three popular statesmen gambled with their personal careers, but even more with the destinies of peoples, little and big, as they sought agreements determining the character of tomorrow.

Four major problems confronted the Big Three at Yalta. Three were regional and one was international in scope. The problem which had haunted the past and which had made Yalta necessary was that of Germany. A force that had newly appeared, that of Russian power in central-eastern Europe, threatened to upset the conference at the outset. The problem of the Far East was important for the immediate future, for the war was not yet won there. And the problem of world order, the search for world peace through international organization, was a continuing one, expressing both the promise and the dilemma of the twentieth century. Other issues, too, arose at Yalta, but in comparison to these they were all subordinate. These were not only the four great issues at Yalta;

they were the four great problems of peacemaking throughout and after World War II. Each of them is discussed in the pages which follow.

The Yalta conference seemed at first to guarantee the continuing unity of the Big Three in peacetime, and thus it bred great optimism. The wartime alliance was indeed a strange one. It had been created against the will of each of the Big Three by the most influential psychopath since Napoleon, Adolf Hitler. So it was that the ability of the Big Three to surmount mutual fears and suspicions was to many of their peoples the most inspiring feature of World War II. Upon the continuance of this unity the future peace of the world seemed to hang. This unity, moreover, never completely achieved, reached an all-time high at Yalta. It enabled President Roosevelt to report to Congress, upon his return from the Crimea, as Cordell Hull had reported in 1943 after a trip to Moscow, that there would be no need for "spheres of influence, for alliances, for balance of power" in the postwar era.

This conclusion was at best unrealistic. The new military balance of power created by the war—as discussed in the first chapter of this book—determined in large measure the political decisions which were made at Yalta, and those decisions, in turn, shaped the postwar political balance. Far from abolishing the balance of power, the Big Three played midwives to a new balance at Yalta.

The new balance of power and the part that personal diplomacy played in shaping it are twin themes that run through the separate essays of this study. The authors have tried to describe not only *how* and *what* and *when,* but also *why* the main decisions were made or, in some cases, postponed. What concessions were made? Who made them? Why? These are the lasting questions about the peace negotiations of every war. Even if Yalta should vanish as a political issue it will remain a problem of interpretation in history. The historian must face the responsibility of showing as impartially as he can "the times and circumstances which made Yalta possible."[2]

[2] Oscar J. Hammen, "The 'Ashes' of Yalta," *South Atlantic Quarterly,* LIII (October, 1954), 477.

In this spirit the authors of Chapters II, III, and IV agreed to present papers before the 1955 convention of the Southern Historical Association meeting at Memphis, Tennessee. This book grew out of the arrangements for that meeting. The authors have made it a small one by design. They have tried to give, in straightforward language, answers to the lasting questions about Yalta, as best these questions can presently be answered. They have written with a sense of responsibility as both citizens and as scholars. The result is neither a polemic nor a noninterpretative compilation, nor yet a record of personal accounts settled or unsettled. Since the authors did not participate in the development of the policies which they describe, they are unhampered in their efforts to achieve an honest, brief, nonpartisan summary of the personal diplomacy of the Big Three in planning for peace in World War II.

Duke University   PAUL H. CLYDE

Preface

THE balance of power which existed in Europe in the nineteenth century was upset by the upsurge of Germany about 1900, and the global balance was radically altered by the emergence of the United States and, in a lesser way, Japan as Great Powers. A readjustment and a new balance has not yet been created, although two world wars have marked the search for a new equilibrium. World War I only created complications for the future, because the peace that emerged from it did not reflect the genuine economic and potential military power of the Great Powers. The military defeat of Germany in 1918 and the chaos in which Russia found herself in the period from 1917 until the mid-thirties artificially and temporarily diminished the part both states previously had played and were destined to play again in world affairs. This combination of circumstances enabled Britain and France to play more dominant parts in international politics between the two world wars than their internal sources of power normally would have permitted. And this unique combination of circumstances made it possible for the United States to remain a Great Power without assuming the responsibilities which have usually been thrust upon Great Powers.

The resurgence of Germany under Hitler, its subsequent collapse, and the upsurge of Soviet Russia after the mid-thirties rudely shook both the global balance of power and the complacence of the American people. Two super powers emerged, the United States and the Union of Soviet Socialist Republics. Hesitantly, complainingly, suspiciously, but on the whole, well, we assumed the responsibilities which our position forced upon us. World War II itself contributed to our military education as a Great Power. Yalta was a valuable lesson in our diplomatic coming of age. Our statesmen were quick to grasp the lessons of Yalta, but as a nation—as citizens —what Yalta has to teach us has been obscured amidst partisan recriminations. The importance of understanding the meaning of Yalta cannot be exaggerated, and it is a sense of this importance that has produced this volume.

Plans to write this book were made in the late spring of 1955, soon after the State Department's intention to publish its collection of records and minutes of the Yalta conference was announced in the press. The authors thought that the State Department papers would surely be available for public distribution by late summer and made their plans accordingly. When it became apparent that they would not, in fact, be publicly available at that time, we were able to work from the uncorrected galley proof of the "Yalta Papers," supplied by Dr. G. Bernard Noble, chief of the Historical Records Division of the Department of State. Dr. Rudolf A. Winnacker, historian, Department of Defense, provided the authors with a copy of his mimeographed report of October, 1955, on the entry of the U.S.S.R. into the Pacific war. We are grateful to both of these fellow historians for their help.

The editor wishes to acknowledge the collective indebtedness of the authors to the following publishers, who have kindly permitted quotation or reproduction of illustrations from their own publications: Department of the Army, for permission to reprint the map from Forrest C. Pogue, *The Supreme Command* (Washington, 1954); Harper & Brothers, for permission to reproduce the map, "Poland and Yalta," from Chester Wilmot, *The Struggle for Europe* (New York, 1952); Houghton Mifflin Company, for permission to make various quotations from Winston S. Churchill, *The Second World War* (6 vols., Boston, 1948–53), and for permission to reproduce the map of Germany from Winston S. Churchill, *Triumph and Tragedy* (Boston, 1953); Curtis Brown, Ltd., for permission to reproduce the cartoon by David Low, "Polish Diplomacy," from David Low, *Years of Wrath: A Cartoon History: 1931–1945* (New York, 1946); The Public Affairs Press, for permission to reproduce the cartoon, "The Shave," from William Nelson (ed.), *Out of the Crocodile's Mouth, Russian Cartoons about the United States from the*

Contents

Illustrations and Maps

CHAPTER I

The Struggle for a New Order

TWO MILES from Yalta, in early February, 1945, the three most powerful leaders in the world sat down to lay the basis for a new world order and a lasting peace. Winston Churchill was reminded that less than a century before in the Crimean Peninsula, of which Yalta was a part, soldiers of his country had fought to halt Russian expansion to the south and west. Livadia Palace, in which the Big Three met, had been built in 1911 by the last of the Romanovs, who died seven years later at the hands of Red Army troops. Marshal Joseph Stalin, whose forces less than a year before had driven the Germans from the palace in which they met, now wanted assurances that his country would not face again the desperate fight for survival of 1941–42. Aware that he now held eastern and most of central Europe in his hands, he hoped to legalize his conquests by agreement of his fellow leaders. Franklin D. Roosevelt, whose armed forces bestrode the globe to a degree known neither to imperial Rome nor Britain, and whose resources contributed mightily to the victories of Great Britain, Soviet Russia, China, and France, hoped not for conquest but for the prize of international peace which had eluded Woodrow Wilson.

Each man sought a new order, but each was in some way disappointed. In less than three months Roosevelt died, knowing that Russia meant trouble for the world. In six months Churchill was out of office, perhaps solaced by the thought that he would not preside over the liquidation of an empire he could defend but could not save. Before Stalin died nearly a decade later, he was aware that in seizing the prizes his own victories had opened to him, he had dissipated the store of good will and respect his country had gained in the West. For, within two years after the great conference, the name of Yalta had become anathema to many peoples of the world.

THE CRUCIBLE OF THE "STRANGE ALLIANCE"

Ten years after Yalta, when the British and American governments were pressing Japan to rearm and firmly urging France to remove her obstacles to German remilitarization, it was sometimes difficult for Americans to recreate the atmosphere in which the western statesmen sat down as friends with Soviet leaders and planned the ruin of the Axis. The compromises with comrades-in-arms of 1945 soon seemed tainted with subversion. It is necessary to recall the events which led to the Yalta conference in order to understand the actions of the participants.

The world order represented by the League of Nations and the collective security system of the twenties and thirties was repeatedly challenged by Japan, Italy, and Germany after 1931. Between the Manchurian "incident" in 1931 and the beginning of war in Europe, the Japanese militarists invaded Manchuria, extended control over northern and eastern China, defied and left the League, assassinated many of their own political leaders who counseled moderation, and carried on a small-scale war against Soviet forces along the borders of Manchuria and Mongolia. Mussolini imposed his will on Ethiopia despite the remonstrances of the League, boastingly intervened in the Spanish Civil War, and threatened France over Nice and Tunisia. These deeds were facilitated after 1933 because of the greater menace of Adolf Hitler, who rearmed his troops and tore up the Treaty of Versailles and the security system erected by the League. European history was reduced to a series of week-end crises. A continuous war of nerves created such a state of tension that many Europeans hailed the Munich settlement as a great victory for peace in their time.

The violence of the three aggressive powers and their formation of an "Axis" pledged to co-operation against communism and common enemies, not all of whom were Communists, helped to rehabilitate Russia in the eyes of the western democracies. As a powerful threat to both Germany and Japan, the U.S.S.R. became a potential ally to the western powers in stopping the aggression of the Axis. The Soviet Union, for its part, was willing to co-operate. Soon after 1933, when Hitler had liquidated the German Communist party, Stalin adopted a policy of international understanding. The U.S.S.R. joined the League of Nations in 1934, concluded defensive alliances with France and Czechoslovakia, conducted a campaign for disarmament, and embarked on a popular front policy by which Communists in every country were supposed to support any government opposed to Germany and "Fascism." Communists thereafter paraded their nationalism and voted for military appropriations in those countries threatened by the Nazis. Soviet Russia was soon looked upon in many circles of the West as the only counterweight to Hitler's Germany.

Admiration for Soviet Russia was diminished or dissipated altogether by the political and military purges of the thirties, which some observers believed to have destroyed the Soviet ability to cope with outside opposition. Partly as a result of this feeling, British and French leaders in the late thirties began to look on appeasement as the only means of gaining an uneasy peace in Europe and drifted apart from the U.S.S.R. in 1938–39. With complete cynicism, Stalin and Foreign Commissar Vyacheslav M. Molotov then bought spoils and temporary peace by the Nazi-Soviet Pact of August 23, 1939. This diplomatic revolution destroyed the balance of power hitherto restraining Germany, however feebly, and made it possible for Hitler to launch his attack on Poland on September 1, 1939.

The remnants of British and American respect and friendship for the U.S.S.R. went out the window as Soviet armies grabbed eastern Poland, declared war on Finland, made satellites out of Latvia, Estonia, and Lithuania, and annexed Bessarabia. Relations were not helped by American and British Communists who, under orders from Moscow, quickly changed from militant patriotism to attacks on "capitalist warmongering." Only the threat of Hitler was strong enough to restore western friendship with the U.S.S.R.

In the spring of 1940 Hitler's armies occupied Denmark and Norway almost overnight and shortly afterwards burst into the Low Countries and France. The quick defeats of the French and British forces, the near catastrophe at Dunkirk, and the fall of France frightened Britain and the United States and made Soviet Russia look less hateful. The Battle of Britain, with its violent attacks on London and other heavily populated cities, made the British more anti-German than ever. The menace of long-range bombing and the later expansion of German power into North Africa, posing a threat to the western hemisphere, made thoughtful Americans aware that they had more than a passing interest in the outcome of the war. The possibility that Hitler might use the governments of occupied countries to control their possessions in the western hemisphere and the rest of the world, the danger that he might seize and use their fleets and military equipment, and the effective submarine activities against commerce off the coast of North America gave the United States a direct interest in stopping the march of German power.

Roosevelt and his advisers thus reluctantly took steps to re-establish the balance of power in Europe. While the President and other American leaders in the course of two world wars sometimes deprecated "balance of power" politics, they actually played it in their efforts to prevent Germany or Germany and Italy from dominating Europe. Great Britain in the eighteenth and nineteenth centuries had placed arms and cash and, sometimes, men on the side of coalitions blocking France or Russia; so the United States in the twentieth century has sought ways of restoring a balance in Europe. To America it was clear that Britain was incapable of such an effort, if, indeed, she could even hold out unaided. The President stretched every legal power he had to provide arms, destroyers, lend-lease, and naval action short of war for the relief of the embattled British. To Roosevelt, Hitler was the enemy of peace and of humanity, and the President was willing to back any power which would help destroy him. As early as January, 1941, he permitted military and naval representatives to hold unofficial conversations with the British relative to mutual action in case the United States should be drawn into the war with Germany, or with Germany aided by Japan. In each case they agreed that the concentrated allied effort would be placed first against Germany.

In June, 1941, Hitler took the step which led to his destruction. Churchill, informed by British intelligence agents of German concentration for an attack on Russia, vainly warned the Soviet leaders of what lay ahead. A week before Hitler's attack, the British Prime Minister alerted Roosevelt, saying that Britain would give every encouragement to the Russian people on the ground that Hitler was the foe they had to beat. Roosevelt replied that if the Germans should attack he would publicly back Churchill's statement welcoming the U.S.S.R. as an ally. Thus before the Soviet Union was driven out of the union with Hitler, Roosevelt and Churchill were laying the basis for collaboration with the Russians. They had accepted firmly the idea that Germany must be beaten, and that they would back anyone who brought the defeat of Hitler nearer.[1]

When on June 22, 1941, Hitler struck with some 164 divisions against the U.S.S.R., Churchill, an ancient and bitter foe of Communist Russia, declared: "If Hitler invaded Hell I would make at least a favourable reference to the Devil in the House of Commons." To the British people he said: "Any man or state who fights on against Nazidom will have our aid. Any man or state who marches with Hitler is our foe." In his conclusion, he sanctified the Russian cause in a way that he could never thereafter completely gainsay:

The Russian danger is, therefore, our danger, and the danger of the United States, just as the cause of any Russian fighting for his hearth and home is the cause of free men and free peo-

[1] Valuable general sources for the introductory pages have included: Herbert Feis, *The Road to Pearl Harbor* (Princeton, 1950); William L. Langer and S. Everett Gleason, *The Challenge to Isolation, 1937–1940* (New York, 1952) and *The Undeclared War, 1940–1941* (New York, 1953); Dwight E. Lee, *Ten Years: The World On the Way to War* (Boston, 1942); C. C. Tansill, *Back Door to War, 1933–1941* (Chicago, 1952); Maurice Matloff and Edwin M. Snell, *Strategic Planning for Coalition Warfare, 1941–1942* (Washington, 1953), in the *United States Army in World War II* series; and Mark S. Watson, *Chief of Staff: Prewar Plans and Preparations* (Washington, 1950), *United States Army in World War II* series.

ples in every quarter of the globe. Let us learn the lessons already taught by such cruel experience. Let us redouble our exertions, and strike with united strength while life and power remain.[2]

To Britain, Russia's entry in the war meant immediate salvation and the ultimate defeat of Hitler. For the United States it meant the chance to re-establish the balance of power in Europe. At the beginning of October the still technically neutral Roosevelt agreed to extend lend-lease to the Soviet Union. His main desire was to help in the fight against Hitler, but it is likely that he also agreed with Joseph E. Davies' remark two weeks after Hitler attacked the U.S.S.R. that it was to our advantage "to have a friendly Russia at Japan's rear."[3]

British and American relief at having the Soviet Union on their side restrained them from putting pressure on the U.S.S.R. when that country was desperate for aid. Churchill, who tried to get a settlement of Polish questions with Stalin in July, 1941, ultimately settled for a mere statement that the Nazi-Soviet Pact of 1939 had lost it validity. Later he explained that the Allies faced a dilemma from the start. Despite a strong sympathy for the Poles, in whose behalf Britain had gone to war in 1939, he felt that he could not force Britain's "new and sorely threatened ally to abandon, even on paper, regions on her frontiers which she had regarded for generations as vital to her security." For him there was no way out and the issue of Polish boundaries had to be postponed to "easier times." This dilemma was never completely resolved and its horns showed plainly in the Yalta settlement.[4]

The United States became a full partner with Britain and the Soviet Union in December, 1941, when Japan struck at Pearl Harbor and Germany and Italy declared war on the United States in support of their Axis partner. Since 1945 some noted historians have held that Roosevelt provoked

[2] Winston S. Churchill, *The Grand Alliance* (Boston, 1950), 370–73.

[3] Robert E. Sherwood, *Roosevelt and Hopkins, An Intimate History* (New York, 1948), 307.

[4] Churchill, *The Grand Alliance*, 390–91.

Japan to war, and they have implied that Japan was not aggressive. But among the American people who had watched Japan march across Manchuria and China and then, after the fall of France, into French Indochina, the reaction in December, 1941, was that Japanese military power must be destroyed if there was to be peace in the Pacific. The attack on Pearl Harbor, Clark Field, Bataan, and Corregidor, stories of the Death March, the menace of the Japanese advance on the Dutch East Indies and Australia all created an impression which was not effaced throughout the war. Even though the public might accept attack against the Germans first, the fundamental feeling was that ultimately "we must settle with the Japs." Americans might talk of vengeance against the Germans, but they felt a burning anger against the "treacherous" Japanese that was not completely satisfied until American troops stood on Japanese soil and hauled up the Stars and Stripes over Tokyo.

The Big Three were now in active partnership, although the U.S.S.R. did not declare war against Japan. For the moment the Americans and the British were content that their hard-pressed ally remain at peace with the Pacific foe. More than nine months before, British and American army and navy representatives had agreed that if the United States and Britain should find themselves at war with Germany and Japan, American operations in the Pacific would be conducted in such a manner as to facilitate the major attack against Germany. Shortly after the war began, the war plans division of the War Department prepared a report, drawn up in part by Brigadier General Dwight D. Eisenhower, which approved this strategy. For the moment, therefore, the emphasis was on British and American efforts to aid the Russians against Germany. The period in which Soviet aid against Japan would be needed was to come later.

AIMS FOR A NEW ORDER

The first general aims for a new world order were laid down by President Roosevelt and Prime Minister Churchill at Argentia in August, 1941. Embodied in a statement known as the Atlantic Charter, these aims—which were not legal agreements—included disarmament and a wider system of general security in the postwar period. Included were three principles which Great Britain and the United States would seek to uphold: (1) opposition to aggrandizement, territorial or otherwise, (2) opposition to territorial changes without the freely expressed wishes of the people concerned, and (3) support of "the right of all peoples to choose the form of government under which they will live."[5] It was these three principles that Roosevelt and Churchill were to be accused of violating in their concessions to the U.S.S.R. at Yalta. The principles of the Atlantic Charter were incorporated into the United Nations Declaration, which the United States, Great Britain, the Soviet Union, China, France, and twenty-one other nations signed at Washington on January 1, 1942. The statement was phrased so that the U.S.S.R. was relieved of any pledge to fight Japan. However, she was not relieved of accepting the general principles of the charter. Critics of Yalta have argued that China's participation in this declaration compounded the degree of betrayal and bad faith at Yalta.

At Moscow on October 30, 1943, Great Britain, the United States, the U.S.S.R., and China signed the Four Nations Declaration on General Security by which they pledged a united effort against the Axis powers with whom they were at war. They called for unanimity on surrender terms, for the formation of an international peace organization, and for postwar regulation of armaments. They agreed that after the termination of hostilities they *would not use their military forces in the territories of other states* except for the purposes envisaged in the declaration and after joint consultation. The importance of the statement lay in Secretary of State Cordell Hull's successful fight to have China included, and in the fact that it reinforced the obligation of the U.S.S.R. to respect the rights of China and, indeed, of other nations its troops might liberate.[6] The communiqué issued by Britain, Russia,

[5] *Ibid.*, 443–44; Sumner Welles, *Where Are We Heading?* (New York, 1946), 4–15.
[6] Cordell Hull, *Memoirs of Cordell Hull* (2 vols., New York, 1948), II, 1274–

and the United States at Teheran on December 1, 1943, supplemented the previous general statements on postwar settlements. Speaking of the peace, the three powers declared: "We recognize fully the supreme responsibility resting upon us and all the United Nations to make a peace which will command the goodwill of the overwhelming mass of the peoples of the world and banish the scourge and terror of war for many generations."[7]

The Great Powers in their various declarations had evoked in general terms a spirit almost Wilsonian in its breadth and idealism. The rights and wishes of the states of the world were to be respected and efforts were to be made to establish the bases for a lasting peace.

Private Visions of Regional Interests, 1941–43

In addition to these general and publicly announced peace aims, more specific agreements or statements, not always in accord with the broad spirit of the general declarations, were made by the Allied statesmen. Several of these included definite commitments which neither the United States nor Britain could later escape. An example may be seen in a British statement made at a time when Churchill could offer little save sympathy to Marshal Stalin. When it appeared that the Germans might take Leningrad, the Prime Minister promised that if Stalin had to sink ships near that city to prevent their capture the British would make compensation after the war. Stalin thanked the Prime Minister, but said that "the damage after the war should be made good at the expense of Germany." Churchill agreed that the German and Italian navies should help make up for Russian losses.[8] This was the sort of "I.O.U." which Stalin took out of the safe at the proper time, and in 1941–42 he sought others.

As 1941 neared its end, Churchill sent the British Foreign

1307; John R. Deane, *The Strange Alliance: The Story of Our Efforts at War-time Co-operation with Russia* (New York, 1947), 23–26; Winston S. Churchill, *Closing the Ring* (Boston, 1951), 290–99; Louise W. Holborn (ed. and compiler), *War and Peace Aims of the United Nations* (2 vols., Boston, 1943 and 1948), II, 8–9.

[7] Holborn, *War and Peace Aims*, II, 12.

[8] Churchill, *The Grand Alliance*, 463–65.

Secretary, Anthony Eden, to Moscow to discuss military plans and postwar organization. The visit took place just after the attack on Pearl Harbor, at a time when the United States was able to furnish only a few supplies to the U.S.S.R. and when the importance of Soviet war efforts was increased. Stalin met the Foreign Secretary with a list of specific demands for postwar settlement. The road to Yalta was plainly marked in his request for an immediate agreement to the incorporation of Estonia, Lithuania, Latvia, and parts of Finland, Poland, and Rumania into the U.S.S.R. Thus Stalin hoped to regain all that Russia held before the beginning of the war in 1939 plus all that he had taken between September, 1939, and the German invasion of the U.S.S.R. in 1941. The shame of 1918 would be wiped away and the Russia of the czars restored.[9]

In addition to these demands, Stalin and Molotov suggested other settlements for the rest of central and eastern Europe: Austria was to be restored to independence; Poland was to get East Prussia; the Czechs were to regain the Sudetenland; Albania should again be made independent; the Rhineland was to be detached from Germany and perhaps be made into an independent state or a protectorate; Bavaria should become an independent state; Germany was to pay reparations in kind; Turkey was to get the Dodecanese Islands and perhaps territory from Bulgaria and Syria; Yugoslavia should be reconstituted and receive territory from Italy; and adjustments were possibly to be made in the Aegean Islands in favor of Greece. This was a list combining some provisions of simple justice, others of a type Disraeli or Bismarck might have suggested, and still others designed principally to gain friends for Russia among her closest neighbors. In a style which Stalin might have crudely copied from Germany's Iron Chancellor, the Russian leader tried to make the demands palatable by promising his support to any arrangement the British might want to make with France, Belgium, the Netherlands, Denmark, and Norway. These Russian proposals, as we shall see, were more far-reaching than anything demanded or conceded at Yalta.

In the demands for incorporation of the Baltic states,

9 *Ibid.*, 630–31; Hull, *Memoirs*, II, 1166–69.

Churchill, Eden, and perhaps Roosevelt, saw clearly enough the rebirth of a czarist dream, and all three reacted strongly against them. Despite the repeated refusal of the western Allies to make concessions, the U.S.S.R. proceeded on the assumption that once she reoccupied the Baltic states they would be hers. Stalin also made clear early in the war that he expected to hold that part of Poland which he had gained after its division in 1939, indemnifying his Slavic neighbor with parts of east Germany. Despite polite arguments by the western Allies and vehement opposition by the Polish government in exile, the Soviet leaders proceeded on the supposition that their seizure of Polish territory in 1939 would be acknowledged by Churchill and perhaps by Roosevelt in the final settlement with the Poles.

Discussions of the future settlement in the Far East matured much more slowly than did consideration of the future of Europe. Roosevelt and Churchill announced their position regarding the postwar settlement with Japan in the Cairo Declaration of December 1, 1943. The Prime Minister thought Roosevelt's treatment of China as a Great Power "a great illusion" and "a great farce" and harumphed about the fact that Roosevelt permitted Allied talks at Cairo to be distracted "by the Chinese story, which was lengthy, complicated, and minor." But he agreed that Chiang Kai-shek should be associated in the Cairo statement. The pronouncement was discussed with the Generalissimo at Cairo, cleared with Stalin at Teheran, and issued at the latter city before the Allied leaders returned to Egypt. By it the United States, Great Britain, and China announced that they were fighting to restrain and punish the aggression of Japan. Denying any desire for territorial gain for themselves, they declared their intention to strip Japan of all islands she had seized in the Pacific since World War I and to restore to China all territories "Japan has stolen," such as Manchuria, Formosa, and the Pescadores. They pledged their efforts to expel the Japanese from all other territories "taken by violence and greed." Mindful of the "enslavement" of the Korean people, they said they were determined that "in due course" Korea should become independent and free.

Also discussed at Cairo was a warm-water port for Russia. Roosevelt mentioned to Chiang Kai-shek the possibility of making Dairen a free port, and the Generalissimo apparently agreed, provided the U.S.S.R. would co-operate with his government and would refrain from impairing Chinese sovereignty. When Churchill spoke of Russia's need for a warm-water port a few days later at Teheran, the President indicated that China might give Stalin access to Dairen but failed to mention the Generalissimo's *quid pro quo.* The question of a free port was not raised again during the meeting, but Stalin outlined nearly all the other Far Eastern concessions he was later to get at Yalta.[10]

So far as peace aims were concerned, certain tendencies were discernible by 1942–43. The U.S.S.R. proposed to proceed along the lines of power politics to get territorial concessions affecting her security as soon as she could. Churchill was inclined, in the early days, to bend in the direction of Moscow, since there was no other way to give the Russians encouragement in their bitter fight against the Germans. Roosevelt, while generally faithful to the spirit of the Atlantic Charter, was willing to make some concessions. Secretary of State Hull wanted nothing to interfere with the establishment of the United Nations organization after the war and stood firmly on the principles of the Atlantic Charter. Churchill's tendencies were to reappear in some of the later negotiations and Roosevelt's sympathies were to cause him to support arrangements of the Prime Minister's which helped to make concessions at Yalta inevitable.

The Search for a Lasting Peace

An important reason for American concessions at Yalta was to be Roosevelt's conviction, nurtured by Hull, that a successful world order could be built only with Soviet co-operation. The President did not initially visualize an organization like the old League of Nations, but from the very beginning of war in Europe he said that the United States

10 United States, Department of State, *United States Relations with China* (Washington, 1949), 558; Sherwood, *Roosevelt and Hopkins,* 792; Herbert Feis, *The China Tangle* (Princeton, 1953), 112n.; Claude A. Buss, *The Far East* (New York, 1955), 426.

would use its influence to seek a final peace which would eliminate the use of force as far as possible. Hull, who had strongly supported Wilson's League, concentrated his efforts on drafting a peace organization which the United States Congress and the Great Powers of the world would accept. Soon after the outbreak of war in Europe, he instituted studies of postwar problems. Under the chairmanship of Undersecretary of State Sumner Welles, the postwar peace organization became one of the State Department's chief projects. Hull established a committee of forty-five members, including representatives from Congress, the press, and labor and business organizations, and asked the Senate Foreign Relations Committee to select members of the major parties to study the draft proposals and suggest changes.[11]

Great emphasis was also placed on the need for Russian collaboration in the establishment of the proposed world organization. The State Department's Subcommittee on Political Problems declared in a report of January, 1943, that "Russian co-operation on the principal international problems was essential and must be obtained." A short time later, Roosevelt, who had been discussing with Churchill the possible establishment of regional councils under a world organization, suggested a four-power arrangement by which the United States, Great Britain, the Soviet Union, and China would police the world until the other powers were disarmed. He thought that these powers had worked well together in prosecuting the war, that personal contacts among the heads of governments were effective, and that "the direct relationship among the chiefs of the four nations would result in efficient future management of the world." While he eventually changed this concept somewhat, the President never gave up his belief that the Big Four or the Big Three must continue to serve as the world "policemen" until the new order was completely established. At various conferences he tended to be impatient with the claims of the lesser powers. More than once in discussing the Poles, Roosevelt said that he would not have them disturbing the peace but would have just settlements worked out for them by the Great Powers.

[11] Hull, *Memoirs*, II, 1649–70.

This idea foretold trouble when Roosevelt coupled it with the notion that he could work out any world problem by sitting down and talking to Churchill and Stalin.

The efforts of Hull and Roosevelt toward four-power cooperation bore fruit in the declaration by Great Britain, the United States, the U.S.S.R., and China at Moscow in October, 1943, that there should be organized as soon as practicable "a general international organization, based on the principle of sovereign equality of all peace-loving states, and open to membership by all such states, large and small, for the maintenance of international peace and security." On his return from the meeting, Hull told a joint session of Congress that, once the provisions of the Moscow Declaration were carried into effect, there would be no need "for spheres of influence, for alliances, for balance of power or any other of the special arrangements through which, in the unhappy past, the nations strove to safeguard their security or to promote their interests."[12]

The passage of the Fulbright Resolution by the House of Representatives in September and of the Connally Resolution by the Senate in November, 1943, gave impetus to the movement to establish the postwar organization. The overwhelming majorities in favor of these resolutions for United States participation in an international organization indicated that Congress had changed since 1920 and, indeed, since 1940. At the beginning of February, 1944, the President approved the State Department's draft charter for a United Nations organization. Shortly afterwards, Secretary Hull invited the British and Soviet governments to exchange ideas on a future peace organization. In April Hull outlined his own view of the proposed international authority, emphasizing that there was no hope of "turning victory into enduring peace" unless the four major powers agreed to work together. "This," wrote Hull, "is the solid framework upon which all future policy and international organization must be built." "Without an enduring understanding between these four nations upon their fundamental purposes, interests, and obligations to one another," the Secretary of State continued, "all organizations

[12] *Ibid.*, 1648.

to preserve peace are creations on paper and the path is wide open again for the rise of a new aggressor."[13]

By late April the State Department decided that the Executive Council of the world organization should contain the four major Allied powers as permanent members plus other nonpermanent members elected by the Assembly. In an effort to settle an old question which had raised trouble in the League of Nations, the planners deliberately sought to protect the interests of the Great Powers by recommending that their concurring vote would be required on all decisions affecting (1) final terms of settlement of disputes, (2) the regulation of armaments and armed forces, (3) the maintenance of peace, and (4) enforcement measures. In this provision that the Council majority vote must include the concurrence of all permanent members was the idea of the veto, a provision of the United Nations Charter sometimes attributed to Soviet Russia and often blamed on the Yalta conference. Some of the members of the State Department committee even objected to the provision that a permanent member could not have its vote counted if it were a party to a dispute before the Council. As a result of their objection to any impairment of the right of veto, the matter was left open for later settlement. It is clear that the veto was one invention for which the Russians cannot claim sole credit; it had strong support in American and British circles before the meeting at Yalta.[14]

In keeping with his policy of avoiding the mistakes which frustrated the work of the League, Hull submitted the finished draft of the State Department's peace organization recommendations to former Chief Justice Charles Evans Hughes, to Nathan Miller, former Republican governor of New York, and to John W. Davis, onetime Democratic candidate for President. All three made suggestions for improving the draft, but gave it their approval. At the Secretary of State's request, the Senate Foreign Relations Committee next named eight of its members to study the draft with him. The group

---

[13] *Ibid.*, 1651.

[14] *Ibid.*, 1652–54; United States, Department of State (Harley Notter, ed.), *Postwar Foreign Policy Preparation, 1939–1945* (Washington, 1949), 247–69.

included eight of the most distinguished members of the upper house: Tom Connally, Alben W. Barkley, Walter George, Guy Gillette, Robert M. LaFollette, Arthur H. Vandenberg, Warren Austin, and Wallace H. White. Hull, after outlining the steps which had been taken, said that the success of the organization would depend on keeping Russia "solidly in the international movement," having an informed public opinion, and preventing the organization from becoming a domestic political issue. Vandenberg, after studying the State Department's draft, found it striking in that it was "so conservative from a nationalist standpoint." Noting that there was no action looking toward the use of force if any one of the Big Four objected, he called it "anything but a wild-eyed internationalist dream of a world State." The Republican Senator's only misgiving was over the possibility that, if established before the peace treaty, the peace organization might have to uphold a bad peace; this point aside, Vandenberg was "deeply impressed (and surprised) to find Hull so carefully guarding our American veto in his scheme of things."[15]

Some of the senators, unnamed by Hull, but apparently including Austin and White, thought the veto to be a serious defect. The Secretary of State replied: "The veto power is in the document primarily on account of the United States. It is a necessary safeguard in dealing with a new and untried world arrangement." Hull added that it was necessary to make the organization palatable to the Big Three, since there was no likelihood that any two of the three Great Powers would undertake another world organization with the third missing. On this point the Secretary added that the United States could not stop in the middle of the war and quarrel with the Soviet Union over peace terms, and could not serve her with ultimatums which might drive her into Hitler's arms.[16]

The senators did not give Hull's draft a complete endorsement, but they told him to go ahead with his planning. Much

[15] Arthur H. Vandenberg, Jr. (ed.), with the collaboration of Joe Alex Morris, *The Private Papers of Senator Vandenberg* (Boston, 1952), 95–99.

[16] *Ibid.*, 105–106; Hull *Memoirs*, II, 1662–68.

of his energies in the summer of 1944 were spent in keeping the proposed peace organization out of the presidential campaign. At Hull's invitation the Republican candidate, Governor Thomas E. Dewey, sent his adviser on foreign affairs, John Foster Dulles, to discuss the draft. After three sessions, Dulles said that Dewey would go along with Hull's proposals. Later, the New York governor sent down three proposed amendments on procedure, two of which were adopted. It was believed that the third was adequately covered in the draft. After the close of the Dumbarton Oaks conference, Dulles wrote Hull that he and Dewey highly appreciated the results of that meeting. He added that while there were many imperfections and inadequacies, the main thing was that the organization had been brought into sight. "For this," he declared, "the world owes you much." Apparently he accepted the veto idea along with the other elements of the peace organization.[17]

In an effort to get broad agreement by the four Great Powers on the draft of the postwar peace organization, conversations were carried on by representatives of the United States, Great Britain, and the U.S.S.R. at Dumbarton Oaks, in Washington, from August 21 to September 28, 1944, and between the United States, Great Britain, and China from September 29 to October 7, 1944. The United States, which had taken the lead in outlining the framework of the peace organization, played host to the delegates. Secretary Hull, who had already by his unceasing efforts established his claim to the title of "Father of the U.N." later bestowed on him by Roosevelt, continued to work as hard as his failing health permitted to eliminate differences at home and abroad which might interfere with the ultimate adoption of the peace organization. In the course of the discussions the title "United Nations," which had already appeared in some earlier drafts, was adopted as the title of the new organization. It appeared in the seventh draft of the text under the date of September 15, 1944.[18]

[17] Hull, *Memoirs*, II, 1694–95, 1709; State Department, *Postwar Foreign Policy Preparation*, 270–90, 321–22.
[18] State Department, *Postwar Foreign Policy Preparation*, 301–308; Hull,

The first differences between the Russians and the western Allies in the conference developed when the British delegation declared that the votes of parties to a dispute before the Security Council should not be counted. The Americans agreed, adding that this was a case in which even a permanent member of the Council could not impose its veto. They made clear that there was no disagreement on the requirement of unanimous consent by all permanent members on nonprocedural matters of peace and security. The Soviet representatives at once disagreed. A second point of disagreement developed on August 28 when Ambassador Andrei A. Gromyko declared that the sixteen Soviet Republics of the U.S.S.R. should be initial members of the new peace organization. This proposal was not entirely unexpected since the Russians had asked for extra seats on the War Crimes Commission in the previous December, and in February, 1944, had announced that the Soviet Republics were autonomous in matters of foreign affairs. President Roosevelt, on being informed of Gromyko's proposal, replied that the United States could "under no conditions accept such a proposal." Both he and members of the State Department delegation talked to the Russian ambassador, who said he would drop the point but that his government would probably raise the question again.[19]

Fearing that the Russian proposal would endanger the success of the whole peace project, the Americans argued that the question of membership for the Soviet Republics should be postponed until after the organization was established. The President cabled Stalin at the end of August, expressing his doubts about Gromyko's suggestion, and received a reply indicating the Marshal's desire for an opportunity to explain the political importance of the proposal. So convinced was the White House of the danger of the Soviet proposition that knowledge of it was closely restricted. It was not known to the entire American delegation until mid-October.[20]

Memoirs, II, 1671–85; Eugene P. Chase, *The United Nations in Action* (New York, 1950), 24–28.

[19] State Department, *Postwar Foreign Policy Preparation*, 318–20; Hull, *Memoirs*, II, 1679–80.

[20] State Department, *Postwar Foreign Policy Preparation*, 326–28.

During the first ten days of September, Hull and Undersecretary of State Edward R. Stettinius discussed the voting
formula with Roosevelt. The President and Secretary both
instructed Stettinius to vote "no" on the Russian proposal for
voting in procedural matters. In writing of this episode, Hull
has noted: "Aside from this, there was no question in our
minds, however, that the vote of the permanent members of
the Council should be unanimous on questions involving
security. This was the so-called veto power. We were no less
resolute than the Russians in adhering to this principle. . . ."[21]
On the remaining, but key, exception Hull tried unsuccess-
fully to get Gromyko to withdraw his proposal for sixteen
seats. Roosevelt intervened with the Soviet ambassador and
urged Stalin by cable to agree to the American and British
views. Despite these efforts, the Russians held firm and announced on September 13 that their government insisted on
a complete veto for permanent members of the Council and
that this position was final.

The American delegation, anxious to break the deadlock
with the U.S.S.R., now began work on possible compromise
solutions. One suggestion, that of empowering the Council to
request, but not require, a major nation to refrain from voting on consideration of a matter to which it was a party, was
dropped as insufficient. Next a compromise formula was
brought forward which would differentiate between the
degree of unanimity required on decisions involving the
pacific settlement of disputes and other decisions made by the
Security Council. This was not presented officially, but was
set down as the maximum compromise the United States
would make. Meanwhile, Marshal Stalin on September 15
cabled the President that the way to a solution might still be
found in some special procedure for voting, but it was felt in
Washington that this gave no real encouragement for a change
in his basic position. Neither Roosevelt nor Churchill at this
juncture appeared favorable to any compromise.

Differences developed between two groups in the American
delegation at Dumbarton Oaks over the need of reaching a

---

[21] Hull, *Memoirs*, II, 1683, 1700–1704; State Department, *Postwar Foreign
Policy Preparation*, 320–24.

compromise. One group held that continued controversy would prejudice the success of the conference, impair military co-operation among the Great Powers, and "adversely affect the prospect of Russia's entering the war against Japan." The other group held that the danger of disagreement was exaggerated. Hull at this point called the delegation together and reminded them of the need for patience and friendliness toward the Russians. He felt in the long run that they would follow the course of international co-operation, since it was the only way in which they could advance their vital interests. The Secretary voiced his anxiety over the effect of the Russian proposals on the attitudes of the small nations, and indicated his concern over the effect on the postwar organization of a "walk out" by any major nation.

The Russians made Hull's position no easier by announcing a few days later, through Gromyko, that Russian agreement upon a date for calling a general conference of the United Nations would depend on British and American acceptance of the Soviet view on voting and on membership for the Soviet Republics. The other delegations made no comment at this point, but turned to the second phase of the conferences, in which they discussed the peace organization draft with the more agreeable Chinese.

Hull's anxiety over the effect of Russian abstention from a postwar peace organization was shared by an old champion of the League of Nations and an adviser of prime ministers and presidents, Marshal Jan Smuts of the Union of South Africa. Smuts was no friend of communism, but he wrote Churchill in September, 1944, when Russia was giving trouble at Dumbarton Oaks: "Should a World Organization be formed which does not include Russia she will become the power centre of another group. We shall then be heading towards a third World War." He also felt that it might be necessary to have Russian help in driving Japan from China. Churchill forwarded this message to Roosevelt, who replied: "I think we are all in full agreement with him as to the necessity of having the U.S.S.R. as a fully accepted and equal member of any association of the Great Powers formed for the purpose of preventing international war." In a significant statement, he added: "It should be possible to accomplish this by adjusting our differences through compromise by all the parties concerned, and this ought to tide things over for a few years until the child learns how to toddle."[22]

In early October the President characterized as "absurd" the Soviet proposal to extend membership to all the Soviet Republics. China's ambassador was informed of the suggestion and was told that Roosevelt, Churchill, and Chiang Kai-shek would probably have to take up the matter with Stalin. Members of the Joint Steering Committee were warned to keep the Russian position secret inasmuch as "the whole civilized world would be shocked by such a proposal" if it were not handled properly. Gossip about the matter, it was feared, would lead to criticism of the Soviet Union and jeopardize the whole movement toward international organization.[23]

The President on October 7, the last day of the Dumbarton Oaks conference, informed the delegates that the matter of voting and membership should be dealt with at the highest level. Soon after the conference adjourned, Roosevelt declared that there was no time to lose in pressing forward the formation of a world organization. "It is our objective," he added, "to establish the solid foundations of the peace organization without further delay, and without waiting for the end of hostilities." Stalin about a month later spoke of differences which existed between the Great Powers, but noted that the surprising thing was not the number of differences, but the fact that there were so few. "What matters," he asserted, "is not that there are differences, but that these differences do not transgress the bounds of what the interests of unity of the three great powers allow, and that in the long run they are resolved in accordance with the interests of that unity."[24]

Six questions relating to the international organization were left open by the Dumbarton Oaks conference for future settlement by a conference of the heads of governments. In addition to voting and membership, these included terri-

22 Winston S. Churchill, *Triumph and Tragedy* (Boston, 1953), 210–16.
23 State Department, *Postwar Foreign Policy Preparation*, 332–34.
24 *Ibid.*, 334–37.

torial trusteeship, the statute of an international court, the location of the international organization, and the means of transition from the League of Nations to the new organization. Of these, voting and membership were most pressing. Both were to have a prominent place on the agenda at Yalta and are commonly associated with the mistakes of that conference.

YALTA AND THE WAR

Stettinius, Byrnes, Sherwood, and others have blamed the President's "concessions" at Yalta on the exigencies, real or imagined, of the military situation just before and during the Crimea conference. It is useful to consider: (1) the extent to which Soviet contributions to the war conditioned the decisions of Roosevelt and Churchill at Yalta, (2) the extent to which the Russian military position in February, 1945, made it impossible for the West to impose conditions unacceptable to the U.S.S.R., and (3) the extent to which Russian help was necessary in the Far East.

The Growing Power of the U.S.S.R.

From June, 1941, until the opening of the Allied attack on North Africa in November, 1942, the Soviet Union bore the brunt of German attacks virtually alone. The British, still reeling from the Battle of Britain and with their forces spread out in the Pacific, the Mediterranean, the Near East, and the home islands, found it impossible to meet Stalin's continued pleas for the opening of a second front in the Arctic and in France. When in September, 1941, Stalin asked the British to send twenty-five to thirty divisions to Archangel or across Iran to his southern front, Churchill had to refuse. Hitler then had more troops in France than the British had in the United Kingdom, and the Prime Minister replied that to put even two divisions into the Caucasus would take at least three months. Nor did the entry of the United States into the war immediately help the situation. With no more divisions in being than Stalin had on the Manchurian border, and with part of these not ready for combat, the United States was in no position to accept Stalin's invitation to fight on Russian soil.

The best the western Allies could offer the Russians in the spring of 1942 was a possible emergency landing in the Cherbourg Peninsula in France to take some pressure off the eastern front. But with only nine divisions available for this task, it seemed unlikely that such an attack would create much diversion from the German offensive. When Churchill journeyed to Moscow to explain that the main Allied offensive in 1942 would be in North Africa, he was bluntly told that it would be of little direct help to the U.S.S.R. When, a year later, the second front in western Europe had still not been opened, Stalin declared that he had not been aided by the fighting in the Mediterranean; in fact, he said, Hitler had transferred thirty-six more divisions from the west to the Russian front. In these circumstances the Prime Minister often hesitated to oppose strongly some of the territorial concessions demanded by the Soviet government.

When at last the second front was opened in Normandy in June, 1944, the U.S.S.R. had passed over from the defensive to the offensive. A few days after D Day, the Red Army began a sweep into Rumania, Hungary, the Baltic states, and Poland, making clear to the world that a new force was now abroad in Europe. It does not detract from the great victories of the British and American forces in the west to state that their conquests were surpassed by those of the Russians. In the three months from June to September, when the forces under Eisenhower fought brilliantly against 700,000 Germans in the west, the much larger Soviet forces inflicted 900,000 casualties on Hitler's armies. When Churchill and American strategists reflected on this fact it became apparent to them that Britain's position would be diminished in the postwar world. The United States, with great manpower reserves and enormous industrial production, might sit down in the future on a basis of equality with the U.S.S.R., but it was clear that the British role would be reduced. And when Roosevelt spoke, as he often did, of taking his troops back home as soon as possible after the war, the Prime Minister felt much alone. However, as a historian and a generous ally, he gave due credit to the Russians in his address to the House of Commons in August, 1944, when he said flatly that the Russian Army had done "the main work of tearing the guts out of the German army."[25]

There can be little doubt that Churchill's desire to build up the British position counted as much as his anti-Russian fears in his much publicized argument for additional operations in the Mediterranean. In June, 1944, as he argued against the launching of the attack against southern France, he angrily declared: "Let us at least have a chance to launch a decisive strategic stroke with what is entirely British and under British command. I am not going to give way about this for anybody. Alexander is to have his campaign."[26] He also spoke of sending troops in Istria at the head of the Adriatic Sea and possibly on to Vienna. When these suggestions went unheeded, he turned from the military to the diplomatic field, seeking to obtain commitments from Stalin in October, 1944, which would guarantee a degree of British influence in eastern Europe. The fact that the Prime Minister took the initiative must have indicated to Stalin that the British now held an uncertain position and under sufficient pressure would retreat in future exchanges. And the agreement to divide the Balkans into spheres of influence was bound to weaken any moral stand Churchill might wish to take at a later conference.

Reverses in the West

Western bargaining power at Yalta was limited by the realities of the military situation which then prevailed. Two German armies, containing a number of divisions shifted from the eastern front, hit General Eisenhower's First Army on December 16, 1944. In the week that followed, Hitler's forces took advantage of surprise, concentration, and bad flying weather to create the "Bulge," forcing American troops back to the Meuse. The attack upset an offensive which had just been launched by the First Army in the direction of the

[25] Hugh M. Cole, *The Lorraine Campaign* (Washington, 1950), 29–43; Forrest C. Pogue, *The Supreme Command* (Washington, 1954), 247–48. (Both of these volumes are in the *United States Army in World War II* series.)

[26] Churchill, *Triumph and Tragedy*, 63, 691–92.

Roer River dams, and disrupted planning for an Allied spring campaign.

The German surprise punch intensified already existing shortages of riflemen and supplies. The British since late summer had been forced to break up some of their regular units to get infantry replacements; the French surplus manpower could not yet be used for lack of equipment. At Eisenhower's call for more men, the Joint Chiefs of Staff moved up the sailing date of all units assigned to the European theater and allocated two other divisions initially intended for the Pacific area. In addition, Washington ordered a "comb out" of all men in Panama, Alaska, and the American defense commands who were fit for infantry duty. Eisenhower started a drastic search for front-line men in his own rear echelon commands and asked if the Marines might be able to send 100,000 men. Among the troops rushed to the front there were many newly inducted eighteen-year-olds with little training. The Joint Chiefs of Staff notified the President that when the units already allocated had sailed, there would not be another division left in the United States. All these actions did not mean that the American position was desperate, but they did indicate that the United States was in no position to dispense with Soviet aid in Europe.[27]

With the possibility that the Russian drive in the east was stalled for weeks or perhaps "for the duration," Eisenhower asked Washington on December 21 to determine Soviet intentions for operations in the coming months. A few days before, Ambassador Averell Harriman had asked about Stalin's intentions and had learned that a Soviet winter offensive would be launched. Unaware of this, Eisenhower reminded Marshall of the shift of German units from the Russian front to his own and stated that, if the trend continued, "it will affect the decisions which I have to make regarding future strategy in the west. . . . If, for instance, it is the Russian intention to launch a major offensive in the course of this or next month, knowledge of the fact would be of the utmost importance to me and I would condition my plans accordingly."

Eisenhower's request for information prompted the Presi-

27 Pogue, *The Supreme Command*, 391–93.

dent to ask Marshal Stalin if he would receive SHAEF representatives to discuss the situation in western Europe and
future plans, adding that the situation in Belgium was not
bad but that it was necessary to see what came next. When
the Soviet chief agreed, Eisenhower sent his deputy commander, his chief of operations, and his deputy chief of intelligence to Moscow. On January 15, soon after their arrival in
Moscow, they were told that the Russian offensive had been
opened three days earlier. Stalin declared that in view of
Allied difficulties the attack, under preparation for more than
a month, had been speeded up despite bad weather. He added
that from 150 to 160 divisions had been thrown into an eight-
to ten-week campaign with orders to reach the Oder. Stalin
was not certain that he could keep the attack going until
May, but he promised to stir up the Germans and prevent
them from shifting from his front to the west. Even though
his attack had come two weeks after the worst of the Ardennes
offensive had been met by Allied troops, Stalin stressed his
benevolent role in aiding Eisenhower. He remarked that it
would be as foolish for him to stand aside while the Germans
annihilated the western Allies as it was wise for the West
to prevent the enemy from crushing the Soviet forces.[28]

General Eisenhower, in outlining future operations, informed General Marshall on January 15 of the importance
of a continued Russian offensive to the success of the Allied
spring offensive. Asked whether or not the eighty-five divisions which would be available in the spring would be sufficient to defeat Germany, he said they might if the Soviet
attack went well. Two weeks later Eisenhower reviewed his
situation with Marshall at Marseilles when the Chief of Staff
stopped briefly on his way to Malta, where he was to discuss
military plans before proceeding to Yalta. At Malta a few
days later, Eisenhower's chief of staff, Lieutenant General
Walter Bedell Smith, told Stettinius there was an outside
chance that the Russian advance might be at an end, and that
there was a possibility that the Germans might retire to southwest Germany and conduct guerrilla warfare for months or
even years. Thus, on the eve of the Yalta conference Marshall

[28] *Ibid.*, 404–407.

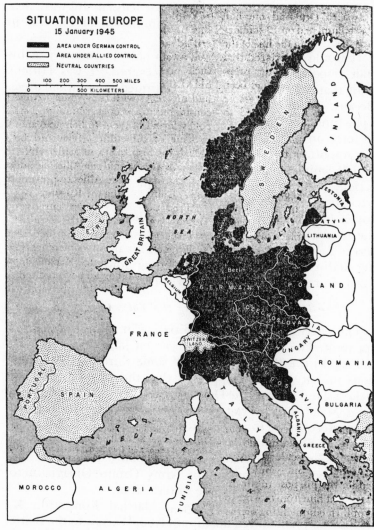

SITUATION IN EUROPE
15 January 1945

AREA UNDER GERMAN CONTROL
AREA UNDER ALLIED CONTROL
NEUTRAL COUNTRIES

0   100   200   300   400   500 MILES
0   500 KILOMETERS

From Forrest C. Pogue, *The Supreme Command* (Washington, D. C., 1954).

and his associates were convinced that Russian aid was essential to a successful and speedy culmination of the war in Europe.[29]

It would be totally misleading to hold Eisenhower or his staff responsible for the Yalta concessions. It was Hitler's fault that Eisenhower needed a continued Russian offensive. Because of the Ardennes counteroffensive, it would be March 24 before the Anglo-American forces could cross the Rhine in force on all fronts. Meanwhile, Eisenhower's emphasis on the importance of the aid by a Russian force, plus General Bedell Smith's anxieties about the future course of Russian action, must have been considered by Roosevelt's military advisers when they suggested at Yalta that he get further Soviet help. Certainly, as far as Eisenhower was concerned, the need to co-ordinate his drive with that of the Russians was of paramount interest. However, his insistence on keeping Stalin informed of his plans drew down on him sharp words from Churchill and the British Chiefs of Staff.

The Russian Front During the Yalta Conference

The effect of the Russian initiative in the east was soon apparent. The Soviet offensive began on January 12, 1945. In two weeks the Red Army cut off some thirty German divisions in Latvia and it appeared that the enemy could not make a stand short of the Oder. On January 20 Hitler ordered Field Marshal Gerd von Rundstedt, commander-in-chief of the western front, to prepare to send the Sixth Panzer Army with four SS armored divisions and two Fuehrer brigades to the Russian front. Reichsfuehrer SS Heinrich Himmler was transferred from command of Army Group Oberrhein to Army Group Weichsel on the eastern front.

At the end of January, 1945, Marshal Konstantin K. Rokossovsky had moved northward from Warsaw to the Baltic and isolated East Prussia from the Reich. Marshal Ivan S. Konev forced his way westward across the south of Poland to the Oder and established several bridgeheads across it during the early days of February—in time for his action to be

---

[29] *Ibid.*, 412–14; Edward R. Stettinius, Jr. (Walter Johnson, ed.), *Roosevelt and the Russians: The Yalta Conference* (Garden City, 1949), 73–74.

announced at the Yalta conference. Poland thus lay in the hands of the Russians or of the Lublin government, which the U.S.S.R. recognized as the government of the liberated area. In the area between Rokossovsky's and Konev's forces, Marshal Georgi K. Zhukov moved westward, sending powerful armored columns in the direction of Berlin. Advance units were within less than one hundred miles of the German capital while the Big Three debated the fate of Poland and Germany at Yalta. (See map, p. 29.) These were facts above which personal diplomacy could not rise.

The War in the Far East

Military needs in the Far East likewise demanded consideration by Churchill and Roosevelt in February, 1945. At the time of the Yalta conference, the Japanese had 2,000,000 to 2,500,000 men under arms in Japan, 1,000,000 in China, and 1,000,000 in Manchuria and Korea. The United States by the end of the war had sent approximately 1,459,000 army and air force men and 187,500 Marines into the Pacific, scattered from Australia to Alaska. "In general," as Admiral Ernest J. King, Chief of Naval Operations, put it at Yalta, "the forward line . . . included Attu, the Marianas, and Luzon." He added that American forces controlled the sea and air beyond that line and up to China, Formosa, the Ryukyus, and even to the coast of Japan itself. Luzon, he might have added, had been under attack for a month, and it was to be nearly five more months before Bataan was cleared and Corregidor was retaken. In this last six-month campaign to clear the Philippines, American forces were to suffer 60,000 casualties while killing 300,000 Japanese.[30]

Between February 19, 1945, and March 16, 1945, two to six weeks after the completion of the Yalta conference and at a time when many experts later claimed that the Japanese had been defeated by air and sea action, the Marine Corps took Iwo Jima, an island two and one-half miles wide by four and two-thirds miles long. In what has been called its bitterest

[30] United States Army, *Biennial Report of the Chief of Staff of the United States Army, July 1, 1943, to June 30, 1945, to the Secretary of War* (Washington, 1945), 78–86.

battle, the Marine Corps killed some 20,000 Japanese at a cost of nearly 7,000 dead and some 20,000 wounded. Just as they were completing this operation, the "greatest sea-air battle in history" was launched against Okinawa by Admiral Richmond K. Turner and General Simon B. Buckner. In eighty-two days of struggle the Japanese force (including Okinawan conscripts) lost more than 100,000 dead. More than 7,800 planes were destroyed. But United States Army and Marine casualties numbered some 39,000, of whom 7,300, including General Buckner, were dead. Naval casualties afloat were 10,000 with 5,000 dead. Japanese planes sank 36 ships and damaged 368 others. American losses were the highest experienced in any campaign against the Japanese. Hanson Baldwin has summarized the results succinctly: "Never before, in so short a space, had the Navy lost so many; never before in land fighting had so much American blood been shed in so short a time in so small an area; probably never before in any three months of the war had the enemy suffered so hugely."[31] Japan was by no means defeated in February, 1945, and Russian participation in the war against her seemed highly desirable to the West.

General Douglas MacArthur was among those who realized this and advocated Soviet entry into the war in the Pacific. On February 25, 1945, Rear Admiral Charles M. Cooke and Brigadier General G. A. Lincoln discussed these matters with the Pacific commander, and shortly afterward Lincoln took them up with General MacArthur and his chief of staff. In a memorandum written on February 25, Lincoln reported: "General MacArthur spoke of the strength of the opposition to be expected in invading the Japanese home islands. He declared that planning should start at once, that heavy fire power would be needed to cover the beachheads, and that as many Japanese divisions as possible should first be pinned

---

31 Roy Appleman, James Burns, Russell Gugeler, and John Stevens, *Okinawa: The Last Battle* (Washington, 1948), 473–74, 488–89, in the *United States Army in World War II* series; M. Hamlin Cannon, *Leyte: The Return to the Philippines* (Washington, 1954), *United States Army in World War II* series; Whitman S. Bartley, *Iwo Jima: Amphibious Epic* (Washington, 1954), 193, 210, 218–21 (a Marine Corps monograph); Hanson Baldwin, "The Greatest Sea-Air Battle in History," New York *Times*, March 26, 1950.

down on the mainland, principally by Soviet forces."[32]

It is understandable that the Pacific commander would want additional help at the time of his landings. Enemy conduct in opposing landings on Luzon, Iwo Jima, and Okinawa in the spring and summer of 1945 provided no grounds for the belief that opposition was getting lighter. American casualty figures in the Pacific jumped from an average of 3,200 per month to 12,750 per month in the first seven months of 1945. Apparently MacArthur's view of the value of a Russian attack did not lessen during the summer months. When news was brought him of the Soviet declaration of war, he declared on August 9, 1945: "I am delighted at the Russian declaration of war against Japan. This will make possible a great pincers movement that cannot fail to end in the destruction of the enemy."[33]

All in all, the military backdrop for the Yalta negotiations, while more favorable to the West than it had been at any

[32] United States, Department of Defense, "The Entry of the Soviet Union into the War against Japan: Military Plans, 1941–1945" (mimeographed report released on October 19, 1955), 1, 51–52, 55–57, 80; Frazier Hunt, *The Untold Story of Douglas MacArthur* (New York, 1954), 385–86; Ray S. Cline, *Washington Command Post: The Operations Division* (Washington, 1951), 307–308, in *United States Army in World War II* series; Walter Millis (ed.), with the collaboration of E. S. Duffield, *The Forrestal Diaries* (New York, 1951), 31; Courtney Whitney, "MacArthur's Rendezvous with History," *Life*, XXXIX (August 15, 1955), 70. The timing of recent allegations and counter-allegations is interesting. The Whitney article in *Life* (August 15, 1955) contained a denial that MacArthur told Forrestal that he wanted Russian help; the Department of Defense report of October, 1955, presented evidence that MacArthur did desire Russian help; and Whitney's book on MacArthur, which appeared at the end of January, 1956, makes no effort to deny Forrestal's statement that MacArthur told him he wanted Russian help. Cf. Courtney Whitney, *MacArthur: His Rendezvous with History* (New York, 1956), 197–203. However, Whitney reports that senior intelligence officers of the War Department on April 12, 1945 (i.e., two months *after* Yalta), presented to General Marshall a memorandum in which they opposed Soviet entry into the war and asked for the recall of MacArthur to present their case directly to the President. On the other hand, Frazier Hunt, an admiring biographer of General MacArthur, has reported that as late as June 10 the Pacific commander stated among associates that if it were necessary for the United States to invade the Japanese home islands, "a prerequisite should be to have the Russian army strike in northern Manchuria." MacArthur allegedly added that Russian intervention would dull the edge of the "Nip Air Force," take up much of the shock of landing, and save thousands of American lives.

[33] New York *Times*, August 10, 1945.

time since 1939, did not yet afford Roosevelt and Churchill the luxury of renouncing or foregoing Soviet military co-operation in Europe and Asia.

THE DECISION TO MEET AT YALTA

As early as July 17, 1944, Roosevelt had proposed to the Russian chief a meeting in September. Apparently his cable was prompted by developments of the two previous days. On July 15 the President had answered an earlier Russian query relative to the American position on proposed Russian and British arrangements concerning Rumania and Greece. Before Roosevelt's reply was received, Stalin cabled Churchill that since the Americans apparently had some questions about the proposals, it would be better to wait for a reply. Churchill thereupon urged the President to call a meeting of the Combined Staffs. On the following day Roosevelt cabled Stalin, suggesting a meeting in northern Scotland in mid-September, apparently with the idea of holding it just before or just after the proposed Combined Staffs meeting. Churchill may have suggested this meeting, for he obviously had one in mind. In a cable to Hopkins on July 19, the Prime Minister had insisted that there was need of another conference since the affairs of the Big Three were getting into a tangled state.[34]

Stalin, unwilling to go any great distance from the Soviet Union, cabled that operational developments prevented him from coming to Scotland at that time. The President was increasingly anxious after the Quebec conference of September to have a tripartite meeting, and he next talked of a possible conference in the Mediterranean in November. This time Stalin's doctors said he could not stand a change of climate. The presidential election intervened and Roosevelt decided that the meeting had better wait until his campaign was concluded. It was then Churchill's turn to press for a meeting. September saw Soviet forces reach the Baltic on a wide front, advance into Yugoslav territory, and drive toward Budapest and Belgrade. With Rumania and Bulgaria in Russia's power, the Prime Minister turned his attention to Poland

[34] William D. Leahy, *I Was There* (New York, 1950), 248; Churchill, *Triumph and Tragedy*, 80–81; Sherwood, *Roosevelt and Hopkins*, 810.

and Greece. He hoped to come to some agreement about these countries and about the unsettled questions relating to the United Nations. Believing that these issues could not be evaded until after the elections, he sounded out Stalin and Roosevelt on the prospect of a visit to Moscow to clear up a few questions which could not wait. Roosevelt approved, but cabled Harriman: "I should hope that this bilateral conference be nothing more than a preliminary exploration by the British and the Russians leading up to a full dress meeting between the three of us. . . . It is of importance . . . that when this conference is over Mr. Hull and I have complete freedom of action." [35]

Roosevelt then began to play about with a number of ideas for possible meeting places, but Hopkins insisted that Stalin would not leave Russia and suggested that the President agree to some place like the Crimea. Hopkins' memorandum on the conference indicates that he raised the question after the November elections. Actually, it was in mid-October that he asked Ambassador Gromyko about the possibility of a meeting on the Black Sea coast of Russia near the end of November. Soon afterward, an enthusiastic and favorable cable was received from Marshal Stalin.

Meanwhile, Roosevelt considered the idea of staging the conference at Athens or Cyprus. Shortly afterward he added Malta to the list. Health reports on poor sanitary conditions in the Black Sea area began to discourage both Roosevelt and Churchill. The former spoke of Piraeus, Salonica, and Constantinople as possible meeting places, and Churchill added Alexandria and Jerusalem. When the advancing Russian forces started pushing toward Belgrade, the President suggested the Adriatic or the Riviera. In mid-November he proposed that the conference be postponed until the end of January or February, since he wanted to be on hand for the opening of Congress. The delay, he said, might make it possible for the Marshal to get transportation through Soviet-occupied territory to the Adriatic. In passing on this sugges-

---

[35] United States, Department of State, *The Conferences at Malta and Yalta, 1945* (Washington, 1955), 4–7 (hereinafter cited as *Yalta Papers*); Churchill, *Triumph and Tragedy*, 206–19; Sherwood, *Roosevelt and Hopkins*, 832–34.

tion to Stalin, Roosevelt added Rome and Taormina to the rapidly growing list of alternate meeting places. Stalin stood firm on his "doctors' advice" and said that he could not travel very far. Churchill and Roosevelt began to waver, the latter proving Hopkins to have been a good prophet, and on December 9 the President cabled the Prime Minister that he could leave just after his inauguration by ship and fly from from Malta or Athens to a meeting place in the Crimea. In this cable Yalta was mentioned as a possible meeting place.[36]

Numerous cables listed the names of an increasingly long list of advisers who would attend, arrangements were made for a stop at Malta so that British and American military staffs could make plans for spring offensives, and arrangements were worked out with the Turks for the passage through the Dardanelles of naval ships which would provide communications for Churchill and Roosevelt while they were away from home. Churchill, looking over the plans, was pleased that the Big Three were to meet again. In a jovial mood, he telegraphed the President on January 1: "No more let us falter! From Malta to Yalta! Let nobody alter!" But considered reflection led Churchill to view the conference pessimistically. In a telegram of January 8, Churchill expressed his misgivings to Roosevelt: "This may well be a fateful Conference, coming at a moment when the Great Allies are so divided and the shadow of the war lengthens out before us. At the present time I think the end of this war may well prove to be more disappointing than was the last."[37]

Much of Churchill's pessimism was caused by the vast shifts in the global balance of power which the twentieth century had ushered in at Britain's expense. It remained to be seen whether personal diplomacy in the Crimea could check the impersonal onrush of history and the sudden expansion of Soviet military power.

[36] *Yalta Papers,* 6–19; Sherwood, *Roosevelt and Hopkins,* 844.
[37] *Yalta Papers,* 26, 31; Churchill, *Triumph and Tragedy,* 341.

CHAPTER II

What to Do with Germany?

THE FUTURE of Germany was not among the major problems which were solved at Yalta, but it was the most fateful European problem discussed there. The problem of German power in Europe was the ultimate cause of the Crimea conference. The very failure of the Big Three to reach agreement on the postwar treatment of Germany undoubtedly conditioned some of the other decisions which they reached in February, 1945. Their negotiations over Germany revealed their divergent interests and foretold sharper clashes which were soon to follow. The balance sheet when the conference was over reflected all the credits and debits of Great Power diplomacy. And, inevitably, the Yalta record carried the imprint of the historical moment in which it was made.[1]

THE PASSIONS OF WAR

In each of the countries of "the strange alliance" relatively few people could think rationally and without emotion about a post-Hitlerian Germany in the winter of 1944–45. Britain, Russia, and the United States had fought together against Germany twice within a single generation. In World War II, as in World War I, the western democracies had little in common with their eastern ally except the disturbing knowledge that each had been goaded into war or directly attacked by the same power and had fought for one common purpose: to prevent the domination of Europe by Germany. Public

[1] The author takes this occasion to express his gratitude to Ernest A. Gross, Professor David Harris of Stanford University, Professor Philip E. Mosely of Columbia University, Professor Harold Zink of Ohio State University, and the former Assistant Secretary for War and United States High Commissioner of Germany, John J. McCloy, all of whom helped the author on points which he could not otherwise have clarified.

sentiment from San Francisco to Liverpool to Magnitogorsk insisted that stern measures should be taken by Roosevelt, Stalin, and Churchill to prevent German aggression in the future. The Germans had opened a Pandora's box, and the floodtide of inhumanity which poured forth threatened to equal the one the Nazis had loosed over the rest of Europe in six years of paranoidal brutality.

In the month of Yalta a public opinion survey in England revealed that 54 per cent of those who were polled either hated or had no use for the German people, not simply the Nazi government. Lord Robert Vansittart was the self-appointed chieftain of the "hate Germany" movement in England, insisting that at least 75 per cent of the German people were "incurably bellicose."[2] In the United States an even harsher sentiment prevailed than in England, although Americans were not so close to the war as were Britons. A national opinion poll indicated that 60 per cent of the people of the United States believed that Germany would begin planning another war as soon as she was defeated. Another national poll showed that 81 per cent of the persons contacted favored the much maligned policy of "unconditional surrender." Even so wise and moderate a commentator as Walter Lippmann admonished his 1944 readers: "Our primary war aim must be unalterable: it must be to make it impossible for Germany to hold the balance of power."[3]

The wartime attitudes of the Russian people toward Germany were recorded in deeds and suffering more than in

[2] H. D. Willcock, "Public Opinion: Attitudes to the German People," *The Political Quarterly* (London), XIX (April–June, 1948), 160–66; Lord Robert Vansittart, *Bones of Contention* (New York, 1945), 46–69 and *passim;* Vansittart's preface to Wladyslaw W. Kulski (W. M. Knight-Patterson, pseud.), *Germany from Defeat to Conquest, 1913–1933* (London, 1945), 5–6; Harold Nicolson, "Marginal Comment," *Spectator* (London), CLXX (April 23, 1943), 382; and CLXXII (June 30, 1944), 590.

[3] See, for example, Donald F. Lach, "What *They* Would Do about Germany," *Journal of Modern History*, XVII (September, 1945), 227–43, which reviews at length many of the anti-German and some of the sympathetic discussions of the German problem in World War II, and Walter Lippmann, *U. S. War Aims* (Boston, 1944), 110–17. The opinion-poll statistics are from a very useful Stanford University dissertation which is available on microfilm from University Microfilms, Ann Arbor, Michigan: Herman Edward Bateman, "The Election of 1944 and Foreign Policy," 137–38.

words. Those that were published must be associated with official propaganda. The very fact that Russia was subjected to a three-year invasion and occupation by the Germans suggests the intensity of hatred toward things German that existed in the U.S.S.R. during the winter of 1944–45. Stalin expressed a common feeling when he told Roosevelt at Yalta that "the Germans were savages and seemed to hate with a sadistic hatred the creative work of human beings." The people of Russia understandably expected that victory would bring a "day of judgment for Germany." Reports abounded in 1944 that the Russians feared that the United States and Britain might let Germany off too easy after the war. To the Russians "the future of Germany appeared as the foremost problem of their national security."[4] Stalin remembered two German invasions of Russia and the humiliating peace of Brest Litovsk which Germany had imposed in 1918. He also remembered that the German working class had failed to curb the excesses of German imperialism in 1918, that it proved to be remarkably cool toward the Soviet brand of socialism, and that it had succumbed or adjusted itself to Nazism without even so much as an attempted general strike in 1933. Stalin believed that there was no hope for Germany.[5]

PRELIMINARY PLANNING, 1941–44

The Soviet leader decided early in the war that what could not be cured should be crushed decisively. The terms of postwar settlement with Germany which he developed during

[4] United States, Department of State, *The Conferences at Malta and Yalta, 1945* (Washington, 1955), 571 (hereinafter cited as *Yalta Papers*). Other material in the above paragraph is based upon I. Deutscher, *Stalin, a Political Biography* (New York and London, 1949), 538; Anna Louise Strong, "Russia's Post-War Policy," *Nation*, CLIX (October 21, 1944), 460–61; Hajo Holborn, *American Military Government, Its Organization and Policies* (Washington, 1947), 23.

[5] Henry J. Tobias and John L. Snell, "A Soviet Interpretation of the SPD, 1895–1933," *Journal of Central European Affairs*, XIII (April, 1953), 61–66; John L. Snell, "The Russian Revolution and the German Social Democratic Party in 1917," to appear in the *American Slavic and East European Review* late in 1956; and Richard W. Reichard, "The German Working Class and the Russian Revolution of 1905," *Journal of Central European Affairs*, XIII (July, 1953), 136–53. See also Wolfgang Steinitz (ed.), *Stalin Spricht: die Kriegsreden vom 3. Juli 1941 bis zum 9. Mai 1945* (Stockholm, 1945), 15–16, 44–45, and 70.

that awful December of 1941, when the *Wehrmacht* was on the outskirts of Moscow, were never abandoned. Then Stalin revealed his aims to Anthony Eden, the British Foreign Secretary, and Eden soon transmitted them to Secretary of State Cordell Hull. Stalin's aims were as follows: Austria must be again made independent of Germany proper; East Prussia must be transferred to Poland; the Rhineland, including the industrial Ruhr and Saar areas, must be detached from Germany and made into an independent state or protectorate; and Bavaria should become an independent state. Hitler's Germany would thus be reduced in size and divided into four parts. Furthermore, the Germans should pay reparations in kind, especially in machine tools. Throughout the war these remained the basic Russian objectives concerning Germany, though they were slightly modified, clarified, or supplemented from time to time, as when it was suggested in 1943 that the U.S.S.R. itself, rather than Poland, would annex the area around Königsberg in East Prussia.[6]

Roosevelt, and to a lesser extent, Churchill, encouraged Stalin to believe that most or all of these Soviet objectives would be realized after the war, but they both managed to avoid formally committing themselves or their governments to any specific program. Instead, they adopted a "policy of postponement" which was extremely frustrating to their expert planners, who were assigned the task of planning the conditions of occupation and peace without being given any broad policy instructions from above. The policy of postponement was both admitted and masked by two very different public statements which Roosevelt and Churchill released during the war. The first was the Atlantic Charter, a humane document which was drafted in August, 1941, at the lowest ebb of western fortune, and before a Russian ally's expansive appetite was made known. The second document was the brief and ambiguous "unconditional surrender" formula, a pledge of good faith given by Roosevelt with Churchill's blessing to an unappreciative Soviet ally in January, 1943, one week before the Russian victory at Stalingrad.

[6] Cordell Hull, *The Memoirs of Cordell Hull* (2 vols., New York, 1948), II, 1165–67. See also Deutscher, *Stalin*, 474, 487, 502; Robert Sherwood, *Roosevelt and Hopkins, An Intimate History* (New York, 1948), 388.

Any western attempt to define more exactly the terms of peace with Germany would either threaten the unity of "the strange allies" or threaten the interests of the West in the postwar era. Harsh terms would give hostages to the future by leaving nothing between "the white snows of Russia and the white cliffs of Dover," as Roosevelt once summarized Churchill's fears. But soft or even moderate terms would convince the Russians that the West hoped to rebuild Germany into a bulwark against the Soviet Union. The decision to speak in radical generalities and to postpone definite policy decisions partly reflected the wavering between reason and wartime passion in London and Washington, but it was also a policy which aimed at preserving the coalition. It was the only sane decision which the President and the Prime Minister could reach under the circumstances, and it dominated their tactics at the first Big Three meeting of the war, which was staged at Teheran in November, 1943.

By the time Churchill and Roosevelt met again their subordinates had already prepared a plan for the occupation of Germany. This plan would allocate the eastern third to the U.S.S.R., the southwestern zone to the United States, and the northwestern zone to Great Britain. This plan made no provision to include France among the occupation powers; France itself was still occupied by the *Wehrmacht* when the European Advisory Commission, meeting in London, recommended the tripartite zonal division of Germany to the three Allied governments. The European Advisory Commission also recommended that Berlin should be placed under joint control and that an inter-Allied Control Commission for Germany should be created to provide and implement uniform policies throughout the separate zones of occupation. Final acceptance of these plans awaited only the approval of the President in September, 1944. He balked at giving his approval, because he wanted the northwestern zone of occupation instead of the less accessible southern zone. But when General Eisenhower's forces approached the German border in September it was obvious that some agreement on the zones of occupation, and other German matters, had to be made.

These and other questions were discussed by Churchill and Roosevelt at Quebec in mid-September.[7]

In the United States, the month before Quebec was one of intense official consideration of the future of Germany, primarily because the Secretary of the Treasury, Henry Morgenthau, Jr., provoked a showdown in the matter. Morgenthau, anti-German to the quick, was aroused by the progress of moderate planning for postwar Germany, and persuaded his friend and neighbor of many years, President Roosevelt, that the peace was about to be lost before victory was won. At Morgenthau's request the President on August 26 created a special cabinet committee on Germany to investigate and recommend possible policies toward that country in the immediate future. Morgenthau himself was named a member of this committee, thus bringing Treasury Department representatives into the preparation of plans for Germany for the first time in any formal and active way. Secretary of War Henry L. Stimson and Secretary of State Cordell Hull also served on the committee, and its work was co-ordinated by the President's intimate adviser, Harry Hopkins.[8]

A preliminary meeting on September 2 of deputies of the three secretaries revealed that the heads of the State and War departments wanted to draft a moderate peace with Germany.

[7] Philip E. Mosely, "The Occupation of Germany: New Light on How the Zones Were Drawn," *Foreign Affairs*, XXVIII (July, 1950), 580–604, provides an excellent survey of the origins of the zones of occupation. Mosely served as political adviser to the United States representative on the European Advisory Commission, John Gilbert Winant.

[8] On the origins of the Morgenthau plan see Morgenthau's own account in the New York *Post*, November 24–29, 1947; Hammond, "JCS 1067 Policy for Germany" (unpublished manuscript; see bibliographical essay for this chapter), 47, 113–17; Carl J. Friedrich and Associates, *American Experiences in Military Government in World War II* (New York, 1948), 219–20; Fred Smith, "The Rise and Fall of the Morgenthau Plan," *United Nations World*, II (March, 1947), 32–38; Dwight D. Eisenhower, *Crusade in Europe* (Garden City, 1948), 287; John L. Chase, "The Development of the Morgenthau Plan through the Quebec Conference," *Journal of Politics*, XVI (May, 1954), 326–28; Forrest C. Pogue, *The Supreme Command* (Washington, 1954), 353–54; E. F. Penrose, *Economic Planning for the Peace* (Princeton, 1953), 244–47, 271; Mosely, "The Occupation of Germany," *loc. cit.*, 595–96; Mosely to Snell, September 21, 1955; Walter Millis (ed.), with the collaboration of E. S. Duffield, *The Forrestal Diaries* (New York, 1951), 10; Hull, *Memoirs*, II, 1602–1608; Henry L. Stimson and McGeorge Bundy, *On Active Service in Peace and War* (New York, 1947), 569.

From the cover of the German magazine *Simplicissimus* (Munich), December 29, 1943.

"THE CONFERENCE VICTOR"

This Nazi comment on the "Strange Alliance" appeared soon after the Teheran conference. The caption, attributed to Stalin, says: "Now that I have defeated my friends I only need to defeat my enemies." It is only coincidental that this cartoon foreshadowed the view of Yalta which many Americans have taken.

But Harry Dexter White, as a special assistant to Morgenthau, presented that day a Treasury Department program which soon became known as the "Morgenthau plan," though White had been instrumental in its formulation. The Morgenthau-White program would break up Germany into at least three separate states; it would eliminate *all* heavy industry throughout the Reich and transfer chemical, electrical, and metallurgical plants and equipment not already destroyed by military action "to Allied nations as restitution"; and it would leave Germany under the long-term occupation of neither Britain nor the United States, but only under powerful Russia, weak France, and the smaller states of Europe. The plan became even more impossibly extreme as Morgenthau himself elaborated upon it in the week that followed its presentation before the deputies of the three secretaries on September 2.[9]

Morgenthau's avowed belief that farmers were always peace-loving ignored the realities of the German past.[10] Yet, there is no gainsaying the fact that Morgenthau's proposals would have left the Germans incapable of waging modern warfare. That it would leave Russia in control of the continent of Europe was pointed out to Morgenthau and White in August, and yet they persisted in pressing their proposals upon the President, seeking to take advantage of his well-known animus toward Germany and his tendency to oppose his own Department of State. These circumstances, plus assertions that Harry Dexter White gave a Soviet spy ring governmental information in World War II, have led some observers to conclude that the plan was a manifestation of Soviet influence in wartime Washington. Others, including men who were associated with Morgenthau from time to time, have attributed the plan to the fact that, as Jews, both White and Morgenthau harbored a special desire for ven-

9 The White-Morgenthau plan is presented in the form in which it was introduced at Quebec in Henry Morgenthau, Jr., *Germany is Our Problem* (New York and London, 1945), frontispiece; and see 23, 50. See also Sherwood, *Roosevelt and Hopkins*, 812, 818, and 832; Hull, *Memoirs*, II, 1304–1309, 1602; Stimson and Bundy, *On Active Service*, 569–74; New York *Post*, November 28, 1947; Riddleberger's account of the meeting of September 2 in *Yalta Papers*, 160–61; and Eleanor Roosevelt, *This I Remember* (New York, 1949), 332.

10 Rudolf Heberle, *From Democracy to Nazism: A Regional Case Study on Political Parties in Germany* (Baton Rouge, 1945), 84–94.

geance against the anti-Semitic Reich. Morgenthau himself
has claimed that his purpose always was to prevent future
German aggression, and it is conceivable that he decided
that this could be accomplished only by leaving Russia dominant on the Continent. In his own self-interest Morgenthau
should provide historians with a full and frank account of
his motives and his actions; he has not yet done so, and judgment about his motives must be suspended until additional
information becomes available.[11]

Apparently in an effort to retain State Department juris-
diction over foreign policy, Secretary Hull compromised with
the Morgenthau proposals during the seven days after White
announced the Morgenthau plan. But no decision was made
on a policy for Germany prior to Roosevelt's departure for
Quebec for his conference with Prime Minister Churchill.
Hull did not attend the Quebec meeting. On September 12
the President telegraphed his Secretary of the Treasury to
come immediately to Quebec, and on the night of September
13 Morgenthau spun out his proposals before the Prime
Minister. Churchill was at first bitterly hostile toward the
proposals and critical of their author. "I have never had such
a verbal lashing in my life," Morgenthau recalled three years
later. Yet, Churchill finally agreed to accept part of the Morgenthau plan. He did so chiefly, it would appear, because
Britain needed postwar credits from the United States and
because he knew that Morgenthau's influence would help
determine how much financial help Britain would get. It is
also possible that both Roosevelt and Churchill accepted
part of the Morgenthau plan out of a desire to reassure their
absent colleague of the Kremlin that Soviet interests were
not being violated in this Anglo-American meeting.

[11] The thesis of Jewish animus is suggested by Hull, *Memoirs*, I, 207–208,
472; Penrose, *Economic Planning for the Peace*, 248, 253; and others. The
thesis of Communist influence is suggested cautiously by M. J. Bonn, "The
Economics of Fear," *Annals of the American Academy of Political and Social
Science*, CCXLVI (July, 1946), 142; and blatantly by Norbert Muhlen, *The
Return of Germany: A Tale of Two Countries* (Chicago, 1953), 10, 12; Felix
Wittmer, *The Yalta Betrayal: Data on the Decline and Fall of Franklin Delano
Roosevelt* (Caldwell, Idaho, 1953), 64, 98; and Whittaker Chambers, *Witness*
(New York, 1952), 500 and *passim*. In contrast to these loose allegations see
White's testimony in the United States House of Representatives, 80th Congress,
2nd Session, *Hearings before the Committee on Un-American Activities* (Wash-
ington, 1948), 877–906.

In any case, the President and the Prime Minister on September 15 initialed an agreement which marked a striking if temporary and partial abandonment of the policy of postponement, and which also marked the high tide of vengeance planning in official circles of the West. The Quebec memorandum provided that Russia and other devastated countries would be authorized "to remove the machinery they require" from Germany to repair their own wartime losses; that the heavy industry of the Ruhr and Saar would be "put out of action and closed down," and these provinces would be placed under international control indefinitely; and finally, that the proposed program for the Ruhr and Saar "looked forward to" the conversion of Germany into a country which would be "primarily agricultural and pastoral in character." Soon after Churchill agreed to the Quebec memorandum (he even dictated it in his own language), Roosevelt finally agreed that Britain should have the northwestern zone of occupation in Germany, including the Ruhr area. The President conditioned this agreement upon British approval of United States control over Bremen and Bremerhaven as enclaves within the British zone, and transportation facilities between these ports and the American zone of occupation.[12] (See map, p. 71.)

It appeared that Morgenthau had scored a total victory as a result of his sudden foray into the field of diplomacy, and in the months that followed both State Department and army planning at the expert level was influenced in varying degrees by the Quebec agreement.[13] Few Washington officials seem to

[12] Mosely, "The Occupation of Germany," *loc. cit.,* 596–97; Morgenthau in New York *Post,* November 28–29, 1947; Morgenthau in "The Morgenthau Diaries," *Colliers,* CXX (October 18, 1947), 75; Morgenthau, "Postwar Treatment of Germany," *Annals of the American Academy of Political and Social Science,* CCXLVI (July, 1946), 126; Hull, *Memoirs,* II, 1613–14; *Time,* LXII (November 23, 1953), 23; Churchill, *Triumph and Tragedy* (Boston, 1953), 156–57, 160, 510, 514; *Yalta Papers,* 134–35; Lucius D. Clay, *Decision in Germany* (Garden City, 1950), 11. See also the *Yalta Papers,* 136–41, for Harry Dexter White's memo of the meeting of September 20, 1944, during which Morgenthau reported on the Quebec conference to Hull and others.

[13] Hull, *Memoirs,* II, 1616; United States, Department of State, *Postwar Foreign Policy Preparation, 1939–1945* (Washington, 1949), 369; Hammond, "JCS 1067 Policy for Germany" (unpublished manuscript), 84–89; and cf. *Yalta Papers,* 143–54, with Holborn, *American Military Government,* 135–43; and *Yalta Papers,* 141, 162–63.

have noticed that the two war leaders had by no means accepted the Morgenthau plan *in toto*. The Quebec agreement made no provision for the partition of Germany, which Morgenthau strongly advocated; the extent to which Germany would be deindustrialized was left completely uncertain, as were the amount and destination of reparations which Germany would be required to pay; and no decision was made upon the amount of territory Germany was to surrender. Possibly most significant of all, the Quebec memorandum was merely an Anglo-American statement of intention, not a contract; since Russia was not a party to it, the memorandum constituted no formal statement of inter-Allied policy toward defeated Germany.

Nonetheless, German propagandists and critics of Roosevelt in the United States immediately capitalized upon the "Morgenthau plan," and it appeared that the Quebec agreement might lengthen the war and become a liability to Roosevelt in his campaign for a fourth term as President.[14] Thus, in the months between Quebec and Yalta, Roosevelt[15] and Churchill[16] both advised their foreign-policy officials that they had retreated from the bold Quebec statement to the time-tested policy of postponement to which they had previously adhered. Roosevelt actually repudiated the statement he had initialed at Quebec, for on December 4 he confidentially advised his new Secretary of State, Edward R. Stettinius, that Germany should be allowed after the war to "come back industrially to meet her own needs," and that the United States would oppose the collection of reparations.[17]

[14] *Yalta Papers*, 134–35, 141–42; Hull, *Memoirs*, II, 1614–18; Stimson and Bundy, *On Active Service*, 578–80; Friedrich and Associates, *American Experiences in Military Government in World War II*, 223; *Spectator* (London), CLXXIII (September 29, 1944), 277.

[15] Stimson and Bundy, *On Active Service*, 580; B. U. Ratchford and William D. Ross, *Berlin Reparations Assignment: Round One of the German Peace Settlement* (Chapel Hill, 1947), 33–38; Holborn, *American Military Government*, 40–42; Bateman, "The Election of 1944 and Foreign Policy" (unpublished Ph.D. dissertation), 138; F.D.R. to Secretary of State, September 29, 1944, *Yalta Papers*, 155.

[16] *Yalta Papers*, 159–60; Churchill, *Triumph and Tragedy*, 240–41, 350–51; and see Eden to Churchill, February 2, 1945, in *Yalta Papers*, 511–12.

[17] Millis (ed.), *The Forrestal Diaries*, 25; Edward R. Stettinius, Jr. (Walter Johnson, ed.), *Roosevelt and the Russians: The Yalta Conference* (Garden City,

Planning for peace with Germany was complicated somewhat by the liberation of France in August and September,
1944. In October General Charles de Gaulle demanded that
France be given representation on the European Advisory
Commission and a zone of occupation in Germany. Churchill
strongly supported de Gaulle's demands, and on November
11 it was agreed that de Gaulle's provisional government
should share in the work of the E.A.C. The French representative to the European Advisory Commission took his
place there on November 27. This move—reflecting French
preoccupation about future relations with their ancient
enemy—marked the first important success in French foreign
policy after the liberation. It only whetted Gallic ambitions.
What France wanted was frankly admitted, as it had been
since the seventeenth century. Foreign Minister Georges
Bidault publicly spoke of the Rhine as "this French river,"
and in speech after speech de Gaulle summed up his chief
desires: "The definite presence of French power from one
end of the Rhine to the other, the separation of the left bank
of the Rhine and the Ruhr basin from the future German
state, or world of states."[18]

A few months earlier the French Resistance movement had
held out hope of more modern and rational approaches to
the German problem. But General de Gaulle insisted that
annexations were both desirable and possible: the way to
the Rhine lay through the gates of the Kremlin. Russia and
France were "united by history and geography in an indis-
soluble community of interests," he told the French people.
In December Stalin entertained de Gaulle with his best
"vodka diplomacy" and agreed to sign with the French a
treaty of alliance. But Stalin proved to be a noncommittal
listener when de Gaulle presented his request for the Rhine,
and he hastened to inform Churchill and Roosevelt that no

1949), 29–30; United States Senate, 83rd Congress, 1st Session, *Hearings before
the Committee on Foreign Relations: Nomination of Charles E. Bohlen, March
2, and 18, 1953* (Washington, 1953), 7, 116; *Yalta Papers*, 174; Philip E. Mosely,
"Dismemberment of Germany: The Allied Negotiations from Yalta to Potsdam," *Foreign Affairs*, XXVIII (July, 1950), 491.

[18] Herbert Luethy (transl. by Eric Mosbacher), *France against Herself* (New
York, 1955), 340; *Yalta Papers*, 303.

bargains had been struck at Moscow. But, all in all, it looked as though Stalin had won a loyal supporter in Charles de Gaulle—if he wanted him.[19]

The French on the eve of Yalta used their position in the European Advisory Commission to clarify formally their immediate postwar desires in Germany. Upon learning of the tripartite zonal plan for Germany, the French requested that it be revised to acknowledge their own Great Power pretensions and immediate interests in Germany. France should be allowed to participate in the signing of the German surrender document, and a French text should be equally as authentic as those in Russian and English; France should be allocated a zone of occupation in western Germany and a zone in Berlin; France should also share in the central Allied control authority in Germany. When it learned unofficially that the Yalta meeting was in the offing, the provisional government of France on January 13, 1945, formally and strongly requested the right to meet with "the other great allied powers," and the de Gaulle government hinted that it might not be bound by decisions affecting Germany which were made in its absence. The French desire to meet with the Big Three was not honored, but, upon recommendation of the Department of State, the President "approved in principle" the French desire to participate in the occupation of Germany.[20]

Meanwhile, Hitler's Reich was showing signs of desperate vigor amidst decay. German forces withdrew under the attacks from east and west, and there were growing signs of weakness within the Reich. On July 20, 1944, the Resistance rose against the fanatical tyrant who ruled Germany. The brutality with which the revolt was put down only intensified the loathing of the Nazi regime among the Allies, and the fact that the revolt occurred at all was a sign of weakness which encouraged the Allies to formulate and insist upon harsh

[19] C. H. Pegg, "Die Resistance als Träger der europäischer Einigungsbestrebungen in Frankreich während des zweiten Weltkrieges," *Europa-Archiv* (Cologne), VII (October 5, 1952), 5197–5206; Churchill, *Triumph and Tragedy*, 258–59; *Yalta Papers*, 219–21, 289, 307. On French aims in postwar Germany see also *Yalta Papers*, 299–300 and 956–57.

[20] *Yalta Papers*, 293–98.

terms of peace.[21] Signs of economic weakness in Hitler's Reich also multiplied in the summer and fall of 1944. Aircraft production reached the highest level of the entire war in September, but insufficient fuel was available to keep the *Luftwaffe* in the air. Tank production slumped seriously during the fall months.[22]

Though conditions were bad, hope and fear still helped greatly to hold together the Hitlerian empire. The hope was that the "strange alliance" would fall apart,[23] and German fear fed upon news of the Morgenthau plan. Even Germans who hated Hitler were horrified by the prospects which the Morgenthau plan opened before them; to many of these the plan seemed "equal to Hitler's own nihilistic fanaticism." What the British, Americans, Bolsheviks, and "international Jews" wanted was clear, Hitler told the German people in his New Year's message: "The complete ripping apart of the German Reich, the uprooting of 15 or 20 million Germans and transport abroad, the enslavement of the rest of our people, the ruination of our German youth, but, above all, the starvation of our masses."[24]

When these words were written, Hitler had already seized

---

[21] John W. Wheeler-Bennett, *The Nemesis of Power: The German Army in Politics, 1918–1945* (New York, 1954), 635–702; Georges Blond (transl. by Frances Frenaye), *The Death of Hitler's Germany* (New York, 1954), 23, 35, 40, 53; Alan Bullock, *Hitler: A Study in Tyranny* (New York, 1953), 672–89. On Hitler's personality and entourage in this period see H. R. Trevor-Roper, *The Last Days of Hitler* (New York, 1947), *passim*. See also Karl O. Paetel, "Der 20. Juli 1944 und das Ausland," *Aussenpolitik* (Stuttgart), V (July, 1954), 438–48.

[22] Pogue, *The Supreme Command*, 246–47; Chester Wilmot, *The Struggle for Europe* (New York, 1952), 554–56; Wilhelm Treue und Günther Frede, *Wirtschaft und Politik 1933–1945* (Braunschweig, 1953), 54–64; Arnold and Veronica M. Toynbee (eds.), *Hitler's Europe* (London, 1954), 186–98; Percy Ernst Schramm, "Die Treibstoff-Frage von Herbst 1943 bis Juni 1944 nach dem Kriegstagebuch des Wehrmachtführungsstabes," in *Mensch und Staat in Recht und Geschichte: Festschrift für Herbert Kraus* (Kitzingen/Main, 1954), 394–421.

[23] Wilmot, *The Struggle for Europe*, 444–45, 578; Pogue, *The Supreme Command*, 249; and see cartoon, Berlin *Völkischer Beobachter*, October 4, 1944.

[24] Berlin *Völkischer Beobachter*, September 26, 30; October 7, 25; and November 14, 1944; Wilmot, *The Struggle for Europe*, 549–50; Bullock, *Hitler*, 693–94; Pogue, *The Supreme Command*, 342; Paul Schmid, *Statist auf diplomatischer Bühne 1923–1945* (Bonn, 1950), 571; Munich *Völkischer Beobachter*, January 2, 27, 1945.

upon the new morale of the German people in order to prepare countermeasures against the Allied military advances.
On the morning of December 16 the Germans struck out of
an icy fog that embraced the sharp hills of the Ardennes like
a halo; the "Battle of the Bulge" was on. For a time the *Wehrmacht* seemed to be irresistible, and the drive engendered
great enthusiasm among the German troops. "We're smoking
American cigarettes and eating American chocolate," one
exuberant infantryman wrote home. But the German drive
was checked two days before Christmas, and on January 9
Hitler ordered a general withdrawal. The "Battle of the
Bulge" cast deep gloom over the West for a time, though by
January 31, on the eve of Yalta, the Anglo-American forces
had regained the positions they had held that awful morning
six weeks before.

One can only speculate about the possible effects upon the
Yalta bargaining in February if Eisenhower's forces had continued their advance into western Germany unchecked in
December and January. As the Yalta conference began, Marshal Stalin confidently—and perhaps pointedly—informed
Roosevelt that the Red Army already held the Silesian industrial complex, and he told Churchill on February 4 that the
Oder River was no longer an obstacle to the Red Army, since
several bridgeheads had already been established and the
German defense was not distinguished. At that time British
and American troops huddled with frozen feet in the snowy
lines which they had just regained after Hitler's December
offensive. But the reality of the December setback should not
disguise the fact that the actual Anglo-American military
power on the continent of Europe was much greater than it
had been in the fall, and this was reflected in the Yalta discussions of the future of Germany. One more fact was clear by
February, 1945: the Nazi *Machtstaat,* of 1938–44 was becoming a power vacuum, slowly but surely. Hitler's refusal to
recognize this reality was only one of his many betrayals of
the interests of Germany.[25]

[25] Wilmot, *The Struggle for Europe,* 575–631; Pogue, *The Supreme Command,* 359–72; *Yalta Papers,* 478–80, 503–504, and 577–88; Blond, *The Death
of Hitler's Germany,* 95–174; Stettinius, *Roosevelt and the Russians,* 304;

YALTA: SUBDUED SHOWDOWN

On January 25 Stettinius and the State Department delegation left Washington by plane for the Crimea conference, reaching the island of Malta in time for conferences with Anthony Eden before the President arrived. At Malta Stettinius informed Eden that the President "was disposed to give France" a zone of occupation in Germany, and he suggested that one might be created out of the southern part of the British zone and the northern part of the American zone. It was agreed that the British and the Americans at Yalta should seek Russian approval of these proposed changes. It was also agreed that France should be integrated into the control machinery over Germany by representation on the proposed inter-Allied Control Council for Germany as a whole. In these pre-Yalta Anglo-American talks Eden frankly voiced his concern about the power of the colossal host who would greet them at Yalta. Eden and Stettinius agreed to limit, if possible, the expansion of Poland at the expense of Germany. Thus, though efforts were made both before and during the Yalta conference to reassure the Russians that they were not confronted by a hostile Anglo-American bloc, it is clear that the British and American diplomats worked out certain problems of teamwork before going to Yalta, and this co-ordination of strategy was to be reflected in the Crimea discussions.[26]

Meanwhile, during the voyage to Malta, the President had rested and had continued his preparations for the Big Three meeting. By the time he arrived at Malta, and throughout the conferences there and in the Crimea, Roosevelt was mentally alert, though physically not well, and he was familiar with the problems that would arise at Yalta. Upon arriving at Malta, Roosevelt met with Churchill, Eden, and Stettinius to

---

Millis (ed.), *The Forrestal Diaries,* 21; Churchill, *Triumph and Tragedy,* 348, 402; William D. Leahy, *I Was There* (New York, London, and Toronto, 1950), 293; Deutscher, *Stalin,* 524; Sherwood, *Roosevelt and Hopkins,* 851. The Nazi press used the German advances in December to reawaken German morale. See Berlin *Völkischer Beobachter,* December 19–28, 1944.

26 Stimson and Bundy, *On Active Service,* 586–87; Stettinius, *Roosevelt and the Russians,* 30, 35, 67; *Yalta Papers,* 498–514, 546.

hear Eden and Stettinius report informally on their discussions of the previous day. Furthermore, before the first meeting of the Big Three at Yalta, State Department officials specifically reviewed for the President the papers which the department had prepared for his use.[27]

Roosevelt and Churchill arrived at Yalta on February 3. At his staff meeting in the morning of February 4 the President learned that the Russians wanted to open the political discussions at Yalta with the problem of Germany. Later that day Marshal Stalin further revealed his preoccupation with the German problem when he greeted the President before the first plenary session.[28] Thus the question of Germany became the first of the great issues to be discussed at Yalta, intruding into a social call even before the plenary sessions began. Stalin was still intent upon ruining Germany. A few months before Yalta he had told the Polish leader Stanislaw Mikolajczyk that communism would fit Germany like "a saddle fitted a cow."[29] This being the case, there seemed nothing to do but butcher the cow.

Dismemberment Postponed

Stalin reminded his colleagues on February 5, the second day of the conference, that they had informally favored the dismemberment of Germany at Teheran, and asked if they still adhered to that principle. "Hasn't the time come for a decision?" he asked. "If you think so, let us make one." He reaffirmed his willingness to accept the kind of partition which Churchill had favored informally, the creation of a north German state, a south German state including Austria, and an internationalized Ruhr and Saar.

[27] James F. Byrnes, *Speaking Frankly* (New York, 1947), 23; Leahy, *I Was There*, 292–93; Stettinius, *Roosevelt and the Russians*, 74; *Yalta Papers*, 567. For comments on Roosevelt's health during the Yalta conference, see Edward J. Flynn, *You're the Boss* (New York, 1947), 188; W. Averell Harriman's 1951 statement in the United States Senate, 82nd Congress, 1st Session, *Military Situation in the Far East: Hearings before the Committee on Armed Services and the Committee on Foreign Relations* (Washington, 1951), Part V, Appendix, 3330; Leahy, *I Was There*, 290; Stettinius, *Roosevelt and the Russians*, 73.

[28] Churchill, *Triumph and Tragedy*, 350; *Yalta Papers*, 566, 570–73.

[29] Deutscher, *Stalin*, 537.

Churchill himself assumed the chief burden of the argument at Yalta against any formal decision to dismember Germany. While agreeing "in principle" to dismemberment, he insisted that he could not commit himself to any definite plan for the dismemberment of Germany until much additional study of the problem could be undertaken. Churchill then tried to change the subject to the more immediate and less fateful question of French participation in the occupation of Germany. But Stalin stuck tenaciously to the question of partition, proposing that the Allies should state their intention to dismember Germany in the surrender document which Germany would sign.

It appeared, that a deadlock existed which could not be resolved, but Roosevelt, hitherto a silent observer, sought to moderate between his two obstinate colleagues. As on many similar occasions the President gave the appearance of supporting Stalin, while proposing action which benefited Churchill. He recalled his experiences as a student in Germany some forty years before Yalta, said that he still thought, as at Teheran, that the dismemberment (or *decentralization*) of Germany into five or seven states "was a good idea," and then suggested that the Big Three refer the matter to the foreign secretaries and ask them to bring in a plan for dismemberment within twenty-four hours. It appeared that the President was with Stalin. "You mean a plan for the *study* of the question," Churchill suggested. "Yes," replied Roosevelt, "for the study of dismemberment."

The effect was not lost upon the Soviet dictator. To salvage what he could of his original hopes, Stalin proposed that the Big Three commit themselves to (1) the principle of partition, (2) the creation of a special commission "to work out the details," and (3) inclusion in the surrender document of a clause calling for dismemberment. Roosevelt again looked for a compromise, saying that Stalin's desire to mention dismemberment in the surrender document was "somewhat my own." Churchill agreed to this, but balked at any attempt to make a binding decision regarding dismemberment. The foreign secretaries were then instructed to study the possi-

bility of including a dismemberment clause among the surrender terms.[30]

The foreign ministers considered their troublesome assignment on the following morning, February 6. Stettinius suggested that final decisions in the matter of dismemberment
would require "much research and study," but proposed that
the surrender document be revised to include the right to
dismember Germany among the other powers which the
Allies would exercise in the defeated Reich. Eden wanted to
provide only for "measures for the dissolution of the German
unitary state," but the Soviet Commissar for Foreign Affairs,
Vyacheslav M. Molotov, proposed a more binding commitment than that which Stettinius suggested.

That afternoon, after a luncheon conference between
Roosevelt and Churchill, the foreign secretaries reported to
the plenary meeting of the Big Three their agreement that
the word "dismemberment" should appear in the surrender
document and their inability to agree how definitely it should
be phrased. The temperature outside the former Romanov
palace was a crisp forty degrees and a log fire blazed in the
great fireplace at the far end of the large hall in which the
plenary meetings were held; Churchill's cheeks reflected the
cozy glow of the fire, and his horn-rimmed glasses slowly and
recurrently slipped down his nose; Stalin sat shrouded in
impassiveness and the high collar of a khaki uniform, his
tunic's drabness relieved by a single decoration. The setting
was congenial. Molotov withdrew his proposal to make the
clause more specific. Churchill indicated that he had not had
an opportunity to secure the approval of the War Cabinet
for the Stettinius proposal, but accepted it "on behalf of the
British Government." The foreign secretaries were again left
to wrangle over the exact wording of the clause and to provide some mechanism for the study of the dismemberment
problem.

At this stage the Russians apparently decided that they had
won as specific a decision on partition as they would be likely
to get at Yalta. When the foreign ministers met again on the
morning of February 7 Molotov was the embodiment of con-

[30] *Yalta Papers,* 611–16, 625–28; Byrnes, *Speaking Frankly,* 25–26.

ciliation. The foreign ministers decided that the problem should be examined in London by a committee which would include Eden himself, United States Ambassador John Gilbert Winant, and Fedor T. Gusev, the Soviet ambassador to Britain. The task of drafting a clause for the surrender document was delegated to a special Yalta committee made up of Andrei Vyshinsky, Sir Alexander Cadogan, and H. Freeman Matthews. The wording these men developed was included in the protocol of agreements which Stettinius, Molotov, and Eden signed on February 11. The revised clause now read as follows:

> The United Kingdom, the United States of America and the Union of Soviet Socialist Republics shall possess supreme authority with respect to Germany. In the exercise of such authority they will take such steps, including the complete disarmament, demilitarisation and the dismemberment of Germany *as they deem requisite* for future peace and security. [Author's italics.]

Five days earlier Molotov had opposed the inclusion of the phrase "as they deem requisite"; its appearance in the protocol left the partition issue almost as muddled as it had been before Yalta. The Russians could console themselves with the knowledge that the surrender text would include the word "dismemberment," but this should not obscure the more important fact that the plans for partition, so boldly discussed at previous informal meetings, were postponed when first considered formally by the Big Three. The clause was bound to disappoint not only Stalin but such active supporters of partition as Henry Morgenthau.[31]

Deindustrialization Through Reparations Delayed

At the very beginning of the Yalta conference the Russians raised the combined questions of reparations and deindustrialization. As it became apparent to them that they might not be able to eliminate German power through permanent partition, they argued all the more fervently and tenaciously —throughout the entire conference—that they be allowed to

[31] *Yalta Papers*, 655–60, 699–709, 936, 978; Stettinius, *Roosevelt and the Russians*, 138.

strengthen their own country and weaken their enemy by a reparations policy which would in large part deindustrialize Germany. With these interrelated policy demands, Molotov coupled yet another on February 5: Russian economic gains from Germany should be discussed in connection with the Russian request for long-term credits from the United States. In the language of diplomacy he was saying in effect: give us credits to buy equipment in America or allow us to take the sinews of industry from the Germans. As "dollar diplomacy" won concessions from Churchill at Quebec, it threatened to win concessions from the West at Yalta.[32]

The Russian interest in reparations was difficult to oppose, for the U.S.S.R. had suffered heavily at the hands of the Germans during the war. Russian estimates have claimed that the U.S.S.R. suffered direct losses of as high as $128,000,000,000 as a result of the German invasion. While this figure is undoubtedly exaggerated, the Russians could state with complete honesty at Yalta that "even direct losses . . . had been so large that no reparations could cover their loss."[33] Yet the British and the Americans put up a stiffer fight on the reparations questions than on the dismemberment issue. The western statesmen were willing to concede that certain key industries should be eliminated, but the President spoke for the others when he insisted that it was impossible to discuss the amount of reparations to be demanded of Germany until "the Allies discovered what was left of Germany after the war." Anglo-American strategy on this question, too, was to seek postponement.[34]

The Russians presented their scheme for reparations and the deindustrialization of Germany at the plenary meeting of February 5. Stalin was flanked by Molotov on one side and the Deputy Commissar for Foreign Affairs, I. M. Maisky, on

[32] *Yalta Papers,* 609–10; Sherwood, *Roosevelt and Hopkins,* 853.

[33] Karl Brandt, Otto Schiller, and Franz Ahlgrimm, *Management of Agriculture and Food in the German-Occupied and Other Areas of Fortress Europe: A Study in Military Government* (Stanford, 1953), 148; Arnold and Veronica M. Toynbee (eds.), *Hitler's Europe,* 632–48; and F. Lee Benns, *Europe since 1914 in Its World Setting* (8th ed.; New York, 1954), 638–39; *Yalta Papers,* 620.

[34] Byrnes, *Speaking Frankly,* 26; Stettinius, *Roosevelt and the Russians,* 41, 230–31.

the other, and at about seven o'clock in the evening he explained that the Russians had worked out a plan for reparations in kind, which he asked Maisky to present. Maisky delivered his report "in a forceful manner" and it was clear to the Americans that he had "the full support of Stalin and Molotov." He was greatly aided by the fact that the essential elements of his proposals had already been advanced by the Secretary of the Treasury of the United States and accepted in principle by Roosevelt and Churchill in the Quebec memorandum of September 15.[35]

The Soviet proposals called for two types of reparations, said Maisky: (1) removal of German heavy industry and (2) annual payments in kind from current production. Sounding more like Morgenthau every minute, Maisky explained that by "heavy industry" he meant "iron and steel, electrical power and chemical industries." Specialized industries which were useful only for military purposes (such as military aviation and the production of synthetic petroleum) should be "100% removed" from Germany. Furthermore, the Allies should "withdraw" 80 per cent of *all* German heavy industry, and Maisky again pointedly clarified his terminology: by "withdraw" he meant "to confiscate and carry away physically." The withdrawals were to be accomplished within two years after the end of hostilities. Reparations in kind would be collected from current German production over a period of ten years. Even beyond this period the three Allies would control the German economy, maintaining British, American, and Russian representatives on the boards of directors of all German enterprises which "could be" utilized for war purposes.

Material taken from Germany under the two types of reparations would be divided, said Maisky, in accordance with two priority indices, both of which would guarantee Russia the wolf's share: "(1) the proportional contribution of any one nation to the winning of the war, and (2) the material losses suffered by each nation." The Big Three should create an inter-Allied Reparations Commission, which would meet in Moscow. This commission, according to Maisky's

---

[35] Byrnes, *Speaking Frankly*, 26; Stettinius, *Roosevelt and the Russians*, 130.

proposal, would be left only to administer the reparations program, not to define policy; for Maisky immediately informed the assembled diplomats that "the total reparations shown in withdrawals and yearly payments in kind which the Soviets required would reach a total of ten billion dollars."

Churchill was the first to speak after Maisky had completed his presentation of the Soviet proposal. Tactfully, the Prime Minister recognized "that the suffering which the Soviet Union had undergone in this war had been greater than any other power." But he recalled the reparations debacle that had followed World War I and said that he believed the Soviet Union "would get nowhere near the sum which Mr. Maisky had mentioned from Germany." He reminded the Soviet delegation that "Belgium, Holland and Norway also had claims against Germany." Finally, he stated frankly that he was "haunted by the specter of a starving Germany, which would present a serious problem for the Allies." "If eighty millions are starving are we to say, 'It serves you right'?" Churchill asked. If not, he wanted to know who was "to pay for feeding them?" With a sharp reference to Soviet demands for annual payments in kind, Churchill remarked that if one "wished a horse to pull a wagon" one must at least "give it fodder." Stalin agreed, but revealed his quick wit in his short retort: "Care should be taken to see that the horse did not turn around and kick you."

The President now recalled that the United States had, by loans to Germany, really financed the reparations program of the twenties. This time, Roosevelt added, "we would not repeat our past mistakes." The President readily offered to support Russian claims for reparations, but quickly qualified his gallantry:

> I envision a Germany that is self-sustaining but not starving. There will be no lending of money. Our objective is seeing that Germany will not starve in helping the Soviet get all it can in manpower and factories and helping the British get all they can in exports to former German markets. Therefore, the time has come to set up a reparations commission. In re-building we must get all we can but we can't get it all. Leave Germany enough industry and work to keep her from starving.

Once again the President thus sought to retain harmony by implementing his policy of postponement. But Maisky had prepared not only a brief but a rebuttal; he argued that Germany could "develop her light industry and agriculture and that since the Germans would have no military expenditures there was no reason why Germany could not give a modest but decent standard of living to her people." Churchill sought at this point to turn the Russian flank by endorsing Roosevelt's policy of postponement. He approved the idea of a Reparations Commission and proposed that such a commission should consider the claims of other countries which had felt the impact of Nazi aggression. Even more significantly, he stated that differences which might arise in the commission "must be referred to and settled by the three governments." Thus this proposal, while immediately postponing the issue, would also make it possible for any one of the Big Three to veto any other's demands in the Reparations Commission in Moscow.

Stalin sought to salvage his reparations dreams by proposing that the Big Three agree at Yalta upon general directives to the Reparations Commission. He repeated that the three Great Powers should "have first claim on reparations," and added in a way that would have deeply wounded de Gaulle that he saw no need for reparations for France, "since she had suffered less than Belgium, Yugoslavia, or Poland." Stalin then suggested that the three foreign secretaries try to work out a set of directives to the proposed Reparations Commission. Churchill and Roosevelt agreed, and the meeting ended after four hours of tactful haggling, with Churchill insisting that reparations should be allotted according to damage suffered, not by extent of war effort against Germany. He urged Stalin to remember the slogan of nineteenth-century socialism: to "each according to his needs." [36]

In a meeting of the foreign secretaries on February 7, Molotov modified Maisky's proposals of February 5 in one most significant respect: his draft of instructions to the Reparations Commission continued to speak of the total dollar

[36] Byrnes, *Speaking Frankly*, 26; Stettinius, *Roosevelt and the Russians*, 168; *Yalta Papers*, 620–23, 630–33.

value of reparations which the U.S.S.R. desired, but contained no provision that 80 per cent of all German heavy industry should either be destroyed or taken away from Germany. Nonetheless, the foreign secretaries reached little agreement in their meetings of February 7–9.[37] On the latter date Stettinius agreed that the Russian figure of ten billion dollars might serve as a "basis for discussion" in the Reparations Commission, but Eden held firmly against this.[38] In his efforts to weaken the obstinate British Foreign Secretary, Maisky weakened the concession he had gotten from Stettinius by stating on February 10 that the proposed Russo-American draft "did not commit the Allies to the exact figure."[39] But Eden was not to be moved. Later that day he submitted in writing the British proposal on reparations. It altered the Russian draft in several ways, among others in insisting that the levy on German capital equipment should be made to destroy "the war potential of Germany," not, as the broader Soviet draft had proposed, "chiefly for the purpose of military and economic disarmament of Germany." The impasse of the foreign secretaries was not broken when the next plenary session was held.

The discussion of reparations was "lengthy and at times somewhat heated" during this plenary meeting of February 10. In one more day the conference would end, and the Russians still had gained little satisfaction in their demands concerning Germany. Eden reported that the British still had reservations on the Russian proposals, and then Churchill moved his heaviest fieldpiece into position: he had received instructions from his War Cabinet in London "not to mention figures." Roosevelt then indecisively drew up on Churchill's flank: if any figures were mentioned, he said, "the American people would believe that it involved money."

According to the minutes taken at Yalta by H. Freeman Matthews, this was "the only time during the conference that Stalin showed some annoyance." This is verified by Stettinius: "Stalin . . . spoke with great emotion. . . . On several occasions

[37] *Yalta Papers,* 702–704, 707–708.
[38] *Ibid.,* 709, 738, 802–16, 843–44, 859.
[39] *Ibid.,* 874–80.

he arose, stepped behind his chair, and spoke from that position, gesturing to emphasize his points. . . . Although he did
not orate or even raise his voice, he spoke with intensity." If
"the British felt that the Russians should receive no reparations at all," said Stalin, "it would be better to say so frankly."
When Churchill emphatically denied this, Stalin urged the
conference to make two decisions in the matter: "(1) that it
was agreed in principle that Germany should pay reparations
and (2) that the Reparations Commission to sit in Moscow
should fix the amount and should take into consideration the
American-Soviet proposal that there should be twenty billion
dollars of reparations, with fifty per cent to the Soviet Union."
But Stalin moderated the Russian claim by adding that the
proposed figure of ten billion dollars was simply to be used
as "a basis for discussions—it could be reduced or increased
by the Commission in Moscow."

At this point, to break the deadlock, Hopkins passed a note
to Roosevelt suggesting the President say that the whole matter should be referred to the Reparations Commission, "with
the minutes to show the British disagree about any mention
of the 10 billion." The President followed this suggestion, but
the British continued to oppose the specification of any figure,
even by the Americans and Russians, in the instructions to
the Reparations Commission. At this point Stalin gave way—
or seemed to give way. He proposed that the Big Three directive should merely instruct the Moscow commission "to consider the amount of reparations." "We bring our figures,"
Stalin told Churchill, "and you bring yours." Churchill agreed
and turned to the President: "How about the United States?"
"The answer is simple," the President replied, "Judge Roosevelt approves and the document is accepted." The Big Three
then took a most timely intermission, which marked another diplomatic concession by the Russians. It seemed that
Churchillian obstinacy had paid off.[40]

But the Russians were not yet ready to admit defeat in
their efforts to present specific figures in the directive to the
Reparations Commission. At dinner that evening Stalin re-

---

[40] *Ibid.,* 885, 901–903, 909–16, 920; Stettinius, *Roosevelt and the Russians,*
263–67; Sherwood, *Roosevelt and Hopkins,* 861 ff.

turned to the matter in conversation with the Prime Minister, emphasizing "the unsatisfactory nature of the reparations question at the conference." The master of the Russians then told Churchill that he "feared to have to go back to the Soviet Union and tell the Soviet people that they were not going to get any reparations because the British were opposed to it." Was this a muted threat or a grim jest? Churchill of course insisted that he hoped Russia would receive "reparations in large quantities." And one final crumb of compromise fell to the Russians from this last Yalta dinner. It was agreed that instructions to the Reparations Commission should state that "the Soviet Union and the United States believed that the Reparations Commission should take as a basis of discussion the figure of reparations as twenty billion dollars and fifty per cent of these should go to the Soviet Union." But these instructions also included as a statement of purpose the proposal which Eden had introduced, "to destroy the German war potential," not the Soviet statement, "for the purpose of military and economic disarmament of Germany."[41] (The final statement on reparations was included in the protocol of the conference, which is reproduced in the Appendix to this volume).

All in all, the reparations decisions at Yalta constituted a thinly disguised defeat for the Russians and a clear-cut rejection of the Morgenthau plan and the Quebec agreement of September, 1944. Nor was there any compensating assurance to the Russians that they would obtain postwar credits in the United States; by agreeing to Stalin's figure as "a basis of discussion," the Americans had successfully sidetracked the Soviet movement for American aid. Once again the policy of postponement had triumphed, and with it, at least temporarily, the policies of the Department of State and of moderation toward Germany.

Postponement of Territorial Limitations

The cup of Soviet disappointment had been filled a little higher, meanwhile, in the discussion of possible reductions

[41] *Yalta Papers,* 921–22, 937, 978–79; Stettinius, *Roosevelt and the Russians,* 274.

in the territory of Germany. Stalin raised the question of the future of the Ruhr and the Saar in the plenary session of February 5, in connection with his proposal to partition Germany. At Moscow in October Stalin and Churchill had informally agreed that these industrial areas should be separated from Germany and placed under international control, but at Yalta Churchill retreated from his earlier position. He was now uncertain whether they should be "handed over to a country like France," be made independent, remain a part of Germany, or be placed under the trusteeship of the world organization. "All this," the Prime Minister said, required careful study, "and the British Government had not yet any fixed ideas on the subject." Churchill terminated this discussion of a reduction of German territory in the west with the statement that he did not "feel it possible to discuss possible frontiers." Another victory for postponement was thus won.[42]

Discussion of Germany's eastern frontier was much more prolonged, but also ended indefinitely and in a way disappointing to the U.S.S.R. Again, it was Stalin who took the initiative, proposing on February 6 that Poland's future frontier should be extended westward to include the German territory east of the Western Neisse and Oder rivers. (See map, p. 71.) This proposed change would separate from Germany not only East Prussia but also a sizeable slice of Pomerania, including Stettin, and Silesia, including Breslau. The Soviet proposal would place some eight million Germans under Polish rule or cause them to be uprooted and transferred to the German rump state (or states) which would survive the defeat. Since much of the eastern territory was already controlled by the Red Army and the rest would soon be under its occupation, the West had no strong position from which to argue this issue. Yet it had been decided in advance that any such sweeping proposals should be opposed, and on February 7 Churchill expressed his conciliatory opposition. He "would always support the movement of Polish frontiers to the west," but he cautioned against giving the Polish nation more German territory than it could handle. Anticipating Stalin's suggestion that the Germans could be moved out of

[42] *Yalta Papers*, 612–25.

the exchanged areas, Churchill observed that British public opinion would "be shocked if it were proposed to move large numbers of Germans." To this Marshal Stalin replied in truthful cynicism that "most Germans in those areas had already run away from the Red Army." The plenary meeting was soon adjourned and the issue was thus postponed for another day.

Roosevelt, in an attempt to achieve compromise in this problem, agreed on February 8 to recognize the westward expansion of Poland's frontier to the Oder River (a territorial change which would affect some 4,500,000 Germans), but the President simultaneously indicated that *"there would appear to be little justification for extending it up to the Western Neisse."*[43] The problem of Germany's eastern frontier again arose on February 10, when Churchill agreed, as had Roosevelt, to grant German territory east of the Oder to the Poles, if they wanted it. But the Prime Minister indicated that this was as far as he was prepared to go. Roosevelt suggested that they should consult the new Polish government before making any public statement about the frontier, and he soon added: "I have no right to make an agreement on boundaries at this time. That must be done by the Senate later." Later in the evening the conference approved a British-American draft for a public statement which would simply declare that Poland "must receive substantial accessions of territory in the North and West," and that the final delimitation of the German-Polish frontier should "await the Peace Conference."

Molotov made one last effort to salvage success for the Russians, however. Seeing that no specific agreement was to be reached, he proposed that the conference agree to promise Poland the return of "her ancient frontiers in East Prussia and on the Oder." The Russian was then chastised by a flurry of western wit. Roosevelt asked how long ago these areas had been Polish. Very long ago, Molotov replied, but he added, dead serious, that "they had in fact been Polish." The President then suggested laughingly that on historical grounds Churchill might "ask for the return of the United States to

[43] *Ibid.*, 669, 716-21, 776. The italicized words are Churchill's: *Triumph and Tragedy*, 377.

Great Britain." Churchill took his cue and quipped back to his friend that the United States "might be as indigestible for us as it might be for the Poles if they took too much German territory." Molotov persisted for awhile, but finally Stalin intervened to "withdraw the Soviet amendment" and accept the Anglo-American draft on the German-Polish frontier.[44] (See page 215.)

Thus there were no decisions at Yalta regarding the future frontiers of Germany. The Russians did not present their demand for Königsberg, and, faced by the combined opposition of Roosevelt and Churchill, they gave up their efforts to define Germany's frontier with Poland. The West and the policy of postponement won an unexpectedly easy victory at Yalta in these frontier questions. But it was only a legal vacuum that the Yalta discussions left, and the Soviet leaders probably did not make another determined effort to fill it because they knew that the power vacuum in eastern Europe was already being filled by the Red Army.

War Criminals

For two years before the Yalta conference informal discussions of the treatment of German war criminals had been held among the Allies, sometimes in a highly frivolous manner. In October, 1943, a formal statement known as the Moscow Declaration threatened dire punishment to the offenders, but there had been no definite decision for action since that statement was issued. It was Churchill who raised the question at Yalta. Stating that the Moscow Declaration was "an egg that he had laid himself," the Prime Minister proposed on February 9 that the Big Three at Yalta draw up a list of the major criminals, those whose crimes had no specific locus. Churchill first stated that "they should be shot once their identity is established," but he quickly added that they should be "given a judicial trial." Stalin agreed. But there was no time at Yalta to draft a list of names such as Churchill had suggested, and virtually no more discussion of the matter occurred during the conference. The final agreements, as embraced in the protocol of the conference, simply stated

[44] *Yalta Papers*, 897–913, 980.

that "the question of major war criminals should be the subject of enquiry by the three Foreign Secretaries for report in
due course after the close of the Conference." On one more
matter moderation seemed to have won out at Yalta, though
it was modestly covered by the camisole which postponement
provided.[45]

France and Four-Power Control

Partition, deindustrialization, territorial reduction, and the
trial of war criminals were all matters which could await the
end of hostilities, but the occupation of Germany had to be
planned in advance of victory. The question of zones of
occupation was, on the other hand, of more than short-term
importance, as events have shown. The present *de facto* partition of Germany rests upon the zonal division, not upon
any formal decision of the wartime Allies to dismember Germany. The power-political potentialities of the zonal arrangements were not naïvely ignored by Roosevelt and others at
Yalta, as has been suggested. At the very outset of the discussion Stalin asked whether the Big Three should create one
occupation government or "three separate governments for
the various parts of Germany." At this same meeting Roosevelt revealed his awareness of the implications of occupation
when he remarked that "as he understood it, the permanent
treatment of Germany might grow out of the question of the
zones of occupation, although the two were not directly connected."[46] Not because they ignored the realities of power
politics, but specifically because they acknowledged them,
Roosevelt and Churchill attached great importance to plans
for the joint occupation of Germany under an inter-Allied
Control Council.

One matter was easy to decide, because the preliminary
negotiations had been thorough and it did not involve Soviet
interests: final approval was given at Yalta to the Anglo-
American zonal arrangement which had been tentatively approved at Quebec. With this done, determination of the part
France should play in the occupation of Germany became the

45 *Ibid.*, 849–50, 938, 979.
46 *Ibid.*, 612.

major remaining occupation issue at Yalta. Its discussion
brought out very fully Churchill's concern over the balance
of power in Europe and the Russian fear that a western bloc
of anti-Soviet states might be in the making. The issue was
twofold: (1) was France to have a zone of occupation? and
(2) was France to be given membership on the inter-Allied
Control Council for Germany as a whole? The first of these
questions proved easier to answer. On both questions Roosevelt overcame his personal antipathy toward contemporary
France to cast his vote against Stalin, and the result was a
positive victory for the West even more impressive than the
victories which had been won through the negative policy
of postponement.

Churchill was the first of the Big Three to state categorically that France should be given a zone of occupation,
though Roosevelt had himself tentatively sounded Stalin on
the matter in a private conference on February 4. At Malta
Stettinius had suggested to Eden that a zone for France might
be carved out of the British and American zones, but it was
Churchill, not Roosevelt, who made the suggestion at Yalta
that the French territory should "come out of the British and
possible the American zones." He especially emphasized the
fact that the zone for France "would not in any way affect
the proposed Soviet zone." Churchill, afraid that American
troops would soon either return home or go to the Far East
after the defeat of Germany, wanted French forces to be on
the Rhine with his own when that time came.

Stalin first balked at the idea, suggesting that to grant
France a zone would create "a precedent for other states."
Warily, he asked if a French zone of occupation would not
call for four-power integrated control of Germany instead of
the tripartite Allied Control Council which had been proposed before the trip to Yalta. Roosevelt approved giving
France a zone of occupation, but he questioned the desirability of admitting France to the Allied Control Council.
Stalin, overlooking his own conduct in 1939–41, argued that
France had "opened the gate to the enemy" in 1940 and had
"contributed little to this war." But Churchill, ever so tactfully, reminded the Soviet leader that "every nation had had

their difficulties in the beginning of the war and had made mistakes." Stalin then agreed that France could be "given a zone within the British and American zones," and with that the first question concerning France was settled at Yalta.[47] (See map, p. 71.) Stalin in the same breath indicated that a long fight lay ahead before the second question could be answered. "I am still against France taking part in the control machinery," he stated in his calm, deliberate fashion. Roosevelt at this point suggested postponement of the discussion of control machinery and agreed with Stalin that France should not take part in the Control Council. But Eden and Churchill "fought like tigers for France," as Harry Hopkins noted, and a complete impasse resulted.[48]

The President himself eventually settled this issue in favor of France. Probably Roosevelt genuinely meant it when, early in the conference, he remarked that he would be "just as satisfied if the French are not in on the control machinery." Possibly because of Soviet intransigence in the Polish problem, possibly because of the strong advice of Hopkins, Harriman, and Byrnes, Roosevelt was won over to French participation. The President abruptly changed his stand in the plenary meeting of February 10. He simply stated that he had "changed his mind." He now agreed with Churchill that it would be impossible to give the French a zone of occupation "unless they were members of the Control Commission." The President's words seemed to have a magical effect upon the Russians, who ceased their opposition with all the suddenness of Roosevelt's shift in position. As Stettinius related: "The Marshal replied to the President's announcement with just two words: 'I agree'."[49]

Thus it was that France began her frustrating efforts to climb back to Great Power status at the expense of her ancient enemy and with the support of Britain and the United States. Within a few months de Gaulle would show his appreciation

[47] *Ibid.*, 616–18, 628–29; Stettinius, *Roosevelt and the Russians*, 63.

[48] *Yalta Papers*, 618–19, 629–33, 701–710, 718–19; Sherwood, *Roosevelt and Hopkins*, 858.

[49] *Yalta Papers*, 629, 899–900, 936–37, 978. See also Byrnes, *Speaking Frankly*, 25; Sherwood, *Roosevelt and Hopkins*, 858–59; Leahy, *I Was There*, 301–302.

to the West by following a German policy which caused no end of grief for his western patrons.

GERMANY AND THE MEANING OF YALTA

Some of the Yalta decisions affecting Germany were summarized in a press report on February 12. This public proclamation embraced certain decisions on which there was such general agreement that they required little or no discussion at Yalta; it included other statements which camouflaged the extent of the Soviet retreat on German matters at Yalta. In it the Big Three announced:

It is our inflexible purpose to destroy German militarism and Nazism and to ensure that Germany will never again be able to disturb the peace of the world. We are determined to disarm and disband all German armed forces; break up for all time the German General Staff that has repeatedly contrived the resurgence of German militarism; remove or destroy all German military equipment; eliminate or control all German industry that could be used for military production; bring all war criminals to just and swift punishment and exact reparation in kind for the destruction wrought by the Germans; wipe out the Nazi Party, Nazi laws, organizations and institutions, remove all Nazi and militarist influences from public office and from the cultural and economic life of the German people; and take in harmony such other measures in Germany as may be necessary to the future peace and safety of the world. It is not our purpose to destroy the people of Germany, but only when Nazism and militarism have been extirpated will there be hope for a decent life for Germans, and a place for them in the comity of nations.

In a moderate bid for German action to shorten the war, the Big Three proclaimed: "The German people, as well as the German soldiers, must realize that the sooner they give up and surrender, by groups or as individuals, the sooner their present agony will be over."[50]

This proclamation veiled the vast indecision of the great

---

[50] *Yalta Papers,* 969–71; United States, Department of State, *The Axis in Defeat, a Collection of Documents on American Policy toward Germany and Japan* (Washington, n.d.), 8–9.

OCCUPATION ZONES OF GERMANY AND AUSTRIA AS FINALLY ADOPTED

Boundaries of Zones ————
National Frontiers, 1937 ———

0   50   100   150   200

From Winston S. Churchill, *Triumph and Tragedy* (Boston, 1953).

Allies in questions concerning Germany. They could not agree, and as long as Germany fought on they could not afford to disagree. But the prospects of Germany's early collapse had brought the western statesmen face to face at last with the greatest European dilemma of the twentieth century: how can the threat of German power be eliminated from Europe without leaving Soviet power dominant throughout the continent? Therein lies the essential meaning of Yalta so far as Germany—and much of Europe—is concerned.

Roosevelt was no conscious advocate of the balance-of-power concept but, like other American statesmen since Wilson, he supported a principle which was its corollary: that it was not in the interest of the United States for any one state in Europe to dominate the whole. Churchill, on the other hand, consciously followed a balance-of-power policy in his negotiations with the Russians concerning the future of Germany. Thus it came about that the discussions of German questions at Yalta revealed beneath the verbiage of conciliation toward Russia the hard rock of Anglo-American solidarity and moderation toward Germany. The Russians failed to win full satisfaction on a single one of the demands they raised at Yalta concerning Germany's future.

The credits and debits of Yalta concerning the German problem read as follows: Stalin demanded a decision to dismember Germany; Churchill and Roosevelt postponed any specific plans, though they agreed in principle to the possibility of dismemberment. Stalin demanded a decision to deindustrialize Germany and rebuild the U.S.S.R. with German equipment; the President and the Prime Minister refused to agree to deindustrialization and postponed consideration of reparations. The Russians hoped that the western boundary of Poland might be drawn by Big Three agreement at the Western Neisse River and that the Ruhr and Saar would be separated from Germany; both Roosevelt and Churchill were opposed. The single set of demands concerning Germany which were met fully at Yalta were those which Roosevelt and Churchill advanced there: France was to have a zone of occupation and to participate in the integrated administration of Germany through the Control Council.

The positive material reconstruction of Germany was not desired at Yalta by any of the participants, nor could it possibly have been planned there; Roosevelt and Churchill avoided committing themselves to the permanent destruction of Germany only at the risk of alienating their Moscow colleague. This situation, so unfavorable for Germany, was of Germany's own creation. Adolf Hitler had sought to conquer Europe while posing as its savior against Bolshevism.[51] Hitler himself had offered Europe its choice of mistresses: Nazism or Bolshevism. But he had shown the opportunistic motivation of his egocentric ideology by outlawing his own nation against the western community. In February, 1945, it seemed certain that Europe would soon be rid of the ruthless and insatiable mistress whom Hitler had forced upon it; the era of German hegemony in European history was almost over, having been desperate in character but brief in duration. Was the second mistress which Hitler had offered, Russian communism, to be the only choice left after the debauchery into which Hitler had led Europe? This was the verdict of the Nazi newspaper *Völkischer Beobachter,* which headlined the Yalta communiqué as the "DEATH SENTENCE FOR EUROPE" and insisted that conference unity had been preserved only by the surrender of Roosevelt and Churchill to every demand Stalin raised.[52]

Ultimately a combination of American and British military and economic power broadened the choices facing Europe, but only after Germany and Japan were defeated and after it became crystal clear that Stalin thought in terms of the same two crude alternatives which Hitler had presented. In February, 1945, this was not fully apparent, and Hitler's Germany still held the Big Three together as it had made them "strange allies" in the first place. "We separated in the Crimea," Churchill has recalled, "not only as Allies but as friends facing a still mighty foe with whom all our armies were struggling in fierce and ceaseless battle."[53]

[51] Paul Kluke, "Nationalsozialistische Europaideologie," *Vierteljahrshefte für Zeitgeschichte* (Tübingen and Munich), III (July, 1955), 240–75.
[52] Munich *Völkischer Beobachter,* February 13–16, 1945.
[53] Churchill, *Triumph and Tragedy,* 510.

The Yalta negotiators had not solved "the German problem." But they had done an essential job of "papering over the cracks" in an alliance which could not be sacrificed until victory was won. This, in essence, was the best the Big Three at Yalta could do when they turned intermittently from the profound problem of Germany to consider the more immediately pressing difficulties which had been created by the Red Army's occupation of central-eastern Europe.

Chapter III

Russian Power in Central-Eastern Europe

ORE TIME was spent at Yalta discussing postwar frontiers and a provisional government for Poland than any other subject. At least in the opinion of Winston Churchill, Poland was the most pressing reason for the conference, and the "first of the great causes which led to the breakdown of the Grand Alliance."[1] And, although it posed by far the most serious dilemma in the area, Poland was but one of the vexing central-eastern European problems which confronted the Big Three in their conflicting efforts to fill the "power vacuum" left in the wake of the retreating *Wehrmacht.*

BACKGROUND OF RUSSO-POLISH RELATIONS

The complete breakdown in the wartime Russo-Polish negotiations which troubled the Big Three at Yalta can be traced ultimately to the legacy of centuries of acrimonious disputes between these Slavic states. Throughout modern history Russo-Polish relations have been embittered by important differences in religious and cultural orientation, conflicting territorial ambitions, and the absence of natural frontiers. Each country has been guilty of aggressive action against the other; Poland took advantage of Russian weakness until the seventeenth century, and Russia more than evened the scales thereafter. In three partitions late in the eighteenth century, Russia, Austria, and Prussia erased Poland from the map; she did not return until 1919, and then only with the aid of the West. In the interval the unhappy Poles developed a sense of romantic patriotism that has few equals in the history of nationalism. Friction between the two great Slavic nations was intensified after 1919 by the subversive

[1] Winston S. Churchill, *Triumph and Tragedy* (Boston, 1953), 366.

activity of the Communist International and the almost in-
credibly tragic experiences of World War II.

The Paris Peace Conference of 1919 was generous to resur-
rected Poland, thanks to President Woodrow Wilson's Fourteen Points program and to the French desire to establish a
strong and friendly state east of Germany and west of Bolshe-
vik Russia. Thus Poland was awarded many of her ancient
lands and was provided with a "corridor" to the sea through
eastern Germany. The conference had a much more difficult
time drawing the Russo-Polish frontier. The Allied diplomats did not bother to ask the views of the Soviet leaders,
but instead appointed a commission of experts to recommend
a boundary based primarily on ethnographical considerations.
The result was the proposed "Curzon Line," which took its
name from the British Foreign Secretary, and which was to
be the subject of hours of bitter debate in World War II. (See
map, p. 121.) To the east of this line, at least in the rural
zones, the population was predominantly Ukrainian and
Byelorussian, although the line would have left a substantial
minority of Poles as well as numerous Jews and some Lithuanians in Russian territory. When neither the Polish nor the
Soviet government would accept the Curzon proposal, the
so-called "Battle of the Frontiers" began in earnest.[2]

Somewhat giddy from the heady wine of freedom and nationalism after long years of enforced abstinence, Poland's
leaders dreamed of gathering into their state the scattered
pockets of Poles living far to the east in the Ukraine and
Byelorussia. This they justified to their own satisfaction on
the basis of historic "rights" and the reasonableness of further
weakening the Soviet regime, which then was confronted with
civil war. In the spring of 1920 Polish forces launched an
invasion of the Ukraine. Not until they reached Kiev were
they finally halted by the Red Army and forced to retreat
all the way to Warsaw. Timely support from the French and
British enabled the Poles eventually to regain the initiative
and push the Russians eastward once more. The war ended

[2] On the general subject of the boundaries, see especially James T. Shotwell
and Max Laserson, *Poland and Russia, 1919–1945* (New York, 1945), 5–16; and
S. Konovalov (ed.), *Russo-Polish Relations: An Historical Survey* (Princeton,
1945), 25–39, and *passim*.

in March, 1921, with the Treaty of Riga, which set the frontier a generous 150 miles east of the Curzon Line, where it remained until September, 1939. (See map, p. 121.)

On ethnic grounds and the Wilsonian principle of "self-determination" the Poles had little right to this eastern territory, for most of the people in this eastern zone were not Polish, except in such cities as Wilno and Lwow. On the basis of the 1931 Polish census it has been estimated unofficially by one Pole that of a total population in this region of 10,768,000 there were perhaps 3,914,000 Poles (36.4 per cent); 4,365,000 Ukrainians or Ruthenians (40.6 per cent); 1,284,000 Byelorussians or White-Ruthenians (11.8 per cent); 102,000 Great Russians (0.9 per cent); 76,000 Lithuanians (0.7 per cent); 899,000 Jews (8.4 per cent); and 128,000 others (1.2 per cent). On the other hand, it should be borne in mind that almost one million Poles, descendants of an earlier expansion, were still strewn east of the Riga frontier in Soviet territory.[3] Clearly, no boundary between the two Slavic states could be ethnographically precise, and a "minority problem" was inevitable there, just as it was on the Polish-German frontier.

Having stabilized her borders by 1921, the new Polish state was ready to play its postwar role as a *cordon sanitaire* against the infectious ideology of Russian communism and as an eastern bastion in the French system of international defenses against Germany. Poland's relations with the Soviet Union could hardly be described as cordial, but they were at least correct during the next decade or so, and the Russians refrained from openly complaining about the irredentist problem. The advent to power of the Nazis in Germany in 1933 led to important changes. In considerable alarm, Poland's leaders decided that their country's safety might best

[3] Statistical estimate of Casimir Smogorzewski, cited in Konovalov (ed.), *Russo-Polish Relations,* 83, on the basis of an unofficial Polish estimate from the 1931 census. No *official* Polish estimate for this region has been published. See also the figures cited by Wladyslaw W. Kulski, "The Lost Opportunity for Russian-Polish Friendship," *Foreign Affairs,* XXV (July, 1947), 667; and those by J. S. Roucek in Bernadotte E. Schmitt (ed.), *Poland* (Berkeley, 1945), 148–66. Cf. also the discussions by Adam Zoltowski, *Border of Europe—A Study of the Polish Eastern Provinces* (London, 1950); and S. Skrzypek, *The Problem of Eastern Galicia* (London, 1948).

be assured by signing a ten-year nonaggression pact with Nazi Germany on January 26, 1934. The Kremlin leaders, for their part, muffled their oft-repeated complaints about hostile capitalist encirclement and joined the very League of Nations which not long before had been denounced as a capitalist "house of ill-fame." In short order Russia signed mutual defense pacts with both France and Czechoslovakia, while Communists in many democratic states busily promoted "popular fronts."[4] The honeymoon rapidly deteriorated after the autumn of 1938, when Soviet representatives were not invited to the Munich conference. The western powers in effect sold out their own interests in central-eastern Europe at Munich; Adolf Hitler and subsequently Joseph Stalin became the arbiters of the fate of this region. Never since Munich have the western democracies, even with American wartime assistance, been able to alter markedly the course of events in this troubled area.[5]

In the spring of 1939 Hitler scrapped the Munich accord and began his "war of nerves" against Poland. Because Poland by herself was patently too weak to withstand a German onslaught, Winston Churchill and others urged Prime Minister Neville Chamberlain to negotiate in her defense a "Grand Alliance" that would include Soviet Russia. In due course, but with considerable diffidence, the British and French began such negotiations, as did the Germans, who desperately needed temporary Russian neutrality. As his price for entry into a "Grand Alliance" with the democracies, Stalin insisted upon having the right to base his troops in Poland and the Baltic states prior to a German attack. Most of the leaders of these border countries, however, had not forgotten past Russian overlordship and preferred to risk a German inva-

---

4 Readable and scholarly surveys of these international developments may be found conveniently in Frank P. Chambers, Christina Phelps Harris, and Charles C. Bayley, *This Age of Conflict: A Contemporary World History, 1914 to the Present* (rev. ed.; New York, 1950), 471–97, and *passim;* C. E. Black and E. C. Helmreich, *Twentieth Century Europe: A History* (New York, 1950), 572–75, 626–29, and *passim;* John A. Lukacs, *The Great Powers and Eastern Europe* (New York, 1953), 35–165; and Hugh Seton-Watson, *The East European Revolution* (London, 1950), 49–61.

5 Cf. the analysis of Hajo Holborn, *The Political Collapse of Europe* (New York, 1951), 138–58.

sion rather than let the Red Army share in their defense. Neither Britain nor France was prepared to force them to accept the Soviet terms.

The German Foreign Minister, Joachim von Ribbentrop, was not bothered by such scruples and succeeded in reaching a cynical agreement with the Soviet Commissar for Foreign Affairs, Vyacheslav M. Molotov, at the expense of Poland, the Baltic states, and Rumania. In secret protocols to their Moscow Pact of August 23, 1939, Ribbentrop and Molotov agreed upon another partition of Poland. Ribbentrop also gave his assent to Russian predominance in Estonia, Latvia, and Bessarabia.[6] Poland's fate was quickly sealed when German *Panzer* divisions roared across the frontier on September 1 and Soviet troops poured in from the east two and one-half weeks later. On September 3 Britain and France reluctantly declared war against Germany, the immediate cause for their intervention being their commitment to help defend Poland.

The most tragic era of Polish history followed, with hundreds of thousands of Jews and Gentiles being herded either into Nazi extermination camps, or on a somewhat lesser scale, into Soviet concentration camps. The Polish government escaped first to Rumania, then to France, and finally to Britain. The presidency of the government in exile passed to Wladyslaw Raczkiewicz, who formerly had been a key official in the authoritarian regime of Joseph Pilsudski, but the premiership was assigned to General Wladyslaw Sikorski, a long-time opponent of the Pilsudski faction. The ministries were held by available representatives of the Nationalist, Socialist, Peasant, and Christian Labor parties, all of which had largely been excluded from the parliamentary arena after the promulgation of Pilsudski's authoritarian constitution of 1935. In the course of time several Polish military units managed to make their way to western Europe to continue the struggle against Germany, while in Poland itself underground

---

[6] Chambers, Harris, Bayley, *This Age of Conflict*, 640–45; Holborn, *Political Collapse of Europe*, 158–61. For full details see R. J. Sontag and J. A. Beddie (eds.), *Nazi-Soviet Relations, 1939–1941* (Washington, 1948); and *Documents and Materials Relating to the Eve of the Second World War* (2 vols., Moscow, 1948).

resistance was fomented by the "Secret State" and "Home Army," which endeavored to maintain liaison with the government in exile.[7]

Meanwhile, the two invaders revised their partition line on September 28, 1939, Germany agreeing to add Lithuania to the Soviet sphere of influence in exchange for Russian renunciation of some Polish territory east of the Vistula River. The Russo-German boundary henceforth ran through Poland along the rivers Pissa, Narew, Bug, and San, a line which, except in the north, coincided pretty much with the Curzon proposal of 1919. (See map, p. 121.) All told, Soviet Russia acquired 76,500 square miles and some 11,000,000 inhabitants of the former Polish state. In this region the Soviets conducted hasty "plebiscites" which purported to show the overwhelming desire of the people to become Soviet citizens. A few weeks later, while the *Sitzkrieg* prevailed in western Europe, Stalin seized borderlands from Finland, and in the early summer of 1940, following the Nazi *Blitzkrieg* in the west, he completed the strengthening of his frontier by annexing through hasty plebiscites Estonia, Latvia, Lithuania, Bessarabia, and Bukovina.

NEW PHASE: 1941 TO 1943

When Hitler put an end to the Nazi-Soviet Pact by his attack against the U.S.S.R. in June, 1941, a new phase of Russo-Polish relations began. Prime Minister Churchill, who was relieved to have a powerful new ally in the war, regardless of its political philosophy, quickly cemented a working relationship with Marshal Stalin and advised Polish Premier Sikorski to do the same. In the ensuing Russo-Polish conversations regarding a treaty of friendship, the Soviet ambassador in London, I. M. Maisky, refused to promise Sikorski restora-

[7] Schmitt (ed.), *Poland*, 100–101, 123–47; Samuel L. Sharp, *Poland: White Eagle on a Red Field* (Cambridge, Massachusetts, 1953), 153–58. Regarding the underground, see especially Jan Karski, *Story of a Secret State* (Boston, 1944); and General Tadeusz Bor-Komorowski, *The Secret Army* (London, 1950). The hardships of the Poles in Soviet Russia are discussed in Anonymous, *The Dark Side of the Moon* (London, 1946), and J. Czapski, *The Inhuman Land* (London, 1951). On early Anglo-Polish relations, see Waclaw Jedrzejewicz (ed.), *Poland in the British Parliament, 1939–1945* (New York, 1946).

tion of the prewar frontier, but to make the agreement more palatable to the Poles he suggested inserting only a vague reference to the eastern frontier. Thus the important Russo-Polish Pact of July 30, 1941, which the Polish government in exile accepted only after a cabinet crisis, stated simply that the Russo-German agreements of 1939 relating to territorial changes had "lost their validity." A few weeks earlier Maisky had advised the British government that his country favored an ethnographical frontier with Poland roughly equivalent to the partition line of September, 1939, although "certain districts and towns occupied by Russia in 1939 might be returned to Poland."[8] Thus there was no doubt that Stalin considered his 1939 annexation of the borderlands irreversible except for minor adjustments. Nevertheless, many Poles unwisely let their emotion govern their reason in hoping that the ambiguous clause in the July 30 pact meant Stalin would consent to restoration of the prewar frontier.[9]

Their hope was strengthened by the announcement in August, 1941, that President Franklin D. Roosevelt, whose nation was not yet in the war, and Prime Minister Churchill had drafted an "Atlantic Charter" of "common principles . . . on which they base their hopes for a better future for the world." Five months later the Soviet Union announced its adherence to the eight principles of the charter. The first three articles of this document were of most interest to the Poles, who determined to keep them fresh in the minds of the Allied leaders:

FIRST. Their countries seek no aggrandizement, territorial or other;

SECOND. They desire to see no territorial changes that do not accord with the freely expressed wishes of the people concerned;

THIRD. They respect the right of all peoples to choose the form of government under which they will live; and they wish

---

[8] William Hardy McNeill, *America, Britain, & Russia: Their Cooperation and Conflict, 1941–1946* (London, 1953), 46–48; Kulski, "The Lost Opportunity," *loc. cit.*, 675.

[9] Jan Ciechanowski, *Defeat in Victory* (New York, 1947), 37–42, 76–80; Kulski, "The Lost Opportunity," *loc. cit.*, 675 *et seq.*; Lukacs, *The Great Powers and Eastern Europe*, 439.

to see sovereign rights and self-government restored to those who have been forcibly deprived of them.[10]

If applied in the future peace settlement, these principles would guarantee the restoration of prewar Poland. But throughout the war years Roosevelt displayed greater public interest in his creation than either of his colleagues, and at one of the Yalta dinners of the Big Three Churchill reminded him rather bluntly that the charter was not "a law, but a star."[11]

For a few months during the autumn of 1941 Soviet-Polish relations seemed relatively amicable. Lieutenant General Wladyslaw Anders and other key Polish military personnel who had been interned in Russia were released and allowed to reorganize Polish combat units to fight alongside the Russians. But their relationship soon deteriorated when the Poles persistently inquired about the fate of several thousand missing Polish officers. In 1942 the half-million Polish troops were permitted to make their way to the Middle East and Italy, where they fought valiantly up the entire length of the rugged peninsula.[12] Meanwhile, toward the end of 1941 Premier Sikorski traveled to Moscow. He had a friendly conversation with Stalin, who intimated that he did not seek the industrial center of Lwow for Russia, and would be willing to see the prewar frontier changed only "a little." Unfortunately for the Poles, Sikorski did not deem it expedient to ask Stalin to set this down in writing.

If the Poles had negotiated an eastern boundary settlement in December, 1941, when Stalin's armies were still hard pressed and he presumably was generously inclined toward Sikorski, would they have achieved a more satisfactory agreement than later was to be the case? Churchill and at least a few Poles have stoutly insisted that they would, with Poland retaining the Lwow zone. Professor Wladyslaw W. Kulski, who was then an official in the Polish government in exile,

10 United States House of Representatives, 77th Congress, 1st Session, *Congressional Record*, LXXXVII, 7217.

11 Churchill, *Triumph and Tragedy*, 393.

12 See General Wladyslaw Anders, *An Army in Exile* (London, 1949), 47–130, and *passim*.

has written that "the Soviet Union would have probably permitted the Polish Government-in-Exile to return to Poland."[13] Whether Stalin's aims with respect to Poland were strictly territorial and not political in nature at this time is of course debatable. Whatever the true situation was, Premier Sikorski could not bring his cabinet to negotiate a boundary agreement with the Russians, and the Slavic honeymoon gave way to years of violent recriminations. The ensuing rift was to affect in the gravest manner the wartime relations of the Big Three, as was revealed during the Anglo-Russian negotiations of 1941–42 over a treaty of alliance. Stalin tried to get Foreign Secretary Anthony Eden to agree in writing to the Curzon Line as the future Russo-Polish frontier, but Eden, at the urging of the American and Polish governments, managed to avoid such a territorial commitment in the pact he signed with Molotov on May 26, 1942.[14]

The United States had insisted from the outset of the war that territorial questions should not be decided until the end of hostilities, when they could be settled in accordance with the freely expressed wishes of the people concerned. But when evidence steadily mounted that the continuation of such deadlocks as that between the Russians and the Poles threatened to imperil the unity of the Great Powers, Roosevelt was gradually forced to modify his "policy of postponement." Thus, on the eve of Churchill's first trip to Moscow in the fall of 1942, the President inquired what he thought of a boundary drawn somewhat east of the Curzon Line, with Lwow remaining in Poland. Churchill, it seems, did not find a suitable opportunity to discuss this proposal with Stalin.[15] Later, during Eden's visit to Washington in March, 1943, it became clear that both the British and American governments hoped that their willingness to accept the Curzon Line might assure Poland's postwar political freedom. And they shared

13 Kulski, "The Lost Opportunity," *loc. cit.*, 676; Lukacs, *The Great Powers and Eastern Europe*, 441, 781; Ciechanowski, *Defeat in Victory*, 103.

14 McNeill, *America, Britain, & Russia*, 178–79; Cordell Hull, *Memoirs of Cordell Hull* (2 vols., New York, 1948), II, 1165–74; Ciechanowski, *Defeat in Victory*, 104–108; Kulski, "The Lost Opportunity," *loc. cit.*, 679; and Lukacs, *The Great Powers and Eastern Europe*, 470–71.

15 Lukacs, *The Great Powers and Eastern Europe*, 474–75.

the belief that Poland ought to be compensated for eastern losses with East Prussian territory.[16]

Whatever may have been Stalin's mood in December, 1941, after his decisive victory at Stalingrad in January, 1943, he was confident of his ability to dictate the key terms of the territorial settlement of eastern Europe. In March, 1943, the world learned of the establishment on Russian soil of a "Union of Polish Patriots," a pro-Communist group which could be counted on to echo Soviet denunciations of the Polish government in London.[17] Evidence that it was being groomed for satellite service was revealed when Stalin broke diplomatic relations with the Polish government in exile in April. The rupture probably would have occurred sooner or later, since there was little likelihood that the London Poles would accept the Soviet frontier demands, but it was precipitated by the revelation of the gruesome massacre of several thousand Polish army officers in the forest of Katyn, near Smolensk. The Germans, who found the bodies, announced over the radio that the deed must have been committed by the Russians in 1940, and the Polish government in exile, which for months had sought information about its unaccounted-for officers in Russia, inopportunely asked for an investigation of the supposed massacre by the International Red Cross. This "unfriendly" action by the Poles provided Stalin with the pretext he needed.[18] As if the Polish situation were not bad enough already, a new misfortune occurred

---

16 Robert E. Sherwood, *Roosevelt and Hopkins, An Intimate History* (rev. ed.; New York, 1950), 710–16; Lukacs, *The Great Powers and Eastern Europe*, 506, 513; and Ciechanowski, *Defeat in Victory*, 149–57.

17 Sidney Lowery, "Poland," in Arnold and Veronica M. Toynbee (eds.), *The Realignment of Europe* (London, 1955), 148.

18 *Ibid.*, 138–47; Joseph Mackiewicz, *The Katyn Wood Murders* (London, 1951), *passim*; Stanislaw Mikolajczyk, *The Rape of Poland* (New York, 1948), 28–65; Ciechanowski, *Defeat in Victory*, 158–66; Winston S. Churchill, *The Hinge of Fate* (Boston, 1950), 757–61; Hull, *Memoirs*, II, 1265–73; William H. Standley and Arthur A. Ageton, *Admiral Ambassador to Russia* (Chicago, 1955), 401–11; Lukacs, *The Great Powers and Eastern Europe*, 503–10; G. F. Hudson, "A Polish Challenge: Review Article," *International Affairs*, XXVI (April, 1950), 214–21; and United States House of Representatives, 82nd Congress, 1st Session, *Hearings before the Select Committee to Conduct an Investigation of the Facts, Evidence, and Circumstances of the Katyn Forest Massacre* (Washington, 1952).

when Premier Sikorski was killed in an airplane crash. In the reorganized Polish government in exile of July, 1943, Stanislaw Mikolajczyk, leader of the powerful Peasant party and native of western Poland, became Premier. In general he was to enjoy very friendly relations with Anglo-American leaders, and he was by no means intransigently anti-Russian.[19]

Reconciliation between the Poles in exile and the Russians was one of the objectives which took Secretary of State Cordell Hull to Moscow in October, 1943, where he held important talks with his British and Soviet colleagues. On the eve of his departure the President informed Hull that at the approaching first meeting of the Big Three he intended to appeal to Stalin on grounds of "high morality" to hold a "second plebiscite" in the disputed territories of Poland and the Baltic states, since the world was not satisfied with the legality of Russia's earlier action. At the same time the President declared that the Russo-Polish frontier should lie somewhat east of the Curzon Line.[20] The Polish ambassador to the United States, Jan Ciechanowski, also saw Hull, and in a long note urged him to postpone any discussion of the frontier.[21] At Moscow Molotov assured the foreign ministers that he desired an independent Poland, provided its government were friendly toward the U.S.S.R. Hull gained the impression that Polish acquiescence in the loss of the eastern lands would pave the way for a resumption of diplomatic relations between the two Slavic governments.[22]

Meanwhile, Churchill tried to persuade the Americans of the advisability of military operations across the northern Adriatic into Trieste and through the Ljubljana gap into the Danube basin, in addition to the major cross-Channel invasion of Normandy.[23] Doubtless the Prime Minister was

[19] Mikolajczyk, *Rape of Poland*, 40–41, and *passim*.
[20] Hull, *Memoirs*, II, 1266.
[21] Ciechanowski, *Defeat in Victory*, 209–21; Hull, *Memoirs*, II, 1271–72.
[22] Hull, *Memoirs*, II, 1305–1306, 1315–17; Ciechanowski, *Defeat in Victory*, 233–43.
[23] On the problem of military strategy, see especially Hanson W. Baldwin, *Great Mistakes of the War* (New York, 1949), 25–44; Winston S. Churchill, *Closing the Ring* (Boston, 1951), 33, 253–54, 350–58, 366–73, and *passim*; Sherwood, *Roosevelt and Hopkins*, 746–47; Lukacs, *The Great Powers and Eastern Europe*, 510–12 *et seq.*

anxious to win greater military prestige for his British forces in the Mediterranean, but undoubtedly he was also motivated by the political desire to liberate as much as possible of south-central Europe before the Russians did. In his protracted arguments with American officials, Churchill carefully refrained from emphasizing political advantages, stressing instead the military benefits that would result from such operations. He couched his arguments in these terms because he did not wish to occasion a rift with Stalin and also, perhaps, because he feared the language of naked power politics would be misunderstood by some Americans who regarded "spheres of influence" as cynical if not sinful methods of international organization. Viewing the problem from the vantage of hindsight, critics have argued that Churchill blundered in not making clearer his real fears.

Churchill was not unwilling to go along with Roosevelt's program for a worldwide "concert of power" to be manifested through a United Nations organization; but in dealing with a "realist" such as Stalin, whose postwar collaboration with the West was by no means certain, he felt more at home when operating on the basis of respective "spheres of influence" and a rough "balance of power." Soviet leaders did their best to block Churchill's Adriatic scheme by harping on the immediate need for a massive second front in France to take some of the pressure off their own armies; and American military strategists opposed the plans mainly because of the logistical difficuties, which certainly could not be minimized, and also because of their desire to strike at Germany's industrial heart as rapidly as possible. The matter had not yet been decided when the Big Three met for the first time at Teheran in November, 1943.

FROM TEHERAN TO LUBLIN

Doubtless to Stalin's relief, the Adriatic operations were rejected at Teheran, and the Soviet leader was reassured that the major western effort would be directed to a cross-Channel invasion by the summer of 1944.[24] By this decision the West

---

[24] Churchill, *Closing the Ring*, 381 *et seq.*

lost its last chance to influence the postwar political fate of at least some of the southeastern European states. It would seem most unlikely, though, that even a successful drive through the Ljubljana gap into the Danubian basin would have enabled the Anglo-Americans to influence materially the course of events in Poland, which lay far inland. And it might have caused Stalin to seek a separate peace with Hitler, a possibility which no western statesman could afford to forget after the surprise of August 23, 1939.

Churchill's Adriatic proposals led also to some discussion of Yugoslavia at the Teheran conference, and it was at this time that Churchill decided British interests would best be safeguarded by transferring military support from General Draža Mihailović's royalist-oriented Serbian guerrillas (*Četniks*) to Marshal Josip Broz Tito's Communist-inclined partisans. The decision, which was based on the belief that Tito's men were killing more Germans than were the *Četniks* and would most likely be the dominant political force at the end of the war, was to have far-reaching effects.[25]

At Teheran Stalin said that if Russia were allowed to gain the East Prussian port of Königsberg, he would agree to Churchill's proposal that the Curzon Line should serve as the eastern frontier of Poland. Roosevelt tacitly approved this suggestion, but qualified it by pointing out the desirability of leaving Lwow and the Galician oil districts with Poland. All three reached informal agreement that Poland should be compensated with German territory as far west as the Oder River. Churchill demonstrated with three matches on the table how Poland might move westward, like soldiers taking two steps "left close." The Big Three apparently did

---

[25] *Ibid.*, 352, 404. A point of departure for study of Yugoslav affairs in this period is provided in the following works: Hugh Seton-Watson, "Yugoslavia," in Toynbee and Toynbee (eds.), *The Realignment of Europe*, 352–71; Robert J. Kerner (ed.), *Yugoslavia* (Berkeley, 1949); Fitzroy MacLean, *Eastern Approaches* (London, 1950); Stephen Clissold, *Whirlwind: An Account of Marshal Tito's Rise to Power* (London, 1949); Jasper Rootham, *Miss Fire: The Chronicle of a British Mission to Mihailovich, 1943–1944* (London, 1946); David Martin, *Ally Betrayed: The Uncensored Story of Tito and Mihailovich* (New York, 1946); Constantine Fotitch, *The War We Lost: Yugoslavia's Tragedy and the Failure of the West* (New York, 1948); and Hamilton Fish Armstrong, *Tito and Goliath* (New York, 1951).

not discuss in any detail the nature of a future Polish government, nor did they talk about any plebiscite in the disputed borderlands.[26] It has been suggested that the President's partial retreat from his earlier "policy of postponement" of territorial disputes may have been motivated by a high-level American military estimate, prepared during the summer of 1943, which recommended that no effort be spared to win the friendship and assistance of Russia in the war against Japan.[27]

On January 4, 1944, Soviet troops crossed the prewar Polish frontier. Before the week ended Moscow made it unmistakably clear to the London Poles that the status of eastern lands was not subject to discussion. In vain, Churchill again urged the government in exile to accept the Curzon Line in exchange for territorial compensation from defeated Germany. He insisted that this would be the only way he could acquire a strong bargaining hand to defend Poland's political independence against the Russians.[28] Meanwhile, Secretary of State Hull publicly modified the American "policy of postponement," observing that it did not mean "that certain questions may not and should not . . . be settled by friendly conference and agreement."[29] But, for the most part, the Poles in London remained adamant.

Early in May Churchill on his own initiative sought to recapture a stake for the West in central-eastern Europe. He asked American diplomatic officials what they would think of a possible Anglo-Soviet agreement that would spell out their respective degrees of "leadership" in Greece and Rumania. Churchill was quickly apprised that the American Secretary of State was passionately opposed to such a resurrection of old-fashioned "spheres of influence." Undismayed, Churchill

[26] Churchill, *Closing the Ring,* 361–62, 394–97, 403; James F. Byrnes, *Speaking Frankly* (New York, 1947), 29; Hull, *Memoirs,* II, 1266. On the subject of the emergence of the Oder line as the proposed new German-Polish frontier, see the monograph by Wolfgang Wagner, *Die Entstehung der Oder-Neisse Linie* (Stuttgart, 1953), 52–84 *et seq.*

[27] Cf. Sharp, *Poland,* 295.

[28] Mikolajczyk, *Rape of Poland,* 284–85; Admiral William D. Leahy, *I Was There* (New York, 1950), 232–33.

[29] *Department of State Bulletin,* XI (December 24, 1944), 836; Ciechanowski, *Defeat in Victory,* 272.

From David Low, *Years of Wrath, a Cartoon History: 1931–1945* (New York, 1946).

"WHOSE SIDE ARE YOU ON—THEIRS OR OURS?"—"MINE"

This David Low cartoon, which illustrates the independent national spirit of Poland, first appeared in January, 1944, soon after the U.S.S.R. announced that it would insist upon having the frontier with Poland that it had won in co-operation with Hitler in 1939.

continued to press Roosevelt in private, scrupulously avoiding the term "sphere of influence." Finally, in June the President, unbeknown to his Secretary of State, reluctantly approved such agreements on a trial basis of three months, in view of the pressing demands of "current military operations" in these countries. The bargain lasted longer, for Churchill and Stalin at their Moscow conference in October, 1944, extended it and reduced to percentages the degree of influence each would exercise. Thus the Soviets, with respect to Britain, would assume 90 per cent predominance in Rumania and 75 per cent in Bulgaria, whereas Britain would exercise 90 per cent of the responsibility for affairs in Greece. In Yugoslavia, where the British were providing Tito with many of his supplies, Anglo-Soviet responsibility would be shared equally. This was supposed to be the case in Hungary, too. To Churchill's amazement, Stalin raised no objection to the proposals and registered his approval by marking with a blue pencil a large tick on the slip of paper on which Churchill had just scrawled the figures. A long minute of silence was broken when the British leader suggested that they perhaps should burn the slip lest historians think that they had been too flippant about a decision which would be "fateful to millions of people." "No, you keep it," was Stalin's quick reply.[30] Since the United States remained on the side lines during the Anglo-Russian negotiations, Stalin may have drawn the conclusion that in any showdown the Americans would not show much concern for eastern Europe.[31]

Meanwhile, in July, 1944, Polish Premier Mikolajczyk had set out to visit Stalin. His trip was made at the behest of President Roosevelt, with whom he had held a cordial conference earlier in the summer. The President had strongly urged him to seek an understanding with Stalin, remarking,

---

[30] Churchill, *Triumph and Tragedy*, 227–28. Cf. Hull, *Memoirs*, II, 1451–59. A lucid discussion of the background and effects of this Anglo-Soviet bargain, particularly with respect to Greece, is to be found in Stephen G. Xydis, "The Secret Anglo-Soviet Agreement on the Balkans of October 9, 1944," *Journal of Central European Affairs*, XV (October, 1955), 248–71.

[31] Mark Ethridge and C. E. Black, "Negotiating on the Balkans, 1945–1947," in Raymond Dennett and Joseph E. Johnson (eds.), *Negotiating with the Russians* (Boston, 1951), 177.

"When a thing becomes unavoidable, one should adapt one-self to it." While en route to Moscow, Mikolajczyk learned that the Russians had announced that they were handing over administration of liberated territory west of the Curzon Line to a recently formed provisional government, the "Polish Committee of National Liberation," headed by Edward Osóbka-Morawski, a left-wing Socialist, and Boleslaw Bierut, a Communist. Despite his anger, the Premier continued his journey, arriving in Moscow on July 30. A couple of days later he was joined by members of the Soviet-sponsored Polish Committee of National Liberation.[32]

While Mikolajczyk was in Moscow the anti-Communist Poles sought to present their case to world opinion by means of a long-planned uprising of their Home Army in Warsaw. They hoped that the Resistance forces of General Tadeusz Bor-Komorowski could drive the Germans from the city and present the advancing Red Army, then only a few miles away, with a *fait accompli* when it crossed the Vistula. But when the uprising began on August 1 the Soviet forces failed to advance and offered virtually no assistance to the Home Army, explaining that the Poles had not co-ordinated with them their "premature" action. For sixty-three days against hopeless odds the Home Army fought the Germans in the rubble and in the sewers. The British and Americans man-aged with great difficulty to drop a number of planeloads of supplies to the insurgents, but all in vain. Elimination of the Home Army left the Communists with no powerfully armed rival political group when the Soviet forces finally entered Warsaw on January 17, 1945.[33]

While the Warsaw uprising was getting under way Miko-lajczyk was presented by Stalin and his advisers with a scheme for a Polish fusion "Government of Unity," to be composed of fourteen Poles from the Soviet-sponsored Committee of National Liberation and only three from abroad. The Com-munist Bierut would be president and Mikolajczyk could

[32] Mikolajczyk, *Rape of Poland*, 56–71; Ciechanowski, *Defeat in Victory*, 291–300.

[33] Sharp, *Poland*, 166–86; Lowery in Toynbee and Toynbee (eds.), *Realign-ment of Europe*, 161–73; Mikolajczyk, *Rape of Poland*, 60–90.

be premier; the authoritarian, "fascistic" constitution of 1935 must be scrapped; Poland must recognize the Curzon Line, and in exchange would receive Silesia and East Prussia, except for Königsberg. The London Poles dismissed all of this as preposterous and Mikolajczyk left Moscow on August 10. Subsequently Mikolajczyk tried to devise a compromise proposal, but his colleagues would not accept it. In September the Committee of National Liberation unilaterally proclaimed Lublin the temporary capital of Poland. The deadlock could not have been more complete.[34]

In the desperate hope of breaking the impasse, Churchill, accompanied by Eden, made a second wartime pilgrimage to Moscow in October, 1944. They quickly agreed upon their spheres in the Balkans, as has been noted, but ran into the usual difficulties regarding Poland. Churchill sent word to Premier Mikolajczyk, Foreign Minister Tadeusz Romer, and Stanislaw Grabski, Speaker of the Polish National Council in London, to join him. Stalin brought in several of the officials of the Lublin committee, whose general impression upon Eden was most "depressing." During this "All Poles Day" Molotov bluntly informed Mikolajczyk, in the presence of both Churchill and United States Ambassador W. Averell Harriman, who sat in as "observer," that the President had orally agreed at Teheran to the Curzon frontier. He asked the westerners to correct him if he was wrong. Mikolajczyk and his colleagues, who had been counting on American support for their territorial claims, were dismayed by the disclosure and looked to Churchill and Harriman for reassurance. There was an embarrassed silence. Although neither Churchill nor Harriman saw fit to correct Molotov at this juncture, Roosevelt had really voiced the opinion at Teheran, as has been noted, that the Curzon Line should be modified to permit Polish retention of Lwow and the Galician oil lands.

For the moment the London Polish delegation remained unbending, and in private talks Churchill passionately insisted that their *"liberum veto"* attitude would "wreck the

---

34 Lowery in Toynbee and Toynbee (eds.), *Realignment of Europe*, 171–73; Mikolajczyk, *Rape of Poland*, 71–79.

peace of Europe." Charging them with irresponsibly seeking a war with Russia in which twenty-five million lives would be lost, the angry Briton shouted, "What are you fighting for, the right to be crushed?"[35] In spite of his unconcealed irritation with many of the London Polish politicians, though, Churchill was deeply conscious of the diplomatic and moral bonds which had linked the British and Poles since the beginning of the war, and he was grateful for the help that a half-million Polish soldiers were rendering the Allied cause on the Italian and western fronts.[36]

By the time the British and Polish delegations left Moscow their relations had somewhat improved again. Churchill had managed to badger Mikolajczyk into tentative acceptance of the Curzon Line, with Lwow going to Russia in return for the possibility of establishing a fusion of the rival governments.[37] But when Mikolajczyk returned to London he was unable to win the support of the other parties in his government and resigned on November 24. His successor as premier was the aged Socialist, Tomasz Arciszewski, who had led the left wing of the Polish underground for five years and had gone to London only in August, 1944. Arciszewski was a much more intransigent nationalist than his predecessor. The new government in exile included no members of Mikolajczyk's Peasant party. While both Britain and the United States continued to recognize the exiled regime, their relations with it can only be described as "correct." Yet, on the eve of the Yalta conference both Arciszewski and Mikolajczyk appealed to Roosevelt and Churchill to safeguard the "legitimate rights of Poland" in their negotiations with Stalin.[38]

---

[35] Churchill, *Triumph and Tragedy*, 235–41; Mikolajczyk, *Rape of Poland*, 93–105; and Ciechanowski, *Defeat in Victory*, 325–45.

[36] Cf. Churchill, *Triumph and Tragedy*, 366.

[37] *Ibid.*, 241.

[38] Sharp, *Poland*, 191–96; Lowery in Toynbee and Toynbee (eds.), *Realignment of Europe*, 186–91; Shotwell and Laserson, *Poland and Russia*, 81–82; Mikolajczyk, *Rape of Poland*, 104–105. See also the diplomatic correspondence between Washington and the United States ambassador to the U.S.S.R., W. Averell Harriman, Prime Minister Churchill, and the Polish government in exile, as published in United States, Department of State, *The Conferences at Malta and Yalta, 1945* (Washington, 1955), 202–25, 950–51, and 953–54 (hereinafter cited as *Yalta Papers*).

THE EVE OF YALTA

Toward the end of 1944 the "tide of Anglo-Soviet-American friendship" was near its crest, and a good many American and British officials were ready to concede that the Russians were going to be predominant in eastern Europe. But this did not mean that they looked forward with pleasure to the prospect or that all of them wore rose-colored glasses when they viewed the problems of future relations with the Kremlin. The recently published American record of the background of the Malta and Yalta conferences reveal growing anxiety on the part of United States Ambassador W. Averell Harriman regarding Soviet foreign policy. Thus on December 28, 1944, he cabled from Moscow that, on the basis of Soviet actions, Russian uses of the terms "friendly" and "independent" governments "appear to mean something quite different from our interpretation." He went on to remark that anyone "who disagrees with Soviet policies is conveniently branded as a 'Fascist.' "[39] And on January 10, 1945, he cabled that Soviet policy in eastern Europe had been clarified during the past few weeks, and that it involved the use of a

. . . wide variety of means at their disposal—occupation troops, secret police, local communist parties, labor unions, sympathetic leftist organizations, sponsored cultural societies, and economic pressure—to assure the establishment of regimes which, while maintaining an outward appearance of independence and of broad popular support, actually depend for their existence on groups responsive to all suggestions emanating from the Kremlin. . . . It is particularly noteworthy that no practical distinction seems to be made . . . between members of the United Nations whose territory is liberated by Soviet troops and ex-enemy countries which have been occupied. The overriding consideration in Soviet foreign policy is the preoccupation with "security," as Moscow sees it. . . . The Soviet conception of "security" does not appear cognizant of the similar needs or rights of other countries and of Russia's obligation to accept the restraints as well as the benefits of an international security system.

[39] *Yalta Papers,* 64–66.

While Harriman sought to alert Washington to the unpleasant features of Soviet policy in eastern Europe, he simultaneously tried to impress upon the Russians the importance of the Polish issue in shaping the future of Soviet-American relations.[40]

But Roosevelt still hoped by "personal diplomacy" and the pursuance of a generous attitude toward Stalin to lay the basis for world peace—for the alternative to Great Power solidarity was division of the world into rival blocs, which he and his advisers felt would be disastrous. Nevertheless, he seemed well aware of the difficulties of dealing with the Soviet leaders, to judge from his correspondence with Stalin and Churchill on the Polish deadlock at the end of 1944. This began when Churchill publicly announced the breakdown of negotiations and intimated that the attitude of the London Poles was based on hopes of American support. Roosevelt at once cabled the Prime Minister that they shared "the same basic objective in regard to Poland," and suggested co-ordinating their measures. He indicated that he was sending a personal message to Stalin, suggesting that the latter "postpone any positive action on the Polish question"—meaning Soviet recognition of the Lublin committee as the provisional government—until their personal meeting.

The cable which Roosevelt dispatched to Stalin on December 16 informed him that the United States stood "unequivocally for a strong, free, and independent Polish state." Questions relating to boundaries "should be left in abeyance until the termination of hostilities," Roosevelt stated, but he added that if the Polish people "decide that it would be in the interests of the Polish state" to transfer "certain national groups" to lessen the number of Poles who might be left beyond the new border, then America would be ready to assist.[41] There is no doubt that the President felt keenly the political pressure of six million Polish-Americans, who expected the full restoration of an independent Poland. Moreover, he had by no means forgotten the idealistic principles about small

[40] *Ibid.*, 450–55. See also Harriman's memo of January 20, 1945, reporting a talk with I. M. Maisky, Assistant People's Commissar for Foreign Affairs, on the Polish problem, *ibid.*, 227.

[41] *Ibid.*, 217–21.

nations which he and Churchill had proclaimed in the Atlantic Charter three and a half years before.

Replying on December 27, Stalin accused "underground agents of the Polish émigré government" of engaging in "criminal terrorist work against Soviet officers and soldiers," and he declared that the emergence of Arciszewski to power in London "had made the situation even worse." Since Russia must consider her own military security, he went on, she would "not have any serious ground for postponement" of diplomatic recognition if the Polish Committee of National Liberation transformed itself into a provisional government.[42]

To this the President replied on December 30: "I am disturbed and deeply disappointed. . . . I would have thought no serious inconvenience would have been caused your Government or your Armies if you could have delayed the purely juridical act of recognition for the short period of a month remaining before we meet." He went on to note "with a frankness equal to your own" that he saw "no prospect of this Government's following suit and transferring its recognition . . . to the Lublin Committee in its present form."[43] Stalin answered by sending a New Year's Day greeting to the President in which he remarked, "I am extremely sorry that I did not succeed in convincing you of the correctness of the position of the Soviet Government on the Polish question." The suggestion to postpone recognition for a month was "perfectly understandable," he continued, but there was "one circumstance which makes me powerless to fulfill your wish." The fact was, Stalin wrote, "that on December 27 the Presidium of the Supreme Soviet of the USSR to an appropriate request of the Poles has already informed them that it intends to recognize the Provisional Government of Poland as soon as it is formed." When he learned of this reply, Churchill commented acidly to the President that it was interesting to see Stalin bring the Presidium "into the line." On January 5, 1945, Moscow extended full recognition to the Lublin provisional government. Two weeks later this regime, headed by "President" Bierut and Premier Osóbka-Morawski and

[42] *Ibid.*, 221–23.
[43] *Ibid.*, 224–25.

including four Communists and four Communist sympathizers, transferred its headquarters to liberated Warsaw, where it came to be known as the "Warsaw government." The position of the West was weakened when, at the end of January, the Czechoslovak government in exile, bowing to Soviet pressure, decided to recognize the Lublin-Warsaw regime as the government of Poland.[44]

It was clearer than ever that Soviet Russia was in control of the destiny of most of eastern Europe and that she had little to gain in this region from any conference of the Big Three. By the time the Anglo-American "Argonauts" reached Yalta, Soviet armies had knocked Finland out of the war, occupied Rumania, Bulgaria, almost all of Poland, driven deeply into Hungary,[45] Yugoslavia, and Czechoslovakia, and had gotten within less than one hundred miles of Berlin. Decisions of an increasingly unilateral nature by Soviet officials in the liberated countries were causing much concern among western statesmen, particularly Churchill, who was frankly pessimistic about the probable results of the war. He cabled the President in January that these "may well prove to be more disappointing than the last."[46]

Recent developments in Greece probably were preying on Churchill's mind. Open fighting had broken out there between the Communist-dominated E.A.M. resistance group and the British occupation forces, and Churchill had made a hurried flight to embattled Athens on Christmas Day to seek a solution. He had received a good measure of criticism from the Labor party and many Americans for his determined intervention, but Stalin had tactfully remained silent, true to his recent bargain regarding spheres of influence. Precarious tranquility ushered in the New Year in Greece when Churchill persuaded the King of the Hellenes to remain abroad a while longer and to appoint a regent to act in his absence.[47]

[44] *Ibid.*, 226. See also the *Yalta Papers*, 507, for Grew to Secretary of State, January 31, 1945.
[45] Chester A. Wilmot, *The Struggle for Europe* (London, 1952), 630–32.
[46] *Yalta Papers*, 31.
[47] Churchill, *Triumph and Tragedy*, 283–325; Sherwood, *Roosevelt and Hopkins*, 837–43. See also R. W. A. Leeper, *When Greeks Meet Greeks* (London,

In Yugoslavia the situation was not much happier. There Churchill was anxious to implement his fifty-fifty bargain with Stalin and promote a fusion of the royalist government in exile with Tito's Anti-Fascist Council of National Liberation (A.V.N.O.J.). He finally persuaded the rival groups to accept a compromise whereby King Peter would not attempt to return until a referendum on the question could be held. The King would meanwhile be represented by a Regency Council, to be appointed jointly by the royalists abroad and Tito's Council. A fusion of the two governments would take place, with an oath to be taken neither to the King nor to the Regency Council but to the "people." The youthful monarch staunchly opposed the slight role of the Regency Council in comparison to Tito's A.V.N.O.J., and his opposition delayed announcement of the accords until late in January, 1945.[48]

In view of the complexity and seriousness of all these problems it is hardly surprising that Churchill was anxious to persuade Roosevelt to hold extensive Anglo-American staff conversations en route to Yalta to co-ordinate strategy. The President was reluctant, ostensibly because of the very limited time at his disposal, but really because he did not wish to give Stalin the impression that he and Churchill were teaming up against him. Thus, only a few brief talks were held between Churchill and Roosevelt at Malta. On the other hand, since several extensive conversations were held in different places by the new Secretary of State, Edward R. Stettinius, and Harry Hopkins with Churchill and Eden, and by Anglo-American military leaders, there probably was enough opportunity for the two governments to exchange views on the major problems. At Yalta separate Anglo-American talks were infrequent, partly because of the considerable distance that separated the British from the American headquarters, an arrangement to which the Russian hosts had given due consideration.[49]

1950), by the British Ambassador to Athens, 1943–46; W. H. McNeill, *The Greek Dilemma: War and Aftermath* (London, 1947); and W. Byford-Jones, *The Greek Trilogy: Resistance, Liberation, Revolution* (London, 1946).

[48] *Yalta Papers*, 250–65.

[49] *Ibid.*, 29–40.

Briefing Papers

All three governments doubtless prepared numerous "briefing" and "position papers" for the guidance of their negotiators at Yalta, but thus far only the American ones have been made public. The Relevant British documents will be published after a lapse of time; meanwhile, historians must content themselves with Churchill's memoirs, official statements in Parliament, and the American revelation of British correspondence. Soviet Russia has given no indication whether or when her documents will be released.

The American briefing papers on central-eastern European affairs were prepared between November, 1944, and early January, 1945. These were assembled in a black binder (the "Briefing Book") and were presented by Secretary of State Stettinius to the President on January 18, shortly before he set sail for Malta.[50] How carefully the President was able to do his "homework" aboard ship is a matter of dispute. Since Stettinius and Hopkins traveled to Malta separately, they were unavailable to carry on intensive briefing sessions with the President, and James F. Byrnes formed the impression that Roosevelt did not find much time to study the papers because of his need to get a thorough rest during the voyage. Byrnes quickly admitted, however, that "only President Roosevelt, with his intimate knowledge of the problems could have handled the situation so well with so little preparation."[51] Whatever the facts, the record of discussions at Yalta suggests that the President was fairly well informed about the problems with which he had been closely concerned throughout the war. Certainly during the grueling week at Yalta he was briefed daily by key advisers.

One of the Briefing Book documents in particular is noteworthy for its concise presentation of American assumptions and general objectives. In it, John D. Hickerson, deputy director of the Office of European Affairs, on January 8, 1945, informed Stettinius: "We have a pretty clear idea of the Soviet objectives in eastern Europe."

50 *Ibid.*, 42.
51 Byrnes, *Speaking Frankly*, 23.

We have the terms of their settlement with Finland. We know that the three Baltic States have been re-incorporated into the Soviet Union. . . . It is not a question of whether we like it; I personally don't like it. . . . The point is that it has been done and nothing which it is within the power of the United States Government to do can undo it. We know that the Russians will insist on the annexation of a substantial portion of East Prussia and a boundary with Poland roughly in accordance with the Curzon Line. The Soviet Union has already re-incorporated Bessarabia. . . .

I would favor using any bargaining power that exists in connection with the foregoing matters to induce the Russians to go along with a satisfactory United Nations organization and the proposed Provisional Security Council for Europe to deal with Poland, Greece and other trouble spots.

Hickerson went on to suggest American acquiescence in Soviet re-incorporation of the Baltic states and Bessarabia, as well as the prospective transfer of much of East Prussia, which the Russians insisted upon having. "I would likewise favor our agreeing to accept as a fact, at the appropriate time, the Curzon line as a frontier . . . and to agree to announce publicly such acceptance," he wrote. "We must have the support of the Soviet Union to defeat Germany. We sorely need the Soviet Union in the war against Japan when the war in Europe is over. The importance of these two things can be reckoned in terms of American lives. We must have the cooperation of the Soviet Union to organize the peace."[52]

Another Briefing Book paper took up the subject of postwar political regimes in liberated countries. It recommended that the Americans pursue a "middle course" between the British and Russians, taking into account "present indications" that the "general mood of the people of Europe is to the left and strongly in favor of far-reaching economic and social reforms, but not, however, in favor of a leftwing totalitarian regime to achieve these reforms." This paper recommended two criteria for American acceptance of any proposed interim government: (1) its dedication to the preservation of civil liberties, and (2) its advocacy of social and economic

[52] *Yalta Papers,* 94–95.

reforms.[53] Yet another memorandum discussed the recent Anglo-Soviet moves to specify in percentages their relative predominance in southeastern European countries. Explaining the limited nature of American agreement, the paper expressed concern lest these camouflaged spheres of influence become permanent and "militate against the establishment and effective functioning of a broader system of general security in which all countries will have their part."[54]

In most of their analyses of Balkan problems, the Americans had a tendency to underestimate the forces of nationalism in this region.[55] Strife-ridden Yugoslavia was the subject of a special paper. "Frankly," it noted, "Marshal Tito and his subordinates have not shown a disposition toward cooperation or even common civility in recent weeks. . . . All indications point to the intention of the Partisans to establish a thoroughly totalitarian regime, in order to maintain themselves in power." The State Department observed that the recent agreement which Churchill had arranged between Tito and Ivan Šubašić, the Prime Minister in exile, "would transfer the effective power of government to the Tito organization, with just enough participation of the Government-in-Exile to facilitate recognition by other governments." The language of the agreement "is in line with our ideas," the paper went on, but "any endorsement of a new administration [should be] contingent on freedom of movement and access to public opinion . . . for our observers."[56]

On the most urgent of all the eastern European problems, Poland, the State Department recommended prevention of any interim regime "which would exclude any major element . . . and threaten to crystallize into a permanent government before the will of the population could become manifest." It advised against recognition of the Soviet-sponsored Lublin provisional government, "at least until more conclusive evidence is received that it does in fact represent the basic wishes of the Polish people." Eventual elections in

[53] *Ibid.*, 103.
[54] *Ibid.*, 105.
[55] Ethridge and Black, "Negotiating on the Balkans, 1945–1947," in Dennett and Johnson (eds.), *Negotiating with the Russians*, 172–73.
[56] *Yalta Papers*, 262–65.

Poland should be supervised by "United Nations arrangements," the paper went on. The vexatious problem of the eastern frontier should be solved by acceptance of the Curzon Line, except in the southern extremity. In that sector the border should follow the eastern edge of the province of Lwow, which would result in leaving to Poland the valuable Galician oil lands. To compensate her for the loss of territory in the east, Poland should be assigned the "bulk of East Prussia, and, in the west . . . a small strip of Pomerania west of the so-called Polish Corridor and Upper Silesia." But the United States should resist the "exaggerated claims" of the Lublin Poles for German lands extending as far west as the Oder and Western Neisse rivers, for this would necessitate the displacement of "eight to ten million Germans."[57]

At Yalta on Sunday, February 4, prior to the formal discussions, President Roosevelt was briefed again on the Polish problem. Present in addition to Stettinius and Harriman were Charles E. Bohlen and H. Freeman Matthews, both key State Department experts on eastern European affairs. Bohlen pointed out the importance of the oil fields to Poland and noted that the Poles stood to receive about one-third less German territory than they would lose to Soviet Russia. The President expressed the hope that Stalin might agree to leave the oil fields in exchange for Lwow. He also mentioned interest in a recent proposal by Mikolajczyk for a presidential council to be composed of members of five political parties (including the Communists). Certain "representative" Poles from the Warsaw provisional government and "moderate" Poles (such as Mikolajczyk) from London would be included. Roosevelt asked his advisers to prepare a short paper expressing the American point of view on this proposal for him to hand to Stalin and Churchill.[58]

At this same briefing session, the President decided not to bring before the conference a State Department project calling for a "Provisional Security Council for Europe," or, as it was also termed, an "Emergency European High Commis-

[57] *Ibid.*, 230.
[58] Edward R. Stettinius, Jr. (Walter Johnson, ed.), *Roosevelt and the Russians: The Yalta Conference* (Garden City, 1949), 84–88.

sion on Liberated Territories," to consist of the three Great Powers and France. According to the planners, this body would supervise elections if necessary and implement the principles of the "Declaration on Liberated Europe," a document which also had been prepared by the State Department. This declaration reaffirmed the ideals of the Atlantic Charter and called for joint action by the Great Powers in meeting the political and economic problems of liberated Europe in accordance with democratic principles. The "Yalta Declaration" was to be adopted by the Big Three with minor changes, but the High Commission was not even proposed. The President objected that it would be another bureaucratic agency of doubtful value and preferred to utilize the existing diplomatic machinery. Stettinius considered this a mistake, and has argued that had such a commission been established, it might have been able to deal effectively with the thorny eastern European issues.[59]

THE YALTA DISCUSSIONS

The Polish question was first raised during the dinner conversation of the Big Three on February 4. The President observed to Stalin that there were "lots of Poles in America . . . vitally interested in the future of Poland," whereupon Stalin immediately rejoined: "But of your seven million Poles, only seven thousand vote." He added with emphasis that he knew because he had "looked it up."[60] If the Soviet dictator was serious, the magnitude of his misinformation is obvious, for American voters of Polish descent were—and are—numbered in the hundreds of thousands. The interchange suggested that he was not likely to modify his objectives in order to mollify Polish-American voters.

Initial Stands

The President, who presided at all the plenary sessions, initiated the formal Polish discussion on February 6 by observing that he had come "from a great distance" and might "have the advantage of a more distant point of view

59 *Ibid.,* 88–89.
60 *Ibid.,* 113.

of the problem." Again he mentioned the pressure he felt from six or seven million Poles in the United States to achieve a satisfactory solution of the problem—an argument which Stalin soon countered with references to the similar pressure he faced from the Ukrainians. "As I said in Teheran, in general I am in favor of the Curzon Line," Roosevelt went on, but then expressed the hope that the Soviet government "would give something to Poland" as a means of saving "face" for the Poles and making "it easier for me at home." "I raised the question of giving them Lwow at Teheran. It has now been suggested that the oil lands in the southwest of Lwow might be given them. I am not making a definite statement, but I hope that Marshal Stalin can make a gesture in this direction."[61] Clearly the President was seeking to be conciliatory.

Far more important than the boundary, the President continued, was the nature of Poland's government. He pointed out that American opinion was against recognition of the Lublin (Warsaw) government, "on the ground that it represents a small portion of the Polish people." He expressed the need for a government representing the five major political parties, but declared that he had an open mind toward the matter of specific individuals to be brought into such a government. Roosevelt commented, though, that he "was greatly impressed" by Mikolajczyk, whom he regarded as "an honest man." "The main suggestion I want to make is . . . the possibility of creating a presidency council made up of a small number of men who would be the controlling force *ad interim*" and who would have the task of forming a cabinet. The President terminated his statement by assuring Stalin that "we want a Poland that will be thoroughly friendly to the Soviet for years to come. This is essential."[62]

In a lengthy statement, Prime Minister Churchill concurred

[61] Matthews minutes, *Yalta Papers*, 677. The stenographic minutes made by H. Freeman Matthews, director of the Office of European Affairs in the State Department, were often somewhat more detailed than those taken by Charles E. Bohlen, assistant to the Secretary of State, who had the additional burden of interpreting for the President. The author has endeavored to cite whichever record seems most complete.

[62] *Ibid.,* 678.

with the President's general views: "I have always considered
that after all Russia has suffered in fighting against Germany
and after all her efforts in liberating Poland, her claim is one
founded not on force but on right. In that position I abide.
But of course if the mighty power, the Soviet Union, made a
gesture suggested by the President, we would heartily acclaim
such action." Churchill's chief interest, however, was "in the
question of Poland's sovereign independence":

> That is an objective which I have always heard Marshal Stalin
> proclaim with the utmost firmness. . . . This is what we went to
> war against Germany for. . . . Great Britain had no material
> interest in Poland. Her interest is only one of honor. . . . Never
> could I be content with any solution that would not leave
> Poland as a free and independent state. However, I have one
> qualification: I do not think that the freedom of Poland could
> be made to cover hostile designs by any Polish government,
> perhaps by intrigue with Germany, against the Soviet.

Churchill expressed his desire that the nature of Poland's
new government be worked out during the conference. Insisting that his most earnest desire was that Poland "be mistress
in her own house" and "captain of her own soul," he indicated that he wanted a place in the new interim government,
pending "free elections," for such London Poles as Mikolajczyk, Stanislaw Grabski, and Tadeusz Romer.[63]

After a ten-minute intermission Stalin presented his views.
Looking straight at Churchill, he declared, "For Russia [the
Polish problem] is not only a question of honor but also of
security." He emphasized that Poland repeatedly had served
as a "corridor for attack on Russia" and recalled that twice
during the last thirty years Germany had marched through it
"because Poland was weak." If for no other reason than her
own protection the Soviet Union sought a "free, independent,
and powerful" Poland, and to this end had repudiated czarist
policies toward her neighbor. Turning to the adjustments of
the Curzon Line recommended by Roosevelt and Churchill,
the Soviet leader pointedly reminded his listeners that "the
Curzon Line was invented not by Russians but by foreigners,"

[63] *Ibid.*, 678–79.

and he asked the British and Americans if they really expected him to be "less Russian than Curzon and Clemenceau." "I cannot take such a position and return to Moscow," he declared emphatically, rising to his feet as he spoke. Stalin then recalled that Mikolajczyk during his recent trip to Moscow had been delighted to learn of the proposed territorial compensation to be obtained from Germany up to the Western Neisse River.[64]

The Soviet leader chided Churchill for what he termed a "slip of the tongue" in talking of creating a Polish government without direct consultation with the Poles. He recalled that a few months before in Moscow they had had an opportunity to create such a government but that the London Poles had repudiated Mikolajczyk's negotiations. After pointing out the difficulties of bringing the two hostile Polish factions together, Stalin said he was ready to "support any attempt to create unity if there is some chance of success." To this end, he suggested that some of the Warsaw Polish leaders be brought to Yalta, or better yet to Moscow later. Then he interjected sharply that in his opinion the Warsaw government's democratic base was as valid as that of de Gaulle in France. Although de Gaulle's regime did not rest on elections, treaties had been signed with it, he noted. The Marshal terminated his long exposition by stressing that "as a military man" he must "demand from the country liberated by the Red Army that there be no civil war in the rear." He accused the London Poles of inciting attacks against Soviet forces and announced: "We will support the Government which gives us peace in the rear."[65] Indirectly, of course, this was a reminder to the West that the Red Army stood in the area which was subject to discussion at Yalta.

Responding, Churchill observed that he and Stalin evidently had different sources of information about Poland. The Prime Minister expressed his desire that no clashes occur between the Polish underground and the Lublin-Warsaw regime, but he reiterated that Britain would not extend recognition to the latter.[66]

[64] *Ibid.*, 679–81; Byrnes, *Speaking Frankly*, 30.
[65] *Yalta Papers*, 669–70, 679–81.
[66] *Ibid.*, 681.

The Maneuvering

That evening after the adjournment President Roosevelt dispatched to Stalin a letter prepared by the State Department and Harry Hopkins. It suggested that the Soviet leader follow through with his proposal to bring some of the Lublin-Warsaw leaders to Yalta, and specifically mentioned Bierut and Osóbka-Morawski. The President also recommended that two or three from the following list of men unconnected with the Lublin-Warsaw regime be brought from Poland: Archbishop Adam Sapieha of Cracow, Wincenty Witos, Zygmunt Zulawski, Professor Stanislaw Kutrzeba, and Professor Franciszek Bujak. A conference with these men might bring agreement on a provisional government, which would also include such Poles from London as Mikolajczyk, Grabski, and Romer. A government of this kind should hold free elections as soon as possible, Roosevelt declared in his letter.[67]

At the February 7 plenary session the President re-opened the Polish question, again stressing the primary importance of the governmental crisis. He suggested a "fresh start" on the subject, observing that he was "not so concerned on the question of the continuity of the government." "There hasn't really been any Polish government since 1939," he went on, rather surprisingly in view of the continued American recognition of the Polish government in exile. "It is entirely in the province of the three of us to help set up a government—something to last until the Polish people can choose. I discard the idea of continuity. I think we want something new and drastic like a breath of fresh air."[68]

Stalin announced that he had received the President's letter only "an hour and a half ago" and had immediately given instructions to telephone Bierut and Osóbka-Morawski, only to learn that they were away from Warsaw, in either Lodz or Cracow; "but they will be found," he added. "I must ask them how to find the representatives on the other side and what they think of the possibility of their coming. . . . If . . . Witos or Sapieha could come here it would facilitate a solution but I do not know their addresses. I am afraid we have

[67] *Ibid.*, 726–28.
[68] *Ibid.*, 718.

not sufficient time."[69] The Marshal then requested Foreign Commissar Molotov to present the Soviet counterproposal. This called for agreement on the Curzon Line, with small digressions of five to eight kilometers here and there in favor of Poland. The Polish western frontier should extend from Stettin up the Oder and Western Neisse rivers. The existing Warsaw provisional government should add to it some democratic leaders from "émigré circles," receive Allied recognition, and call for elections quickly to form a permanent government. The British and American ambassadors in Moscow should meet with Molotov to take up in the first instance the question of enlarging the provisional government and then should submit their proposals to the three Great Powers. Concluding his statement, Molotov announced that the Warsaw leaders still could not be reached by telephone. There really was no time for them to get to the Crimea in any case, he added.[70]

The President and the Prime Minister indicated that they wished to study Molotov's proposals overnight, but meanwhile would object to usage of the term, "Polish émigrés." They insisted that the word "émigrés" bore the connotation of men driven out by their fellow citizens, which certainly was not the case in Poland. Churchill also objected to the Western Neisse River as a frontier because of the hardships that mass transfers of population would entail. And, he added, "I do not wish to stuff the Polish goose until it dies of German indigestion." Before the meeting of February 7 adjourned Churchill succeeded in persuading Stalin to add to Molotov's plan a clause entitling the broadened government to include not only members of the Lublin-Warsaw group and certain Poles from abroad, but also others "from inside Poland."[71]

The next morning Roosevelt sent a counterproposal to Churchill and Stalin in which he acquiesced in Molotov's plan for the eastern frontier but objected strongly to pushing back the German frontier to the Western Neisse. The President proposed instead that Polish compensation from Germany

[69] *Ibid.*, 719.
[70] *Ibid.*, 716.
[71] *Ibid.*, 717, 720.

include only East Prussia to the south of Königsberg, Upper Silesia, and the land east of the Oder. As for the political question, he suggested that Molotov and the two Western ambassadors in Moscow invite Bierut, Osóbka-Morawski, Sapieha, Witos, Mikolajczyk, and Grabski to form a provisional "Government of National Unity" in the following way: (1) first, appoint a presidential committee of three—perhaps Bierut, Grabski, and Sapieha; (2) then have this committee form a ministry composed of representative members of the present Warsaw government, other democratic elements inside Poland, and Polish democratic leaders abroad; (3) when such a "Government of National Unity" was formed the three Great Powers would recognize it as the provisional government of Poland; and (4) have this interim government hold free elections as soon as conditions permit for a constituent assembly to establish a new Polish constitution, under which a permanent government would be elected.[72] At the plenary session that same day Molotov asked the President if the Polish government in London would disappear as soon as Big Three recognition was extended to the "Government of National Unity." Both Roosevelt and Churchill answered affirmatively.[73]

After a recess during the February 8 plenary session Churchill observed that while he had already circulated a British proposal for Poland, discussion had begun on the American proposal and he was willing to accept the latter with slight modification. Churchill's document agreed to the Curzon Line with the adjustments indicated by Molotov, but it objected to the Western Neisse line. Poland should limit its acquisitions to Danzig, regions in East Prussia west and south of Königsberg, the district of Oppeln in Silesia, and any lands as far west as the Oder River which it might desire. Churchill suggested that an exchange of populations be made in the areas affected. He called for a fully representative provisional government based on all the democratic and anti-Fascist forces in Poland and including democratic leaders from abroad. Representative Polish leaders should consult on

[72] *Ibid.*, 792–93.
[73] *Ibid.*, 776, 786.

the composition of this provisional government, and the British and American ambassadors in Moscow together with Molotov should talk with these leaders and submit their proposals for consideration by the Big Three. Churchill insisted upon "free, unfettered elections" as soon as possible.[74]

In his response Molotov asserted that neither of the western proposals took into consideration the existing Warsaw government, which should be "enlarged" by adding to it other democratic elements from within Poland and abroad. Expanding his argument, he insisted that the Warsaw government enjoyed popularity because of its close identification with the liberation. Molotov expressed happiness over agreement on the Curzon Line and declared there was no doubt whatever that Warsaw leaders desired the Western Neisse frontier. He said he would be willing to go along with the proposal that the Polish leaders meet with him and the two Western ambassadors. Turning to the American proposal for a Polish presidential council, he declared that he preferred a government made up of three members from the Warsaw regime and two from the list the President had suggested the day before, but he remarked that he was not at all sure about including Mikolajczyk. The Soviet spokesman noted in passing that all three powers were in agreement on the need for free elections.[75]

Confronted with the divergent views regarding a Polish government, Churchill declared that the conference had now reached its crucial point. The Warsaw regime did not have the support of the mass of Poles, he insisted, and he had no intention of brushing aside the London Poles and the Polish Army of some 150,000 men who were fighting in Italy and on the western front. The Prime Minister pointed out that he had conceded to the Russians on the frontier but that he could not capitulate on the governmental issue. The British must be convinced that a new government, representative of the Polish people, was being created and pledged to unfettered elections. After such elections Britain would disre-

[74] *Ibid.*, 869–71; and summarized in Stettinius, *Roosevelt and the Russians*, 211–12.
[75] *Yalta Papers*, 786–87.

gard the London government and salute the new one, he promised.[76]

In an effort to relieve the tension, Roosevelt remarked that since all three agreed on the need for free elections, the problem was how to govern Poland in the interim. Stalin then reaffirmed Molotov's contentions and declared that it would be best to "enlarge" the existing Warsaw government. He repeated the argument about de Gaulle—if the Allies could deal with him, why not also with an enlarged provisional government of Poland? The lengthy session was drawing to a close when the President inquired of Stalin how long it would be before elections could be held. Stalin answered that they could take place within a month. The three then decided to refer the problem overnight to their foreign secretaries.[77]

The Foreign Secretaries Negotiate

When the foreign ministers met in the morning of February 9, Secretary of State Stettinius commented that if the Polish matter were not solved satisfactorily at Yalta it might prevent American participation in the United Nations. To speed up the solution, he offered to drop the proposal for a presidential committee. Voicing the conviction that only the Poles could really decide the problem of their government, Stettinius suggested a new formula which combined parts of the proposals put forward by each of the Great Powers. It called for "reorganization" of the existing Warsaw regime into a "fully representative" one, thereafter to be termed the "Provisional Government of National Unity," which would include representatives of "all democratic forces" in the country and democratic leaders from abroad. Molotov and the two western ambassadors in Moscow would consult with members of the existing Warsaw regime and other democratic leaders from within and without the country about the "reorganization" of the government along these lines. When such a "Provisional Government of National Unity" was satisfactorily formed, the Big Three would recognize it; it would

[76] *Ibid.*, 787–88.
[77] *Ibid.*, 788–90.

then hold "free elections" in accordance with the definition made in the British proposals. The ambassadors of the three Great Powers accredited to such a Polish government would observe and report officially on the "carrying out of the election pledge for free and unfettered elections."

Emphasizing Britain's concern over the problem, Foreign Secretary Eden informed his opposites that he had just received a telegram from London insisting upon an entirely "new start" rather than mere "addition" to the Warsaw regime and demanding inclusion of Mikolajczyk in the new government. Molotov conceded that Mikolajczyk might be included, if the Poles were agreeable, but he insisted that revision of the governmental organization must be based on mere "enlargement" rather than "reorganization" of the "existing Warsaw Government" and that the Poles must be consulted. The Soviet Commissar repeated that elections could be held within a month or two, but that even in that interval Russian military needs must be safeguarded. At this point Eden stated bluntly that if the elections were conducted by the present officials in Warsaw he was sure that they would not be free. Finally, Molotov expressed his willingness to confer with Stalin about Stettinius' modified proposal, but he objected strenuously to the section calling upon the ambassadors to observe and report on the elections, for this would "offend" the Poles. Unable to reach agreement, the three foreign ministers decided to refer the entire problem back to their superiors.[78]

The Big Three Resume Talks

When the plenary session convened in the afternoon, Molotov suggested the following revision of the Stettinius proposal: "The present Provisional Government of Poland should be reorganized on a wider democratic basis with the inclusion of democratic leaders from Poland itself and from those living abroad, and in this connection the government would be called the National Provisional Government of Poland." He recommended elimination of the sentence about the three ambassadors' observing and reporting on the elec-

[78] *Ibid.*, 803–807; Stettinius, *Roosevelt and the Russians*, 224–29.

tions, and in one passage he suggested that participation be restricted to "non-Fascist and anti-Fascist" parties.[79]

Churchill was pleased by Molotov's concession but cautioned both the Americans and Russians against excessive haste in handling the "most important question" before the conference. A half-hour recess was called to permit the western delegations to study Molotov's amendments. When the group reconvened the President observed that they were nearer agreement and that it was now mainly "a matter of drafting." He preferred that Molotov call the Warsaw regime not the "Provisional Government" but the "Government now operating in Poland." Roosevelt emphasized again that millions of Polish-Americans were deeply concerned with the decisions they were making and he underlined the importance of retaining the clause calling upon the ambassadors to observe and report on the elections. This statement was echoed and amplified by Churchill, who also asked Stalin pointedly if Mikolajczyk and the Peasant party would be allowed to participate in the elections. Stalin promised that they would. Roosevelt at this point remarked, "I want this election in Poland to be the first one beyond question. It should be like Caesar's wife. I did not know her but they said she was pure." "They said that about her," Stalin interrupted, "but in fact she had her sins." "I don't want the Poles to be able to question the Polish elections," the President continued. "The matter is not only one of principle but of practical politics." He then suggested that the foreign ministers work out the details of the governmental agreement that night. Stalin remonstrated that it should be discussed in the presence of the Poles, but Churchill insisted that it must be finished at Yalta. The matter was again referred to the ministers for action and report.[80]

Meanwhile, the plenary session took up the "Declaration on Liberated Europe" which the Americans had drafted. Stalin recommended addition of the provision that Big Three support would be given to political leaders who had "taken an active part in the struggle against the German invaders,"

79 *Yalta Papers*, 842.
80 *Ibid.*, 842–55.

a clause which was obviously designed to justify Soviet support for Communist puppets. Mischievously, Stalin told Churchill that he need not worry about the implications of this clause for Greece, whereupon the two premiers engaged in some banter about recent developments in that British-occupied and revolt-torn land. Roosevelt avoided a showdown on Stalin's new proposal and observed that the declaration would apply to Poland as well as to other areas. He noted that in an earlier draft France was to be included as a signatory, but was dropped since that country was not represented at Yalta. Stalin expressed his pleasure that France was not included, but Churchill observed that it would be well to have France sign the declaration. Roosevelt recommended that the foreign ministers discuss the matter overnight.[81]

Again the Foreign Secretaries

When the three ministers met later that evening Eden announced receipt of another urgent cable from the War Cabinet insisting that there be agreement to something like the Polish formula he had presented on February 8. In this connection he submitted a "Revised Formula," which thereupon gave rise to what Stettinius termed a "long, grueling discussion." Eventually the three ministers reached the following agreements: (1) a new situation had been brought about by the Red Army's liberation of Poland; (2) there was need for a fully representative Polish government, to be called the "Provisional Government of National Unity," based upon the provisional government then functioning in Poland, and to include other democratic Polish leaders from within and abroad; (3) Molotov, British Ambassador Archibald Clark Kerr, and American Ambassador Harriman in Moscow would consult with Poles from the three sources mentioned in order to "reorganize" the existing government along more representative lines; (4) such a "Provisional Government of National Unity" would hold free elections; and (5) when such a government was formed the Great Powers would recognize it. The section of the formula that had called upon the three ambassadors to observe and report on the elections

81 *Ibid.*, 849.

aroused so much Soviet opposition that it was tossed back to the Big Three. At the same session of the foreign ministers, Stalin's proposed amendment to the Declaration on Liberated Europe came up for discussion, but neither westerner would agree to its relevancy and it was referred back to the plenary session.[82]

Saturday morning, February 10, Secretary Stettinius reported to the President about the session of the previous evening. On this occasion Roosevelt, in order to hasten the negotiation, agreed to withdraw the sentence that spelled out in detail the function of the ambassadors during the Polish elections, provided it remained clearly understood that the ambassadors would in any event observe and report.[83] Stettinius then informed the other foreign ministers of Roosevelt's concession, which did not at all meet with Eden's acceptance. Thereupon Molotov attempted to get the British and Americans to state that they would "establish diplomatic relations with the Polish Government as has been done by the Soviet Union." Both Eden and Stettinius refused, insisting that recognition would be accorded only to a new government.[84]

Next, the foreign secretaries turned to the Declaration on Liberated Europe. In the face of American objections, Molotov agreed to withdraw Stalin's proposal about supporting leaders who had taken an "active part in the struggle against the German invaders." Instead of providing that the Big Three should "immediately establish appropriate machinery for the carrying out of the joint responsibilities set forth in this declaration," Molotov insisted upon substituting the weaker clause, "They will immediately take measures for the carrying out of mutual consultation." The westerners concurred. At Russian insistence, the question of France's signature of the declaration was left for the plenary session to answer.[85]

---

[82] Stettinius, *Roosevelt and the Russians*, 246–49; *Yalta Papers*, 867–71; 883–84.

[83] Stettinius, *Roosevelt and the Russians*, 251–52.

[84] *Ibid.*, 252; *Yalta Papers*, 872–73.

[85] *Yalta Papers*, 873; Stettinius, *Roosevelt and the Russians*, 253.

Final Agreements

Early Saturday afternoon an Anglo-Russian subcommittee met to discuss the wording of sections regarding diplomatic recognition of the new government and observation of the elections, and in mid-afternoon Churchill and Eden went to see Stalin and Molotov at the Yusupov Villa. There they obtained Soviet agreement to the phraseology worked out by the subcommittee. The Prime Minister was able to get Stalin to agree to a statement that recognition of a new Polish government "should entail an exchange of Ambassadors by whose reports the respective governments would be informed about the situation in Poland." "This was the best I could get," Churchill has declared.[86]

Late in the afternoon the plenary session convened as usual in Livadia Palace. Both Churchill and Stalin were tardy. They apologized to Roosevelt for their delay and then informed the group of their agreement, which avoided any reference to the Polish government in London:

> When a Polish Provisional Government of National Unity has been properly formed in conformity with the above, the Government of the U.S.S.R., which now maintains diplomatic relations with the present Provisional Government of Poland, and the Government of the United Kingdom and the Government of the U.S.A. will establish diplomatic relations with the new Polish Provisional Government of National Unity, and will exchange Ambassadors by whose reports the respective governments will be kept informed about the situation in Poland.[87]

Churchill observed that thus far the Polish agreement did not mention boundaries. Everyone agreed upon the eastern frontier and upon the right of Poland to compensation from Germany, he noted, but he for one could not approve establishment of the German frontier along the Western Neisse.[88] At this point Hopkins passed a note to the President, recommending only a general statement in the communiqué to the effect that the Big Three were considering essential boundary

[86] Churchill, *Triumph and Tragedy*, 385.
[87] *Yalta Papers*, 898.
[88] *Ibid.*, 898–99, 907.

changes. He suggested that precise wording of the statement might be left to the foreign ministers.[89] Roosevelt did not follow Hopkins' advice. Instead he declared that the Polish government should be consulted before any statement was made regarding the western frontier. Molotov then recommended that the foreign ministers draft the statement on the eastern frontier and observed that it was unnecessary to be so specific about the western one. Churchill interposed that the opinion of the new "Government of National Unity" should be ascertained on the German boundary but reiterated his agreement that Poland should receive a good slice of territory. The President concurred and asked Churchill to draft a statement.[90]

Next, the heads of government turned to the Declaration on Liberated Europe. Eden reported that both the British and Americans now wished France to be associated with the declaration and that the Soviets wished to add a paragraph to the effect that the three governments should take steps immediately to carry out mutual consultation. As in the discussion of French participation in the occupation of Germany, Roosevelt confirmed his changed opinion with respect to French participation in the signing of the declaration, whereupon the Big Three speedily registered their approval of the additions.[91]

The problem of achieving amalgamation of the Yugoslav government in exile with Tito's government was next discussed. It had been explored in previous plenary sessions and in those of the foreign ministers. As the result of strong British pressure, ostensible agreement between Tito and Premier Šubašić had been reached a few weeks before, but Šubašić had not yet gone to Belgrade, and King Peter was displeased with some aspects of the accord. To improve matters Churchill at Yalta asked for Soviet approval of two amendments to the Tito-Šubašić agreement: (1) expansion of the Anti-Fascist Assembly of National Liberation (A.V.N.O.J.) to include members of the last Yugoslav legislature who had

[89] Stettinius, *Roosevelt and the Russians,* 260.
[90] *Yalta Papers,* 898–99, 907.
[91] *Ibid.,* 899, 908.

not compromised themselves by collaboration with the Germans, the enlarged body to serve as a temporary parliament; (2) subjection of its legislative actions to subsequent ratification by a constituent assembly. Roosevelt supported Churchill's amendments, but Stalin and Molotov for some time endeavored to sidetrack them in favor of putting the Tito-Šubašić fusion government into operation first. Churchill's unyielding attitude led to Stalin's acquiescence at the final plenary session. Stalin not only accepted the two amendments but agreed to their publication in the Yalta communiqué and their immediate delivery to Tito and Šubašić.[92]

By this time it was six o'clock and everyone was weary. A brief recess was taken for tea, after which the plenary group turned to the subject of the Dardanelles. Stalin considered the Montreux Convention, which regulated the Straits, outdated, remarking that it was part of the now defunct League of Nations machinery, that it enabled Turkey to exercise a stranglehold on Russia, and that Japan had played a bigger role in drafting it than had the U.S.S.R. Anxious as any czar to win free access to the Mediterranean, Stalin suggested that the subject be placed on the agenda of the first meeting of the foreign ministers after Yalta. The westerners agreed, after observing that Turkey should be informed and assured that its independence would be guaranteed.[93]

The President then reverted to the problem of Polish boundaries, as the result of a memorandum handed to him by Hopkins prior to the recess. His advisers, aware of the storm of criticism that would be forthcoming from Polish-Americans, had raised the question whether the President had constitutional power to commit the United States to a treaty establishing boundaries. During the intermission the President hit upon his own solution to this problem. Suddenly he remarked, "I've got it." He suggested substituting "three Heads of Government" for "the three powers," and the words "consider" and "feel" for "agree." In this way the statement would not be a binding and official commitment but simply an expression of views. Thus it read:

92 *Ibid.*, 900–901, 908–909. The telegram as sent is *ibid.*, 919–20.
93 *Ibid.*, 903–905, 909–11.

The three Heads of Government consider that the Eastern frontier of Poland should follow the Curzon Line with digressions from it in some regions of five to eight kilometres in favour of Poland. It is recognized that Poland must receive substantial accessions of territory in the North and West. They feel that the opinion of the new Polish Provisional Government of National Unity should be sought in due course on the extent of these accessions and that the final delimitation of the Western frontier of Poland should thereafter await the Peace Conference.[94]

It was this vague formula that was finally approved by the plenary session.

Sunday morning, the last day of the conference, the Big Three hastily edited and approved the public communiqué, which was to be released the next day. The President, who was very tired after the long series of exhausting conferences, banquets, and decisions, was especially anxious to be on his way, and he jokingly reminded the group that he had a date with "three Kings" in the Middle East. The foreign ministers lingered on to draw up the protocol, which included both the communiqué and certain documents not then published. The agreements regarding Poland and the Declaration on Liberated Europe were the same in both the communiqué and protocol. Such topics as the operation of the Allied Control Commissions and the Montreux Convention were not mentioned in the communiqué, since no decision was reached except to refer them back to the ambassadorial level for further discussion.[95]

EASTERN EUROPEAN EPILOGUE

Early in the war Poland had emerged as the roughest testing ground of the possibility of maintaining amicable relations between East and West. Harry Hopkins once told Stalin that "the question of Poland *per se* was not so important as the fact that it had become a symbol of our ability to work out problems with the Soviet Union."[96] Uppermost in the

[94] Stettinius, *Roosevelt and the Russians*, 269–71; *Yalta Papers*, 905, 911.

[95] For the communiqué, see *Yalta Papers*, 968–75. The protocol appears as the Appendix to this volume.

[96] Sherwood, *Roosevelt and Hopkins*, 898.

American delegation's thoughts was winning Soviet acceptance of the United Nations blueprint and Russian participation in the Pacific war. Churchill declared at Yalta that his
country "had no material interest in Poland." Britain's interest, he said, was "only one of honor" toward an allied state
whose invasion had precipitated the war.[97] Stalin, on the
other hand, took the uncompromising stand that for his country the Polish problem was not just a "symbol," nor a "question of honor," but one of "security."[98] Because of the relative
weight which each of the Big Three assigned to the Polish
issue, the nature of their prior agreements, and the realities
of Russian military power in eastern Europe, there was little
room at Yalta for successful bargaining against the U.S.S.R.

Nonetheless, Churchill and Roosevelt argued the Polish
problem with Stalin for six days and nights. Obviously, it was
not a question of what they would permit him to do but what
they could persuade him to accept. In the protracted, exhausting discussions, Churchill, whose previous diplomatic en-
gagements involved him in this region much more deeply
than was the case with Roosevelt, doggedly carried the burden
of western argumentation. He marshaled his points carefully
and often eloquently, and in the drafting of the final agreements he endeavored, insofar as the limited time permitted,
to weigh the import of every word. President Roosevelt preferred to play the role of moderator, but in the showdowns
he usually aligned himself with Churchill. Roosevelt's exposition was not always so skillful, energetic, or persistent as that
of the Briton, but it fully evidenced his concern for a really
independent Poland as well as for lasting world peace. For
his part, Stalin set forth with bluntness Soviet Russia's strategic interests, and he cleverly seized upon the weak points in
the westerners' case. He reminded them that they should not
expect him to be any less Russian than Clemenceau and Lord
Curzon; he skillfully equated the legitimacy of his Lublin
regime with that of de Gaulle in France; and employing the
same arguments that Churchill had used recently in Greece
to justify British measures, he argued persuasively that noth-

[97] *Yalta Papers,* 678-79.
[98] *Ibid.,* 679-81.

From Chester Wilmot, *The Struggle for Europe* (New York, 1952).

POLAND AND YALTA

ing must be allowed to jeopardize the security of the Soviet armies in Poland. The Russian leader was impervious to arguments based either on "high moral" principles or on the need for placating Polish-American voters. But sometimes he was willing to accept phraseology that enabled the West to "save face," especially if he felt certain that in the execution of the agreements he could have his own way.

Thus Roosevelt and Churchill were able to win a moral victory when they persuaded Stalin to agree with minor changes to the pledges contained in the somewhat loosely phrased Declaration on Liberated Europe. Certainly there was nothing reprehensible in the terms of this American-sponsored document, which called for "free" and "democratic" regimes in eastern Europe. But the present-day observer is inclined to marvel at the optimism of the Big Three when they declared: "We reaffirm our faith in the principles of the Atlantic Charter, our pledge in the Declaration by the United Nations, and our determination to build in cooperation with other peaceloving nations a world order under law, dedicated to peace, security, freedom and general well-being of all mankind."[99] At the time of the Crimea conference there was still reason to hope that Stalin might honor his promises. Had he not scrupulously refrained from criticizing the British military operations in Greece, in accordance with his recent bargain with Churchill? When the evidence of Soviet lack of good faith in Rumania and other eastern countries was forthcoming a few weeks after Yalta, the United States and Britain were in an excellent position, thanks to the "Yalta Declaration," to make it clear to the world who was at fault.

On the subject of the Yugoslav agreements between Tito and Prime Minister Šubašić, the British were able to win Soviet acceptance of pledges for a more parliamentary and constitutional type of government than then existed under Tito. What was regrettable in this was not the Yalta agreement but its violation.

The discussions of the perplexing Polish territorial prob-

[99] The Declaration on Liberated Europe is quoted in its final version in the Appendix of this volume.

lem ended by assigning to Soviet Russia the land east of the Curzon Line, except for minor rectifications in favor of Poland. No plebiscites were called for, and the action was taken without the consent of the Polish government in exile, although hardly to its surprise. The agreement thus violated the spirit of the Atlantic Charter. But it is impossible to see how the western statesmen could have prevented Soviet acquisition of this land, short of armed conflict with Russia, for the military balance of power in eastern Europe had shifted entirely in her favor by 1945. To ratify the shift or to repudiate the eastern ally? Therein lay the meaning of Yalta so far as the Polish problem was concerned.

Because of firm western opposition to "overstuffing the German goose" with millions of displaced people from Silesia, Stalin was forced to agree to leave the western frontier of Poland undefined. But in assenting to this, he undoubtedly foresaw that he could at a later time unilaterally assign a wide strip of the Soviet zone in Germany to Poland, thereby tightening his grip on a grateful Polish government. This he did a few months later, when he handed to Poland the territory east of the Oder and Western Neisse rivers.

On the issue of the Polish government, Churchill and Roosevelt could barely budge Stalin, in view of the Soviet recognition of the Lublin-Warsaw Committee of National Liberation a month before Yalta. There seems to be no reason to dispute the contention of Charles E. Bohlen, who was present at the conference, that on this subject only three courses of action were open to the western leaders: (1) they could have accepted the *fait accompli*, doing nothing, which is what Stalin doubtless would have preferred; (2) they could have stood uncompromisingly behind the Polish government in exile, in which case probably no member of it would have returned to Poland; or (3) they could have attempted to get as many members as possible of the London group into a "reorganized" government.[100] Realistically, they chose the third course.

[100] United States Senate, 83rd Congress, 1st Session, *Hearings before the Committee on Foreign Relations: Nomination of Charles E. Bohlen, March 2, and 18, 1953* (Washington, 1953), 2–113.

The crux of the negotiations was whether the Lublin-Warsaw regime should simply be "enlarged," as the Russians insisted, or completely "reorganized," as the West demanded. After six days of haggling, the agreement that emerged on paper was ambiguous at best. In deference to Stalin, no mention was made in the document of the government in exile, but reference repeatedly was made to the "Provisional Government which is now functioning in Poland." On the other hand, the western phrasemakers were able to insert a clause explaining that this provisional government would be "reorganized on a broader democratic basis . . . with the inclusion of democratic leaders from Poland itself and from Poles abroad."[101]

Admiral William D. Leahy commented to the President at the time that the Polish agreement was so elastic that the Russians could "stretch it all the way from Yalta to Washington without ever technically breaking it." Roosevelt readily conceded this. "I know, Bill—I know it. But it's the best I can do for Poland at this time."[102] Upon his return from the 14,000-mile trip, the President, in his last personal report to Congress, endeavored to put forth the best possible interpretation of the Polish compromise, but he scarcely concealed from his listeners that it was not entirely to his liking.[103] In the House of Commons Churchill was confronted with a full-dress debate on the Crimea conference between February 27 and March 1, and vigorous opposition was raised by some three dozen members who regarded the agreements as inconsonant with Britain's written and moral obligations to her Polish ally.[104] Most of the Poles abroad were in a rage, and on the Italian front General Anders threatened for a time to pull his Polish forces out of the line.[105] A great number of his soldiers decided to live permanently in western Europe.

101 *Yalta Papers*, 973–74.
102 Leahy, *I Was There*, 315–16.
103 For the text of President Roosevelt's speech, see Leland M. Goodrich and Marie J. Carroll, *Documents on American Foreign Relations, 1944–45*, VII (Boston, 1947), 18–28.
104 Churchill, *Triumph and Tragedy*, 401–402. Excerpts from the debate in the House of Commons are reprinted in R. Umiastowski, *Poland, Russia, and Great Britain, 1941–1945: A Study of the Evidence* (London, 1946), 509 *et seq*.
105 Anders, *An Army in Exile*, 247–54.

From the vantage point of hindsight and an absolute standard of morality, one can readily concede the cogency of many of the criticisms levied against the agreements. But a fairer historical approach has been suggested by Churchill, notwithstanding the fact that he was an "interested party." He has reminded the world to judge the actions of statesmen on the basis of the limited knowledge available to them at the moment of their decisions and the over-all objectives that they considered to be pre-eminent.[106]

If the western leaders cannot escape responsibility for certain miscalculations, neither can many of the Polish politicians abroad. The war had left them "men without a country," yet they unrealistically and stubbornly insisted that virtually no political or territorial changes could be acknowledged in a region in which a great change in power relationships had, in fact, occurred. Clearly they could not hope to maintain an independent, viable state between the U.S.S.R. and the Soviet zone of Germany unless they were willing to collaborate with their all-powerful neighbor. Still, it is hard to blame the Poles for having been reluctant to give up a vast portion of their prewar state without a plebiscite and in the mere hope that the Communists would not attempt to subvert a fusion government. Churchill has stoutly insisted that if the Poles had been willing in 1941 or even as late as the autumn of 1944 to agree to the Curzon Line, Stalin might have been persuaded to permit the establishment of a truly independent but friendly government, much as he did in the case of Finland. This may be true, but the historian can not write in the subjunctive case.

Like the other decisions, the Yalta agreement on the Polish government rested on the assumption that the Kremlin would honor it. Instead, the dispute over "reorganization" as opposed to mere "enlargement" resumed almost at once, bedeviling the last weeks of Franklin D. Roosevelt's life and adding to the headaches of Harry S. Truman's first months in office. From Moscow, Ambassador Harriman in March informed Washington that Molotov refused to live up to the Yalta agreements regarding the future Polish government;

[106] Cf. Churchill, *Triumph and Tragedy*, 402.

and on April 7 Stalin protested to Roosevelt that the United States and British ambassadors in Moscow had departed from the principles of Yalta.[107] Just before his death in April, 1945, Roosevelt cabled Churchill with respect to the Polish controversy: "We must be firm . . . and our course thus far is correct."[108] However, the "reorganized" Polish government that eventually was formed and recognized by the Great Powers retained a majority of the cabinet seats for former members of the pro-Soviet Lublin committee. The elections which Stalin had promised within a few weeks after Yalta were postponed until January, 1947, and were of course neither "free" nor "unfettered."[109]

The Soviet Union failed to live up to the Yalta agreements concerning central-eastern Europe, and western statesmen, especially Roosevelt, have been denounced as traitors or bemoaned as babes in the diplomatic woods for having accepted Stalin's promises. But the historical moment must be remembered and Yalta agreements on eastern Europe must be viewed as part of an entire complex of wartime problems. The fact that Roosevelt and Churchill had blocked Soviet pretensions in Germany made it difficult for them to resist all of Stalin's Polish demands and neither was ready to let the Polish problem rupture western relations with the Soviet Union; Japan remained to be defeated even after Nazism was crushed. Consideration of strategic problems in the Far East undoubtedly conditioned the Yalta bargaining of the West on all European questions. By the time the final agreements on central-eastern Europe were signed, Stalin had delighted both Roosevelt and Churchill by promising to enter the war against Japan. Diplomacy has ever been a "give-and-take proposition," and the global proportions of the Yalta give-and-take must be considered if the historical meaning of Yalta is to be understood.

---

[107] See *Yalta Papers,* 989–93, for the exchange of Russian and American protests of bad faith during March and April, 1945; cf. Harry S. Truman, *Year of Decisions* (Garden City, 1955), 15–16, 23–26, 37–39, 50, 71–79, 84–86, 107–109, 254–55, 263, 280–81, 320–22, 347–410, and *passim.*
[108] Churchill, *Triumph and Tragedy,* 454.
[109] Mikolajczyk, *Rape of Poland,* 180–202; Arthur Bliss Lane, *I Saw Poland Betrayed* (Indianapolis, 1948), 276–88.

CHAPTER IV

Yalta and the Far East

WHILE THE European decisions at Yalta were rooted in the imperialism of Germany, the Far Eastern agreements devolved from the imperialism of Germany's ally, Japan. Ironically, it had been the United States and Russia that, ninety years earlier, had forced Japan to abandon her policy of peace through isolation. Pulled into the maelstrom of international relations, Japan had plunged feverishly into intensive, defense-geared industrialization, which eventually provided her not only with the means but, because of its lopsidedness, also with some of the causes of renewed imperialism.

THE ROAD TO YALTA

Since 1854—throughout Japan's "Modern Century"—the United States and Russia have commanded the attention of Japanese policy makers. To keep these Western neighbors from making common cause against Japan has been the guiding principle of Japanese diplomacy. Only twice in her history —in 1854–55 and in 1945—has Japan had to bow to foreign dictation. Both times American and Russian arms were joined against her.

Russian Interests in the Far East

Russian interests in the Far East, aside from the usual considerations of commerce, land, raw materials, and political domination, have included such strategical aspirations as convenient access to the sea and unhindered use of the Pacific Ocean. Northern Manchuria bounded and seemed to the Russians to threaten the vital Amur River; southern Manchuria, like Korea, contained ice-free harbors; and through the middle of Manchuria there passed after about 1900 the Russian-controlled Chinese Eastern Railway, a short cut to

Russia's Maritime Province and Vladivostok. Sakhalin Island offered control over the mouth of the Amur River. The Kurile Islands, Japan, the islands in Tsushima Strait, and Korea together formed a net which could block or guarantee Russian entry into the open Pacific. Thus from the Russian point of view the possession or domination by Russia of Manchuria, Korea, Tsushima Island, the Kurile Islands, and all of Sakhalin seemed highly desirable; and the conquest of these bordering areas and of Mongolia by a powerful Japan would constitute an immediate and serious threat to Russia. (See map, p. 151.)

Through Japanese spectacles, on the other hand, Japanese expansion looked no less defensive. Japanese fishermen and hunters had pushed northward from island to island in the Kuriles even before the Russians penetrated southward and established contact with them at about the halfway mark. Japanese explorers had surveyed Sakhalin Island before Russian surveyors came, although five Russian sailors had been left still earlier on Sakhalin by a naval officer who had marauded Japan's northern territories in an attempt to frighten her into commercial relations with Russia. The rival "finders-keepers" claims in no way altered the fact that in foreign hands Sakhalin and the Kuriles would be a constant source of anxiety both to Japan and to Russia. Korea was not only a bridge for Japanese expansion to the continent, it was at the same time "a dagger pointed at the heart of Japan." And to Japan Manchuria seemed the breadbasket without which Japan's dense population and industry could not be fed.

Thus the century after 1854 witnessed diplomatic friction and war between Russia and Japan, as both sought to dominate the same territory. Sakhalin Island was occupied and annexed to the Russian empire by Cossacks and sailors in 1853–54, but the Treaty of Shimoda in 1855 put Sakhalin back under joint occupation. This same Treaty of Shimoda divided the Kurile Archipelago. Uruppu and the islands to the north were recognized as Russian; Etorofu and the islands to the south were designated as Japanese. Then in 1875, without war or military pressure, the Russians and the Japanese voluntarily negotiated an agreement whereby Japan ceded to

Russia her interests in Sakhalin in exchange for the northern Kurile Islands. As a result of the Russo-Japanese War of 1904–1905 Japan regained southern Sakhalin and the right to fish in Siberian waters, retaining, of course, all of the Kurile Islands. Thus the situation remained until the Yalta conference.

The Russo-Japanese War of 1904–1905 also checked Russian aspirations in Manchuria and Korea. Manchuria, which was part of the Manchu Chinese empire, had fallen increasingly under Russian influence at the turn of the twentieth century. This Russian influence was exercised chiefly through the construction of the Chinese Eastern Railway, the leasing of Port Arthur and Dairen, the building of the Manchurian Railway connecting Port Arthur with the Chinese Eastern Railway, and the actual military occupation of Manchuria from 1900 to 1902. Russia spent much effort on the development of Manchuria. Port Arthur became a strong naval base and fortress with docks, breakwater, and an artificial harbor in an inland lake, connected with the sea by a canal; Dairen became an important commercial center and port. Japan had been willing to recognize Manchuria as a Russian sphere of interest, if Russia would recognize Korea as a Japanese sphere of interest. This Russia refused to do. Japan, having assured herself by an alliance with England (1902) that Russia would stand alone, attacked the Russian fleet at Port Arthur in February, 1904. President Theodore Roosevelt, impressed by the Japanese victories over the Russians, helped to arrange the peace conference at Portsmouth, New Hampshire, which terminated the Russo-Japanese War in 1905.

By the Treaty of Portsmouth, Russian rights in the Liaotung Peninsula (including Port Arthur, Dairen, and the southern section of the Manchurian Railway) were transferred to Japan. The treaty provided for the withdrawal from Manchuria of both Russian and Japanese troops, but not the railway guards. Finally, the Treaty of Portsmouth recognized Japan's "paramount political, military, and economic interests" in Korea. Like the Russians before them, indeed at an accelerated pace, the Japanese set about the economic development of Manchuria. Dairen became the third most important port in Asia, and Manchuria in general eventually became the breadbasket of Japan. It must be remembered that the Manchurian railways were not just so much trackage, but centers of manifold economic, political, and military activities. By the time of World War II, Japan had openly annexed Korea (1910), and in consequence of her invasion of Manchuria in 1931 had displaced Russia from that region as well, purchasing over Chinese objections the Chinese Eastern Railway through the puppet government of Manchukuo.

One more area of contention, Outer Mongolia, was to figure in the Yalta agreement. Russia had shown an active interest in this region even before World War I. In 1924 Russia publicly recognized Chinese sovereignty over Outer Mongolia, but by 1933 Soviet "advisers" were in control of the territory's army and economy; the so-called Mongol People's Republic had become part of the Russian sphere. When the Japanese during the 1930's conquered China's three Eastern Provinces and Jehol and penetrated into Inner Mongolia, they gave birth to a series of Mongol-Manchurian and Manchukuo-Siberian border incidents which involved Russian and Japanese forces. The determination with which the Russians repelled the Japanese in the late 1930's was a factor in deflecting Japanese expansion southward into ultimate conflict with the United States.

American Interests in the Far East

American interests in the Far East date from the eighteenth century. Until World War II American interests, unlike those of Russia and Japan, were in large measure economic. The dream of four hundred million customers fired American imagination, even though the persistent refusal of the dream to come true made of China what Winston Churchill has called "the Great American Illusion."

Unwilling to participate in "the slicing of the Chinese melon," yet anxious lest the mad scramble for concessions lead to discrimination against and eventual exclusion of American business, Secretary of State John Hay formulated the Open Door policy, which, quite simply, insisted on equal opportunities and rights for American businessmen throughout China. Two conditions were essential for the preservation of this Open Door: the territorial integrity of China and a strong Chinese government. These also became American aims. These three related policies—the Open Door, the territorial integrity of China, and a strong Chinese government—became the mainsprings of American actions in the Far East. They inclined the United States against Russia before 1904, when the latter sought to exploit Manchuria on an exclusive basis; similarly, they set the United States against Japan when that country abandoned the Open Door policy and instead followed in Russian footsteps. Japan's southward push ignited the Pacific war in 1941, but American demands that Japan withdraw her troops from China and recognize the Nationalist government as *the* government of China played a part in the coming of hostilities.

Japan's Decision to Expand Southward

Japan's decision to expand southward represented a major policy decision. For years Western observers had predicted a thrust to the northwest and the inevitability of another Russo-Japanese War, and certainly there were those in Japan who desired such a conflict. Foreign Minister Yosuke Matsuoka, for example, in 1941 urged that Japan join Germany in her war against Russia in order to rid herself of the Soviet menace once and for all. But when the Imperial conference of July 2, 1941, considered the implications of the Russo-German war, a different conclusion was reached: Japan would take advantage of the Russian struggle for survival by expanding into Thailand, French Indochina and beyond, "even at the risk of an armed conflict with Great Britain and the United States." Pleas by Adolf Hitler that Japan invade Siberia went unheeded.

Ironically, Hitler himself had done much to improve Russo-Japanese relations. Japan's alliance with Germany in 1940, concluded in the wake of the Nazi-Soviet Pact of 1939, was intended as a step in the direction of a German-Italian-Russian-Japanese four-power alignment. To preclude rivalry among the four and to protect them from each other, Hitler developed the theory of the *Südmotiv*, giving a southerly direction to their respective imperialisms. When Matsuoka left Japan for Europe in March, 1941, he planned to negotiate a nonaggression pact with Russia in conformity with this four-power alignment plan. The deterioration in Russo-German relations which he found upon his arrival actually played into his hand, and he had little difficulty in concluding a Russo-Japanese Neutrality Pact, which was supplemented by a declaration of the mutual recognition of Manchukuo and the Mongolian People's Republic. Joseph Stalin appeared so elated that, contrary to his habit, he saw Matsuoka off, hugging and kissing the Japanese foreign minister on the platform, in the presence of all the Axis ambassadors.

Still, Matsuoka three months later urged an attack against the Soviet Union. Why did his views not prevail? The reasons were various and strictly Japanese. In terms of climate and raw materials, Siberia was not so attractive to the Japanese as was Southeast Asia; the southern drive provided greater opportunity for the full employment of both naval and military forces; and the Japanese Army profoundly respected the Red Army. Nor was this respect purely military. Although the dominant extremists among the Japanese military leaders shouted that Japan's major enemies were both capitalism and communism, morally and ideologically they had much more in common with the latter. The young officers' "native militarism and nationalism" met "the impact of Marxism" and "Marxism and Japanism fused into an Imperialist-Socialist amalgam," as Hugh Byas reported in his book, *The Japanese Enemy*. Thus Japan moved southward. With the European powers involved in the West, the United States was left to meet the new Japanese challenge almost singlehandedly.

At the time of Yalta, traditional American and Russian interests in the Far East remained basically unchanged, and they were intensified by one consideration: the inevitable defeat of Japan threatened to create a power vacuum into which neither the United States nor Russia could afford to let the other step. Therein lay the key to Roosevelt's insistence that China be treated as one of the Big Four and to his long and costly support of Chiang Kai-shek as the symbol of a strong central government. Therein also was the key to

Russia's insistence upon concessions and to Soviet opposition
to Nationalist China, which even to Winston Churchill
seemed but a "faggot vote" of the United States.

PREPARATIONS FOR THE YALTA CONFERENCE

The Yalta conference was not a sudden spasm of unpre-
meditated diplomacy. It was one of a series of wartime "summit" conferences of statesmen who were linked together by
the urge of self-preservation. Immediate military requirements and the desire to attain victory in the shortest possible
time with the least possible casualties tended to overshadow
other considerations.

Russian participation in the war against Japan—the crux
of the Far Eastern agreement at Yalta—had been discussed
repeatedly at earlier meetings. The Japanese seemed determined to fight until their last breath, and United States military planners, therefore, wanted the Russians to engage Japan's continental forces to facilitate an American invasion
of the Japanese home islands. As early as December 8, 1941,
the day after the Japanese attack on Pearl Harbor, Russian
participation was suggested to Soviet Ambassador Maxim M.
Litvinov by both President Roosevelt and Secretary of State
Cordell Hull. Generalissimo Chiang Kai-shek that same day
made a similar proposal to the Soviet government. And General Douglas MacArthur on December 10 recommended
Soviet participation to General George C. Marshall. At the
Quebec conference in August, 1943, Harry L. Hopkins had
with him a military report which pointed not only to savings
in time, life, and resources that would result from Russian
co-operation, but warned that "should the war in the Pacific
have to be carried on with an unfriendly or a negative attitude
on the part of Russia, the difficulties will be immeasurably
increased and operations might become abortive."[1]

At the Moscow conference in October, 1943, during a
banquet in the Kremlin, Marshal Stalin "astonished and de-

[1] United States, Department of Defense, "The Entry of the Soviet Union into
the War against Japan: Military Plans, 1941–1945" (mimeographed report
released on October 19, 1955), 1; Robert E. Sherwood, *Roosevelt and Hopkins,
An Intimate History* (New York, 1948), 748–49.

lighted" Cordell Hull by saying clearly and "unequivocally" that, upon the defeat of Germany, Russia would join in defeating Japan. Stalin's promise was "entirely unsolicited," and as far as Hull could judge "had no strings attached to it." It was repeated in December at Teheran to both President Roosevelt and Prime Minister Churchill, though by then some "strings" had become discernible in Stalin's expressed interest in Dairen and Soviet use of the Manchurian railways.[2] In June, 1944, Stalin overcame deep-seated Soviet sensitivity about foreign troops on Russian soil to advise the American ambassador, W. Averell Harriman, that he had arranged for the construction of twelve airdromes, suitable for heavy bombers, in the Vladivostok-Sovietskaya Gavan area, of which six or seven would be available for United States use against Japan.[3]

It was in October, 1944, that the foundations for the Yalta agreement were definitely laid. Taking advantage of a visit by Churchill to Moscow, Harriman and United States Military Attaché General John R. Deane pressed for specific Russian commitments. The role which Deane and the American Chiefs of Staff envisaged for Russia in the Pacific war was a major one. Russia would (1) secure the Trans-Siberian Railroad and the Vladivostok Peninsula, (2) base Russian and American strategic air forces in the Maritime Province for operations against Japan, (3) interdict or interrupt Japanese shipping and air traffic between Japan proper and the Asiatic mainland, (4) defeat the Japanese Army in Manchuria, and (5) help safeguard the Pacific supply route between the United States and the U.S.S.R. To safeguard the supply route, the Soviet Union would make Petropavlovsk available to the United States as a naval base, neutralize southern Sakhalin and Hokkaido through air attacks, improve Amur port facilities, seize and militarily occupy Sakhalin, and provide the necessary Soviet-American naval co-operation which all these measures implied.

2 Cordell Hull, *The Memoirs of Cordell Hull* (2 vols., New York, 1948), II, 1309–1310; Edward R. Stettinius, Jr. (Walter Johnson, ed.), *Roosevelt and the Russians: The Yalta Conference* (Garden City, 1949), 4; United States, Department of State, *United States Relations with China* (Washington, 1949), 113.

3 John R. Deane, *The Strange Alliance: The Story of Our Efforts at Wartime Cooperation with Russia* (New York, 1947), 231.

General Deane bluntly asked Stalin how soon after the defeat of Germany the United States could expect Soviet-Japanese hostilities to commence, how much time would be required to build up the Soviet forces in the Far East so that they could initiate and sustain an offensive, and how much of the capacity of the Trans-Siberian Railroad could be devoted to the build-up and support of an American strategic air force. In reply to these searching questions and additional queries by Harriman, Stalin on the evening of October 14 stated that the strengthening of Russian forces in the Far East would begin soon, but that three months would be required after the defeat of Germany to increase the number of the Red Army divisions in the East from thirty to sixty. Then Russia would join the war against Japan, provided that two conditions were met: First, the United States would assist in building up a reserve of supplies for sixty divisions, supplies which the Trans-Siberian Railroad, in spite of its capacity of thirty-six trains a day, would not be able to transport. Secondly, Soviet participation would be contingent upon clarification of the political aspects of Russia's participation —the recognition by China of Russian claims against the Japanese in the Far East. Stalin did not elaborate on his conditions, but they already had been suggested at Teheran the previous December, when the internationalization of Dairen and Soviet use of the Manchurian railways had been considered. Stalin promised to provide the United States with air bases in the Maritime Province and access to Petropavlovsk as a naval base.[4]

But all these promises were oral only. When Harriman upon the urging of Anthony Eden drew up a written agreement and submitted it to Commissar Vyacheslav M. Molotov, Stalin was outraged. Any leak of Russian intentions would almost certainly invite a Japanese invasion, he complained. Stalin cautioned Harriman the next day, "Stenographers and secretaries are eager to exaggerate their own importance by telling news to their friends, and thus military secrets no longer remain military secrets." "I am a cautious old man,"

[4] *Ibid.,* 241–42, 246–47.

he added.[5] It was left for the Yalta conference to translate oral promises into written commitments.

The United States representatives went to the Yalta conference after having given much thought to Far Eastern matters. The military planners had spent hours in outlining American military needs in the Far East, including Russian entry into the war against Japan, and the State Department had prepared a special Briefing Book for the President setting forth United States political objectives in Asia. Stalin's Far Eastern demands, as presented at Yalta, had been reported to the President by Harriman after a talk with Stalin in December, 1944, and the Briefing Book took them into consideration. Unfortunately, State Department memoranda concerning the recommended disposition of the Kurile Islands and Sakhalin were not included.[6]

THE YALTA CONFERENCE

Unlike European problems, Far Eastern matters, and in particular Russian entry into the war against Japan, were not discussed during the large and formal sessions at Yalta. They were not even the subject of joint deliberation by the Big Three, and, of course, were omitted from all official press releases. It was feared that any leak of Russian intentions would precipitate a Japanese invasion of Siberia.

Military Considerations

The Far East was discussed instead in a series of meetings that were predominantly military: meetings of the United States Joint (Army and Navy) Chiefs of Staff and meetings of the Joint Chiefs of Staff with the British and Russian Chiefs of Staff and with the Russian Chiefs alone. Even at the meetings of the Joint Chiefs of Staff with the President and his civilian advisers and at the so-called political meetings between Roosevelt and Stalin the military approach prevailed.

On the very day of President Roosevelt's arrival at Yalta,

5 *Ibid.,* 248.
6 United States, Department of State, *The Conferences at Malta and Yalta, 1945* (Washington, 1955), 378–79 (hereinafter cited as *Yalta Papers*); Stettinius, *Roosevelt and the Russians,* 130.

Saturday, February 3, 1945, the Joint Chiefs of Staff communicated to Stalin's "second in command," General of the Army Alexei I. Antonov, their desire to discuss with the Soviet Staff details of possible Russian participation in the war against Japan. At the Joint Chiefs's meeting on the morning of February 4 General George C. Marshall stressed the importance of keeping the consideration of military matters alive throughout the conference, while Fleet Admiral William D. Leahy, Chief of Staff to the President, promised to attempt to have military matters presented first when Roosevelt met with his advisers later that morning. In this way the President would be briefed on military considerations prior to his talks on political matters with Churchill and Stalin.[7]

The Joint Chiefs of Staff did not debate at Yalta whether Russia should or should not enter the war against Japan. Since 1941 they had considered Russian participation militarily desirable, and attention at Yalta was focused on the ways and means of making such participation most effective. On Monday, February 5, the Joint Chiefs of Staff approved a memorandum to the Russians designed to facilitate the work of a special United States planning staff in Moscow. Simultaneously, they agreed to formulate another memorandum which Roosevelt should give to Stalin, asking whether the Russians would require a Pacific supply line upon the outbreak of hostilities and whether they would provide American air bases in eastern Siberia.[8]

On Tuesday, February 6, the American military leaders briefed the British and Russian Chiefs of Staff on American operations in the Far East. In the Pacific, the then existing forward line included Attu, the Marianas and Luzon, but American control of the sea and air extended beyond, to China, Formosa, the Ryukyus, and to the very shores of Japan itself; dates had been set for operations against the Bonin Islands and Okinawa; plans were under way for an invasion of the Chusan Archipelago off the China coast. Even an effort to capture one of the Kurile Islands had been considered in order to secure safe sea passage, though the project had to be

[7] *Yalta Papers*, 562–64.
[8] *Ibid.*, 593–94.

shelved for the time being in favor of the other operations. But occasional naval bombardments were being carried out against some of the northern Kurile Islands. In China, American forces were also active, and their supply by the Air Transport Command across the Himalayas was especially noteworthy. It was the objective of the United States, Fleet Admiral Ernest J. King reported, to bring about the defeat of Japan at the earliest possible date. Germany was the principal enemy, but unremitting pressure would be maintained against the Japanese in order to obtain positions from which a final attack could be staged after forces in Europe were available for Pacific duty. When the Russians asked whether greater emphasis on the European front might not have hastened the over-all end of the war, Marshall answered that the United States had placed great importance on the maintenance of the present regime in China and that the conquest of all of China by Japan would have been a serious military matter.[9]

This exposition of American plans in the Pacific failed to bring forth reciprocal Russian information, much less commitments, in the Far East. As Antonov had warned quite frankly the day before, the Soviet General Staff would not engage in the discussion of Pacific affairs until after the governmental leaders had considered the war in the Far East. In order to learn more about Russian intentions, therefore, the Joint Chiefs of Staff asked Roosevelt to secure Stalin's approval for an American meeting with the Soviet General Staff to discuss details of possible Soviet participation in the war against Japan. On February 7 Leahy sent a written statement to Antonov proposing "a most secret discussion" the following afternoon, assuring him that no one was to be present except "the Chiefs of Staff and one interpreter, your Russian interpreter being satisfactory for our purpose."[10]

Antonov agreed, and on the morning of Thursday, February 8, the Joint Chiefs of Staff met to prepare for the conference. They examined and approved two memoranda as a basis for their afternoon meeting. One, prepared by Major

9 *Ibid.*, 650–54.
10 *Ibid.*, 607–608, 698.

General John R. Deane, Commanding General of the United States Military Mission in Moscow, listed eight questions which Deane wanted raised:

(1) Have there been any changes in Soviet projected plans of operations in the Far East from those described to Mr. Harriman and General Deane in October?

(2) Will the Soviets require a Pacific supply route after Soviet-Japanese hostilities start?

(3) Will agreement be given for operation of U. S. air forces in the Komsomolsk-Nikola[y]evsk area? [See map, p. 151.]

(4) Will U. S. forces be required for defense of Kamchatka?

(5) Will the Soviets make pre-hostility preparations including construction, and reception and storage of U. S. stockpiles in Kamchatka and Eastern Siberia?

(6) Can the Kamchatka survey party depart from Fairbanks by 15 February 1945?

(7) Will the Soviets occupy southern Sakhalin and when? If so, will they cover passage of LaPerouse Strait? [Between Sakhalin and Hokkaido.]

(8) Are we assured that combined planning in Moscow will be vigorously pursued?

The second memorandum, in essence a synthesis of previous papers prepared by the Joint Staff planners, included the same questions in somewhat more elaborate phraseology plus additional queries. One was a request for increased weather information for American use from more stations in eastern Siberia than were currently in operation; the second asked how weather conditions would affect the beginning of Russian actions in eastern Siberia, "on the assumption Russia can be ready to enter the war against Japan three months after the end of the German war as indicated by Marshal Stalin in October." The Joint Staff planners' memorandum recommended that it be made clear to the Russians that American amphibious operations against Japanese islands in the North Pacific (the Kuriles, for example) were unlikely in 1945; furthermore, that if the Russians desired a supply route across the Pacific, the United States would require strategic air bases in Siberia. Appended to the memorandum were two notes to the Russians, one of which restated American wishes for the admission into Kamchatka of an American reconnaissance party. (It had been contemplated that the men in this group would wear Russian uniforms to fool the Japanese on Kamchatka; their names and measurements had already been submitted.) The second of the proposed notes would request a "full, free and frank exchange of information" between Russian and American planners in Moscow.[11]

The highly important Russo-American military conference was held during the afternoon of February 8. At the outset General Antonov made it absolutely clear that he had no authority to give definite answers or promises or to make decisions on Far Eastern matters. His reply to the American questions would reflect only his own personal opinions. But Antonov's comments indicated that he was well briefed about Soviet political objectives in the Far East, for when he brought "definite and official" replies the following day, they differed but slightly from the replies he had given informally.

This is what Antonov communicated: (1) There had been no changes in projected Soviet Far Eastern operations since the previous October; (2) a maximum effort would be made to keep the Trans-Siberian Railway in operation; air and sea routes across the Pacific must also be kept open; (3) American help in the defense of Kamchatka and eastern Siberia would be "useful"; (4) Russian supply problems made it impossible to promise the construction and storage of materials for American forces; indeed, American materials might be required to build fuel storage for Soviet forces; (5) Russian forces would occupy southern Sakhalin "as quickly after the beginning of hostilities as possible"; they would do so without American help; (6) the Soviet Navy would deny LaPerouse Strait, which separated Sakhalin from Hokkaido, to the Japanese, but would find it "difficult" to permit American passage there until a Russian naval base and shore battery could be established; (7) an effort would be made to co-ordinate more closely American and Russian military operations in the Far East; (8) weather conditions in Siberia would be most difficult for ground forces during the thaws and floods in April and May, favorable in June, but again unfavorable in July and

11 *Ibid.*, 730–34, 762–66; Deane, *The Strange Alliance*, 252–53.

August; September, October, and November would be most favorable for operations on land; July, August, and September would be best for naval operations; and (9) only Stalin could answer the questions concerning the basing of United States air forces in Siberia, the entry of an American survey party into Kamchatka, and the increase of Siberian weather stations for American information.[12]

The Stalin-approved replies, presented by Antonov on February 9 at a second Russo-American military meeting, modified the statement that there had been no change in Soviet plans since the previous October. There had been no change in intent, but there had been minor changes in operations. The only change in the basic plan was a delay in the redeployment of Russian troops to the Far East because of requirements on the Russian front in Europe. The official reply also upgraded possible American assistance in the defense of Kamchatka from "useful" to "very useful." In addition, the reply contained Stalin's approval of the immediate entry of American advance reconnaissance and survey parties to the Komsomolsk-Nikolaevsk area in preparation for United States air force operations there, of the establishment of additional weather-reporting stations for American information in Siberia, and of pre-hostility preparations of United States stockpiles in eastern Siberia and in Kamchatka for American air units to be stationed there. But the Americans were informed that the departure of an American survey party to Kamchatka must be deferred "until the last moment" because the presence of Americans there could not be kept secret from the Japanese.

Both the American and Russian Chiefs of Staff agreed that all Far Eastern matters must be veiled by "a high order of security" lest the Japanese beat the Russians to the punch. According to Antonov, the Russians did not expect to be strong enough to meet a Japanese attack until at least three months after the initiation of redeployment.[13]

When the military meeting officially adjourned, two of the officers stayed behind to work out in detail some of the agree-

[12] *Yalta Papers,* 757–66.
[13] *Ibid.,* 834–41.

ments that had been reached in general, thrashing out specific requirements of American bases in Siberia, Russian requests for transport and training planes, and even the possibility of exchange visits of a United States Army Air Force band and a Russian military choral group.[14]

The American and Russian officers had gotten along well. Their intimacy was, of course, professional and human rather than political. The Americans were impressed by the fact that Stalin and his generals and all of his staff worked every night at Yalta until five in the morning, keeping up with the campaigns in Europe in addition to the business at hand. And General Deane has noted that General Antonov, "by far the coldest but at the same time the most capable Russian officer" with whom he had come in contact, gained the respect, if not the affection, of the American Chiefs of Staff.[15]

Wartime operations, and thus responsibilities, in the Pacific were predominantly American, and the British did not participate directly in these Russo-American talks. But the British were not left out entirely. It was a joint recommendation that the Combined (Anglo-American) Chiefs of Staff presented to Roosevelt and Churchill at noon on February 9. Drafted in the main as an interim report aboard the U.S.S. *Quincy* at Malta on February 2 and supplemented by additional paragraphs at Yalta, this final report, approved by Roosevelt and Churchill without amendment, became formally the military basis upon which the political decisions at Yalta were built.

The Anglo-American military recommendation opened with a general statement of the over-all objective: "In conjunction *with Russia* and other Allies, to bring about at the earliest possible date the unconditional surrender of Germany *and Japan*." (Author's italics.) It then reviewed the steps necessary for the attainment of this end: (1) unremitting Allied pressure against Japan in order to reduce her military might and to attain positions from which her ultimate surrender could be forced; (2) continuing military aid to China

14 *Ibid.*, 836–41.
15 Stettinius, *Roosevelt and the Russians,* 115; Deane, *The Strange Alliance,* 32–33.

as an effective ally and as a base for operations against Japan, while the war in Europe was still in progress; and then, upon the defeat of Germany, (3) almost immediate transfer of troops from Europe to the Far East; and (4) full-scale attack by Anglo-American forces "in cooperation with other Pacific Powers and with Russia." Envisaging the seizure of objectives in the industrial heart of Japan, the Combined Chiefs "took note" of the plans and operations proposed by the American Joint Chiefs of Staff at Malta, plans which called for an attack on Kyushu in September, 1945, and for the invasion of the Tokyo plain in December of the same year, providing that the defeat of Germany could be accomplished in time for the shift of troops to the Pacific.

The American Chiefs of Staff had calculated that they would need four to six months for the redeployment of troops from Europe to the Pacific. The Combined Chiefs now recommended that the planning date for the end of the war against Japan should be set tentatively at *eighteen months* after the defeat of Germany. The importance of this estimate can not be overemphasized in explaining the concessions which were made to the Russians at Yalta. The military planners had agreed that the war in Europe would not likely end before July 1. Even with Russian aid they now expected that the war in the Pacific might last another year and a half (that is, until about December, 1946). No one knew how long it might last *without* Russian aid.[16]

Political Commitments

No aspect of the Yalta negotiations reflected the dominance of "personal diplomacy" so clearly as did the Far Eastern political discussions. The State Department delegation did not participate in the political talks concerning the Far East at Yalta. Yalta was still a wartime conference, and, as Charles E. Bohlen testified in 1953, the war was run very much from the point of view of the military considerations. The State Department had no representatives who sat with the Joint Chiefs of Staff, and until late in 1944 the State Department

[16] *Yalta Papers,* 518–21, 540–46, 799–800, 825–33; William D. Leahy, *I Was There* (New York, 1950), 8.

did not even have a liaison officer with the White House. Only once did Secretary of State Edward R. Stettinius have the floor concerning the Far East at Yalta. On February 4, at a meeting of the President with his military and civilian advisers, in line with traditional American support of a strong Chinese central government, Stettinius recommended that Roosevelt seek British and Russian backing for American efforts to bring about a Kuomintang-Communist agreement, on the ground that "cooperation between the two groups will expedite conclusion of the war in the Far East and prevent possible internal conflict and foreign intervention in China." At the same meeting Ambassador Harriman repeated what he had cabled the President from Moscow in December, 1944, after a meeting with Stalin, namely that the Russians would demand in return for their participation in the war against Japan the southern half of Sakhalin, the Kurile Islands, maintenance of the *status quo* in Outer Mongolia, and control over the railroad to Dairen. Harriman's statement elicited from Roosevelt the comment that he would like to have Chiang Kai-shek's views before dealing with Mongolia, but that he was prepared to discuss the other points.[17]

The most crucial of the Yalta talks were held in much more limited surroundings. The military recommendations of the American and British Chiefs of Staff were kept in mind, and the Briefing Book papers of the State Department were still at hand, but neither the Chiefs of Staff nor the State Department participated directly in these discussions. In fact, the crucial conferences were essentially personal talks between Roosevelt and Stalin. The only other persons present at the first of these meetings were Harriman and Charles E. Bohlen, assistant to the Secretary of State, on the American side, and Molotov and Vladimir N. Pavlov on the Russian side. Bohlen and Pavlov acted only as interpreters.

The first of these "private" talks was held at the American headquarters on the afternoon of Thursday, February 8,

17 United States Senate, 83rd Congress, 1st Session, *Hearings Before the Committee on Foreign Relations: Nomination of Charles E. Bohlen, March 2, and 18, 1953* (Washington, 1953), 7; Stettinius, *Roosevelt and the Russians*, 84–87; *Yalta Papers*, 564–69.

while the American and Russian Chiefs of Staff were having their first meeting at the Russian headquarters. Manila had just been taken by American forces, and Roosevelt observed, therefore, that the time had come to discuss additional bombing of Japan. He said that he would actually invade the Japanese islands "only if absolutely necessary." He hoped to destroy Japan and its army of four million men by intensive aerial bombardment, and thereby save American lives. Stalin replied that he had no objection to the establishment of American bases at Komsomolsk on the lower reaches of the Amur River or at Nikolaevsk at its mouth. But the presence of a Japanese consul on Kamchatka precluded similar arrangements there for the time being. Stalin agreed to permit the Soviet General Staff to enter into planning talks with the American General Staff concerning these and other problems.

It was also Stalin who initiated discussion of the political conditions under which Russia would enter the war against Japan, noting that he had already talked about these with Harriman. Roosevelt replied that he had received a report of this conversation and that he foresaw "no difficulties whatsoever in regard to the southern half of Sakhalin and the Kuril Islands going to Russia at the end of the war." Roosevelt also recalled that he himself had suggested at Teheran that the Russians be given the *use* of a warm-water port at the end of the South Manchurian Railroad, possibly at Dairen, but reported that he had not yet had an opportunity to discuss this matter with Chiang Kai-shek, and thus could not speak for the Chinese. There were two methods whereby the Russians could obtain the use of this port, said Roosevelt: by outright leasing from the Chinese, or by making Dairen a free port under some form of international commission. He preferred internationalization.

Stalin then raised the question of Russian use of the Manchurian railways. He indicated that Russia wanted long-term leases on the Manchouli-Harbin-Dairen-Port Arthur and Harbin-Nikolsk-Ussurisk lines. Stalin justified his claim to these lines on the grounds that they had once been used by the czars. Again Roosevelt sought to ward off Russian demands by replying that he had not discussed the matter with

Chiang Kai-shek. He pointed out that there were two possible ways of giving Russia the use of these railways: leasing under direct Soviet operation, or leasing under a joint and equal Sino-Russian commission. His comment in itself indicated to Stalin that he preferred the latter arrangement, which would guarantee China a voice in the affairs of the all-important railway zones in Manchuria. But Stalin declared that if his conditions were not met "it would be difficult for him and Molotov to explain to the Soviet people why Russia was entering the war against Japan . . . a country with which they had no great trouble."

Once more Roosevelt stated that he had not talked to Chiang and complained semi-apologetically that anything said to the Chinese "was known to the whole world in twenty-four hours." Stalin agreed and said that it was not yet necessary to speak to them. But he could guarantee the security of the Supreme Soviet, and asserted that it would be well at this meeting to put the political conditions and their acceptance by the three powers in writing. Roosevelt said he thought that this could be done. Stalin remarked that when Soviet troops could be spared in the west and twenty-five Russian divisions were moved to the Far East, then it would be possible to speak to Chiang Kai-shek. In an impressive, if insincere, gesture, Stalin assured Roosevelt that the Russians would not be difficult about a warm-water port—that an internationalized free port would not be objectionable.

After a discussion of possible trusteeships for Korea and Indochina, the conversation turned to the internal conditions of China. Roosevelt stated that for some time the United States had been trying to keep China alive. Stalin opined that China would remain alive, but that she needed some new leaders around Chiang Kai-shek. There were some good people in the Kuomintang; why were they not brought forth? Roosevelt knew, of course, that what Stalin really wanted was the entrance of Chinese Communists into the national government at Chungking, and commented that General Albert C. Wedemeyer, the American Chief of Staff to Chiang, and General Patrick J. Hurley, American ambassador to China, had made more progress than their predecessors in arranging such a merger of the Communists in the north with the Kuomintang government. He stated that the fault lay more with the Nationalists than with the "so-called" Communists. Stalin chimed in that he could not understand why the Chinese did not join against the Japanese in a united front which, he stated, should be under the leadership of Chiang Kai-shek.[18]

Thus, while the American Chiefs of Staff were meeting with the Russian Chiefs to make plans concerning Soviet entry into the war against Japan, Stalin reminded Roosevelt of Russian conditions for such entry. There was little discussion of these conditions. Roosevelt tried to leave final responsibility in Chiang Kai-shek's hands and to safeguard Chinese sovereignty and the Open Door, but not with great eloquence. According to the minutes of the meeting, Roosevelt and Stalin took less than a quarter of an hour to consider Russian desires in the Far East. Stalin made no mention of the *status quo* in Outer Mongolia. Instead he demanded, with the exception of the Kurile Islands, somewhat less than what Japan had taken away from Russia in 1905, for he had indicated his willingness to use Dairen as an internationalized free port, not insisting on a unilateral Soviet administration. Stalin not only agreed to American bases in Siberia, but recognized Chiang Kai-shek as *the* leader of China.

Roosevelt was less anxious to deny Stalin's demands than to confine him to those he had mentioned. Like the Chiefs of Staff, Roosevelt wished to avoid a premature Russian entry which might necessitate American involvement on the mainland of Asia;[19] and, like the Joint Chiefs, the President deemed it important to secure Soviet entry in time to facilitate an American invasion of the Japanese home islands. But unlike the Chiefs of Staff, his motivation was not exclusively military. He apparently was fully aware of the danger that the Soviet Union might stand by until the United States crushed Japan, at great cost in American lives, and then march into

[18] *Yalta Papers,* 766–71.

[19] Department of Defense, "The Entry of the Soviet Union into the War against Japan," 40.

Manchuria and northern China and establish "People's Republics" in Manchuria and Inner Mongolia.[20]

The Roosevelt-Stalin talks of February 8 had been exploratory in nature. The conditions of Russian participation in the war against Japan were shaped into final form on Saturday, February 10. At two o'clock that afternoon Molotov handed Harriman a draft, in English, of Stalin's demands. These were the same terms which Stalin had given Roosevelt two days before, and it was obvious that the President's efforts to achieve modifications had failed. Harriman objected in the name of the President to the provision that "possession of Port Arthur and Dairen on lease should be restored" and proposed in its stead the statement that "lease of the port areas of Port Arthur and Dairen should be restored, or these areas should become free ports under international control." Molotov's draft stipulated the restoration of former Russian rights to the operation of the Chinese-Eastern Railroad and the South Manchurian Railroad, though it recognized Chinese sovereignty in Manchuria; Harriman suggested adding: ". . . or these railroads should be placed under the operational control of a Chinese-Soviet Commission." These modifications would not guarantee an American victory in the interests of China, but they would certainly postpone Soviet victory at China's expense.

Whether by previous arrangement with Stalin or not, Molotov readily agreed to these modifications, but it took Harriman some time to explain the need for one more clause, that "it is understood that the agreement concerning the ports and railways referred to above requires the concurrence of Generalissimo Chiang Kai-shek." Yet, on this point, too, Molotov finally agreed. Harriman then transmitted the Russian draft and his amendments to Roosevelt. With the Yalta conference nearing its end, the President quickly approved

20 "Statement of W. Averell Harriman, Special Assistant to the President, Regarding Our Wartime Relations with the Soviet Union, Particularly as They Concern the Agreements Reached at Yalta," in United States Senate, 82nd Congress, 1st Session, *Military Situation in the Far East, Hearing before the Committee on Armed Services and the Committee on Foreign Relations,* Part V, Appendix (Washington, 1951), 3332 (hereinafter cited as "Statement of W. Averell Harriman").

them and authorized Harriman to resubmit them to Molotov.[21] It remained to be seen whether or not Stalin himself would approve the concessions to Roosevelt.

Later in the afternoon Stalin had a private talk with Churchill, which quite possibly made up his mind for him. Churchill asked about Russian wishes in the Far East. Stalin replied that Russia wanted a naval base such as Port Arthur; that the Americans preferred the ports to be under international control, but that the Russians wanted their interests safeguarded. Churchill commented that the English would welcome the appearance of Russian ships in the Pacific, and agreed that Russia's losses in the Russo-Japanese War should be made good.[22]

Thus reassured, Stalin approached Harriman at the end of that day's plenary session and told him that he had no objection to Dairen becoming a free port under international control, but that Port Arthur was another matter. Since it was to be a Russian naval base, a lease was required as before 1905. Harriman suggested that Stalin discuss this matter at once with the President.

Roosevelt, in the face of Russian persistence, then consented to Stalin's proposal regarding Dairen and Port Arthur. Stalin in turn agreed that the Manchurian railroads should be operated by a Chinese-Russian commission. He also agreed that these arrangements were conditioned upon Chiang Kai-shek's consent. Having made these concessions, Stalin requested one from Roosevelt: Chiang should give concurrence to the *status quo* in Outer Mongolia. Roosevelt offered to take this and the other matters up with the Chinese, and Stalin readily agreed. Since he was an interested party, he would prefer that Roosevelt do it, he said. Roosevelt then asked, in view of the need to keep all this from the Japanese, when the subject should be discussed with Chiang. Stalin said that he would inform the President when he was prepared to have this done. Roosevelt promised that, to insure secrecy, he would send a letter of instructions to Ambassador Hurley by courier from Washington through Moscow to Chungking.[23]

[21] *Yalta Papers*, 894–97.
[22] Winston S. Churchill, *Triumph and Tragedy* (Boston, 1953), 388–89.
[23] *Yalta Papers*, 895–97.

The military advisers had not participated in these political discussions. But with the President's approval Harriman had shown the agreement to General Marshall and to Admirals Leahy and King individually for comment. None of them voiced any objections, though Leahy personally did not consider the entrance of Russia into the Pacific war desirable.[24]

The final agreement, as redrafted by the Russians, was signed the next day, Sunday, February 11, by Stalin, Roosevelt, and Churchill, in that order, and was entrusted to the care of Admiral Leahy for safekeeping in his secret files at the White House. As finally worded, the top secret agreement read as follows:

The leaders of the three Great Powers—the Soviet Union, the United States of America and Great Britain—have agreed that in two or three months after Germany has surrendered and the war in Europe has terminated the Soviet Union shall enter into the war against Japan on the side of the Allies on condition that:

1. The *status quo* in Outer-Mongolia (The Mongolian People's Republic) shall be preserved;

2. The former rights of Russia violated by the treacherous attack of Japan in 1904 shall be restored, viz:

(a) the southern part of Sakhalin as well as all the islands adjacent to it shall be returned to the Soviet Union,

(b) the commercial port of Dairen shall be internationalized, the preeminent interests of the Soviet Union in this port being safeguarded and the lease of Port Arthur as a naval base of the USSR restored,

(c) the Chinese-Eastern Railroad and the South-Manchurian Railroad which provides an outlet to Dairen shall be jointly operated by the establishment of a joint Soviet-Chinese Company it being understood that the preeminent interests of the Soviet Union shall be safeguarded and that China shall retain full sovereignty in Manchuria;

3. The Kuril Islands shall be handed over to the Soviet Union.

It is understood, that the agreement concerning Outer-Mongolia and the ports and railroads referred to above will require concurrence of Generalissimo Chiang Kai-shek. The President

24 Herbert Feis, *The China Tangle* (Princeton, 1953), 248; Leahy, *I Was There*, 312.

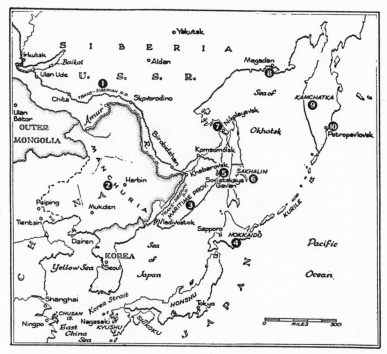

From the New York *Times*, October 20, 1955.

THE FAR EAST

The Joint Chiefs of Staff's aim in 1944 for the Soviet role in the Pacific war was to secure the Trans-Siberian Railroad (1); to set up bases for air operations against Japan from the Maritime Provinces (3) and Kamchatka Peninsula (9); to cut the lines of communication between Japan and Asia; to destroy Japanese forces in Manchuria (2), and to secure the Pacific supply route by getting Petropavlovsk (10) and Kamchatka (9) for United States bases, neutralizing Southern Sakhalin (6) and Hokkaido (4) with air attacks, improving port facilities at Nikolayevsk (7), Magadan (8), Petropavlovsk (10), and Sovietskaya Gavan (5), occupation of Southern Sakhalin (6), and Soviet naval co-operation.

will take measures in order to obtain this concurrence on advice from Marshal Stalin.

The Heads of the three Great Powers have agreed that these claims of the Soviet Union shall be unquestionably fulfilled after Japan has been defeated.

For its part the Soviet Union expresses its readiness to conclude with the National Government of China a pact of friendship and alliance between the USSR and China in order to render assistance to China with its armed forces for the purpose of liberating China from the Japanese yoke.[25]

Presented somewhat more graphically, the "balance sheet" of the Roosevelt-Stalin negotiations, as reflected in this agreement, was as follows:

What Stalin asked for:	*What Stalin got:*
1. *Status quo* in Outer Mongolia	1. *Status quo* in Outer Mongolia
2. Southern Sakhalin and adjacent islands	2. Southern Sakhalin and adjacent islands
3. Lease of Dairen	3. Internationalization of Dairen
4. Lease of Port Arthur	4. Lease of Port Arthur
5. Operation of Chinese-Eastern and South Manchurian railroads	5. Russo-Chinese operation of these railroads
6. Kurile Islands	6. Kurile Islands

What Roosevelt asked for:	*What Roosevelt got:*
1. Russian participation against Japan soon after end of war in Europe	1. Russian participation against Japan soon after end of war in Europe
2. Conditioning of Outer Mongolia and railway agreements on Chiang Kai-shek's concurrence	2. Conditioning of Outer Mongolia and railway agreements on Chiang Kai-shek's concurrence
3. Promise of Russian support for Nationalist government	3. Promise of Russian support for Nationalist government

THE AFTERMATH OF YALTA

The realization on the part of Roosevelt, Churchill, and Stalin that allied co-operation was essential if the problems

25 *Yalta Papers,* 984.

of peace were to be met in the postwar world was reflected in
the harmony and seeming good-fellowship of Yalta. Perhaps
this harmony was only superficial. Certainly it did not last.
The Russians hedged on American bases in Siberia. They
went substantially beyond the Yalta understanding in demands which they put to representatives of the Chinese government in Moscow in June and August of 1945; ignoring
American protests, they then asked for a controlling Soviet
interest in the Chinese-Eastern and South Manchurian railways, Soviet domination of Dairen, and recognition of the
loss of Chinese influence in Outer Mongolia. They stripped
Manchuria of its industrial resources. Most important of all,
they subsequently withdrew their support of Chiang Kai-shek
and assisted the Chinese Communists instead.[26]

Various explanations have been advanced for this shift in
Soviet policy. Perhaps it had been planned all along. Perhaps
Stalin's concessions encountered opposition in the Politburo
upon his return to Moscow.[27] Perhaps the withdrawal of
American troops encouraged Stalin to forget the restraining
commitments of Yalta. No doubt the very creation of a power
vacuum as a result of Japan's defeat stimulated renewed
Russo-American rivalry in the Far East. The totality of this
power vacuum was accentuated by Allied, especially American, insistence upon the unconditional surrender of Japan.
Theodore Roosevelt had acted more wisely when he had
furthered the termination of the Russo-Japanese War by
negotiation before the balance of power had been destroyed
in the Far East. Weakened by Japanese aggression and by
internal strife, Nationalist China was not strong enough to
fill this vacuum. The United States was not willing to do so.
The way was left open for Russia and the Chinese Communists to close the Open Door in China.

But in February, 1945, the secret Far Eastern agreement
seemed "very reasonable." Indeed, to some it appeared to
usher in "the dawn of the new day we had all been praying for
and talking about for so many years." Shortly after the Yalta

[26] "Statement of W. Averell Harriman," 3339; State Department, *United
States Relations with China*, 116–26.
[27] Stettinius, *Roosevelt and the Russians*, 310.

conference General MacArthur was quoted as having stated that Russian seizure of Manchuria, Korea, and possibly part of northern China was inevitable, and that to deny Port Arthur to Russia would be impractical. Less than a decade later the Yalta agreement was branded not only as a betrayal of American principles, but as downright "treason," and General MacArthur in 1955 characterized as "fantastic" concessions which in 1945 seemed "inevitable."[28] In 1948 and especially in 1952 the Far Eastern agreements at Yalta became major issues in American presidential elections.

The controversy over these agreements may well last as long as the Far East remains important in world affairs; it is likely to be reopened whenever the careers of Roosevelt, Churchill, and Stalin are evaluated. The whole controversy hinges on two basic questions, one of power and one of morality. The first: Was Russian entry into the war against Japan necessary? The second: Did Roosevelt and Churchill willfully and lightly sacrifice the interests of a third power and a friend, China?

Did defeat of Japan depend on Russian help? This question is examined in the last chapter of this volume. Suffice it to state here that in February, 1945, no one could count upon the effective use of the atomic bomb in the war against Japan,[29] and that American planners estimated that eighteen months of fighting after the not yet attained German surrender and at least 500,000 American casualties—perhaps one million—might be required to subdue the Japanese, even with Russian help.[30] In the circumstances it is understandable that United States and British military strategists sought the

[28] Leahy, *I Was There*, 318–19; Sherwood, *Roosevelt and Hopkins*, 870; Felix Wittmer, *The Yalta Betrayal: Data on the Decline and Fall of Franklin Delano Roosevelt* (Caldwell, 1953), 76; Letter from Col. Paul L. Freeman, Jr., to General Marshall (February 13, 1945), and memorandum from General George A. Lincoln to General Marshall (March 8, 1945), as cited in Department of Defense, "The Entry of the Soviet Union into the War against Japan," 50–52; statement of General MacArthur, New York *Times*, October 21, 1955.

[29] Churchill, *Triumph and Tragedy*, 388–89; *Yalta Papers*, 383; Stettinius, *Roosevelt and the Russians*, 90.

[30] Churchill, *Triumph and Tragedy*, 388–89; Sherwood, *Roosevelt and Hopkins*, 867; Stettinius, *Roosevelt and the Russians*, 8–9; Harry S. Truman, *Year of Decisions* (Garden City, 1955), 265.

destruction or at least the diversion of the Japanese forces on the Asian continent by Russian action. As late as July 24, 1945, the Combined Chiefs of Staff recommended Russian entry into the war against Japan "to assist in the execution of the over-all strategic concept." Roosevelt's successor, Harry S. Truman, has stated emphatically in his memoirs that even on this date, seven days after he had received news of the successful test explosion of the A-bomb, it was still of great importance to the United States to secure Soviet participation in the war against Japan.[31] In February, 1945, it was up to the President and the Prime Minister to make the political arrangements which the military needs seemed to require, and this they did. This may have been a mistake; quite clearly it was not "treason."

Had the Joint Chiefs of Staff and the President decided that Russian entry into the war against Japan was not desirable, would the Soviets have come to the same conclusion? Admiral William H. Standley, upon his return from ambassadorial duties in Moscow in October of 1943, had told Roosevelt: "I don't think you can keep Stalin out." During World War I Japan had invoked the Anglo-Japanese Alliance ostensibly to come to Britain's aid, but actually to conquer the former German possessions in China for herself. In 1945 Russia was America's ally in Europe; she might well have entered the Pacific war uninvited to help herself, with or without the pretext of aiding the United States. Then the sky would have been the limit. The conditional entry, negotiated at Yalta, put at least a paper restraint on Russian ambitions, and this was the only restraint anyone could have put on Stalin at Yalta in February, 1945.

The alternative to refusal of Russian help or failure to bargain for it would not simply have been to fight without Russian assistance; the exclusion of Russia would have aroused Russian apprehension if not hostility. Stalin was in a stronger bargaining position than the Joint Chiefs of Staff

---

[31] Walter Millis (ed.), with the collaboration of E. S. Duffield, *The Forrestal Diaries* (New York, 1951), 51; Department of Defense, "The Entry of the Soviet Union into the War against Japan," 90–91; Truman, *Year of Decisions*, 236, 265, 381–82, 411.

or Roosevelt realized, for Japan was ready to offer much to
keep Russia neutral. As Japan's position grew more desperate
during the war, so did the plans of her leaders. Expecting
the co-operation of Communist Russia and the capitalist
states to deteriorate if not end upon the defeat of Germany,
Japanese admirals wanted their diplomats to negotiate a
coalition or alliance with the Soviet Union and "apparently
also hoped eventually to draw the Soviet Union into the
Japanese war effort as a fighting member in good standing."
Marquis Koichi Kido, the Lord Keeper of the Privy Seal,
whose duty it was to advise the Emperor, looked to Russia
for a possible alignment because she was "Oriental" in outlook. As Stalin had said to Matsuoka in April, 1941, "You
are an Asiatic. So am I." Other Japanese felt that "the Soviet
Union would want to see Japan retain a fairly important
international position so that the two countries could ally
themselves in the future against America and Britain." Stalin
had asserted in 1941 that "the whole world can be settled" if
Japan and Russia co-operate. In June, 1945, Koki Hirota,
a former prime minister and onetime ambassador to Moscow,
suggested to Jacob A. Malik, then Soviet ambassador to
Japan, that "if the Soviet Army and the Japanese Navy were
to join forces, Japan and the Soviet Union together would
become the strongest powers in the world."[32]

The Japanese were prepared to make substantial concessions to Russia in order to bring her into the war on their
side or, if this were not possible, to restrain her from taking
up arms against Japan. Foreign Minister Shigenori Togo,
for example, went so far as to suggest that Japan might have
to return to her pre-1904 boundaries. Others would have
given up even more. In the words of a former Japanese diplo-
mat, the Japanese military leaders were "frightened out of
their wits" at the thought of a new war with Russia and were
willing to pay a heavy price to avoid one. After all, "If a ship
is doomed what matters its cargo, however precious? Jettison

[32] William H. Standley and Arthur A. Ageton, *Admiral Ambassador to
Russia* (Chicago, 1955), 499; Robert J. C. Butow, *Japan's Decision to Surrender*
(Stanford, 1954), 77, 86–87, 121–22; Toshikazu Kase (David Nelson Rowe, ed.),
Journey to the Missouri, 131; Otto D. Tolischus, *Tokyo Record* (New York,
1943), 107.

the cargo as fast as possible, if only doing so may save the ship."[33]

Having been promised what they wanted at Yalta, the Russians rebuffed Japanese overtures. Had their conditions been rejected at Yalta, Stalin conceivably might have made his bargain with the Japanese instead of with Roosevelt. True, Russian entry into the war against Japan enabled Soviet historians to boast that "the Armed Forces of the Soviet Union played the decisive role in the crushing of the Japanese imperialism, in the final liberation of China from the Japanese usurpers," but had Russia chosen to attain her ends by acting as a peace-loving mediator, her propaganda stock in these days of smiling imperialism would have been even higher in the Far East.[34]

There are other questions. Granted that Russian entry into the war against Japan was desirable, was the price paid for Soviet help too high? Were the concessions justified? Did Roosevelt "sell out" Nationalist China? Did Yalta pave the way for Russian domination of China? The best way to answer these questions is to take a closer look at the agreements.

The stipulation in the Yalta agreement that "the *status quo* in Outer-Mongolia (The Mongolian People's Republic) shall be preserved" implied Soviet domination of this area. This was contrary to the Sino-Soviet Treaty of 1924, which recognized Chinese sovereignty over Sovietized Outer Mongolia. But this sovereignty ceased to exist in the middle 1920's, and by the time of Yalta the Soviet Union had exercised *de facto* control there for about twenty years. The parenthetical inclusion of "the Mongol People's Republic" in the Yalta agreement merely strengthened later Russian

---

[33] Kase, *Journey to the Missouri*, 169; Butow, *Japan's Decision to Surrender*, 84; Tolischus, *Tokyo Record*, 107.

[34] G. Efimov, *Ocherki po novoi i noveishei istorii Kitaia* [Account of the Modern and Contemporary History of China] (Moscow, 1951), 401; V. Avarin, *Bor'ba za Tikhii Okean* [The Struggle for the Pacific Ocean] (Leningrad, 1947), 419; E. M. Zhukov (ed.), *Mezhdunarodnye otnosheniia na Dal'nem Vostoke (1870–1945)* [International Relations in the Far East (1870–1945)] (Moscow, 1951), 610–11.

arguments vis-à-vis the Chinese for Outer Mongolia's formal "independence."[35]

The provision that "the southern part of Sakhalin as well as all the islands adjacent to it shall be returned to the Soviet Union" provoked no American discussion. Professor Hugh Borton, then of the State Department, recommended that southern Sakhalin be treated as an international trusteeship, in view of its importance to both Russia and Japan. But somehow his memorandum had not been included in the Yalta Briefing Book.[36] Postwar disillusionment in America in the Yalta agreements led to the devaluation of experts, particularly professors. Actually, the Yalta records show that it was not the advice of the academicians which was taken that caused trouble, but that which was ignored.

The agreement that "the commercial port of Dairen shall be internationalized, the preeminent interests of the Soviet Union in this port being safeguarded and the lease of Port Arthur as a naval base of the USSR restored" has been criticized severely as a reversion to nineteenth-century imperialism. Harriman has tried to meet these objections by pointing out that "there is no reason from the discussions leading up to the Yalta agreements to presume that the safeguarding of the 'pre-eminent interests of the Soviet Union' should go beyond Soviet interests in the free *transit* of exports and imports to and from the Soviet Union," and that "President Roosevelt looked upon the lease of Port Arthur for a naval base as an arrangement similar to privileges which the United States has negotiated with other countries for the mutual security of two friendly nations." Be that as it may, the Russian desire to get back from the Japanese what they had lost in the Russo-Japanese War seemed on the whole reasonable.[37]

The provision that the Chinese-Eastern Railroad and the

35 Gerald H. Friters, *Outer Mongolia and its International Position* (Baltimore, 1949), 149; State Department, *United States Relations with China*, 113, n. 2, and 117, n. 7; Charles Patrick Fitzgerald, *Revolution in China* (New York, 1952), 235.

36 *Yalta Papers*, 385–88; Ernest J. King and Walter Muir Whitehill, *Fleet Admiral King, A Naval Record* (New York, 1952), 591–92.

37 State Department, *United States Relations with China*, 114, n. 3, 4; Leahy, *I Was There*, 318–19; Werner Levi, *Modern China's Foreign Policy* (Minneapolis, 1953), 240–41.

South Manchurian Railroad, which provides an outlet to Dairen, should be jointly operated by a Soviet-Chinese company—with the understanding that "the pre-eminent interests of the Soviet Union shall be safeguarded and that China shall retain full sovereignty in Manchuria"—has encountered less criticism. China had never recognized Russia's sale of the Chinese-Eastern Railroad to Japan in 1935 and still clung to the Sino-Soviet agreement of 1924, which provided that the manager of the railway be a Soviet citizen. Furthermore, the curious geographical conformation of Russia's Maritime Province made joint operation highly logical. Last but not least, Roosevelt and other Allied leaders were still preoccupied with the thought of future security against Japanese aggression. Japan had put down roots in southern Manchuria that could not be destroyed by military defeat alone. China did not seem strong enough to neutralize this area. As one historian has put it: "To recognize Russia's legitimate economic and strategic stake in Manchuria under conditions that specified 'that China shall retain full sovereignty' was a solution far more conservative than to abandon the 'cradle of conflict' to the winds of fate."[38] It must also be remembered that Roosevelt was not "giving away" any Chinese territory which he or even the Chinese actually held, but what the Japanese had in fact conquered. The concessions at Yalta seemed the most effective way of winning Manchuria back for the Chinese, at least politically.

But whatever historical arguments there may have been for the cession of southern Sakhalin, Dairen, and Port Arthur, there were none to justify the transfer of the whole Kurile Archipelago to the Soviet Union. A State Department memorandum by Professor George H. Blakeslee, which unfortunately, like the memorandum by Professor Borton, was not included in the Briefing Book, recognized that Russia had "a substantial claim" to the northern Kurile Islands and a strategic interest in the central group. "There would seem, however, to be few factors which would justify a Soviet claim to the southern islands," the memorandum continued. "This

[38] William Appleman Williams, *American-Russian Relations, 1781–1947* (New York, 1952), 277.

transfer to the Soviet Union would create a situation which a future Japan would find difficult to accept as a permanent solution. It would deprive Japan of islands which are historically and ethnically Japanese and of waters which are valuable for fishery. If the southern islands should be fortified they would be a continuing menace to Japan." In view of the proximity of the Kurile Islands to the Aleutians and their consequent importance to the United States as a land bridge between Japan and Alaska, the memorandum recommended that the northern and central Kuriles should be placed under the projected international organization.[39] The advice of Professor Blakeslee was not considered at Yalta, where Stalin was assured that all the Kurile Islands "shall be handed over to the Soviet Union."

The Roosevelt-Stalin agreement qualified the provisions concerning Outer Mongolia, Dairen, Port Arthur, and the railroads by making them subject to concurrence by Chiang Kai-shek, but then proceeded to nullify this qualification by stating that "these claims of the Soviet Union shall be unquestionably fulfilled." Was this a "sell-out" of the Chinese government?

It is relevant to remember in this connection that Chiang Kai-shek's own policy from the middle of 1943 on was directed toward a *rapprochement* with the Soviet Union. For this he sought American mediation, suggesting to Vice-President Henry A. Wallace in June, 1944, that Roosevelt act as "middleman" between China and the U.S.S.R. Chiang was willing to go "more than halfway" to obtain a friendly understanding with the Soviet Union, partly because he hoped that this might induce the Russians to continue recognizing his government as *the* government of China and deprive them of incentive to support the Chinese Communists, and partly because he felt that obligating Russia to something by a treaty was better than leaving her a free hand.[40] It was only in later years, when the Nationalist government began to shift the blame for its own shortcomings upon the shoulders

39 *Yalta Papers*, 379–83.

40 Levi, *Modern China's Foreign Policy*, 243–44; State Department, *United States Relations with China*, 550; Max Beloff, *Soviet Policy in the Far East, 1944–1951* (London, 1953), 29; "Statement of W. Averell Harriman," 3339.

of the United States, that Nationalist officials "demanded American support as an atonement for the betrayal at Yalta."[41]

Postwar accusations of betrayal ignored the stipulation in the Yalta agreement that "the Soviet Union expresses its readiness to conclude with the National Government of China a pact of friendship and alliance between the USSR and China." The pact of friendship and alliance was not intended to betray China, but to strengthen it. As a Briefing Book paper stated, "The American Government's long-range policy with respect to China is based on the belief that the need for China to be a principal factor in the Far East is a fundamental requirement for peace and security in that area." And another paper, considering the "political and military situation in China in the event the U.S.S.R. enters the war in the Far East," recommended that the British and American governments "should make every effort to bring about cooperation between all Chinese forces and the Russian military command in order to prevent military developments from further widening the gap between the Communists and the Chinese Government and increasing the possibility of a disunited China after hostilities." In point of fact, the treaty which eventually was concluded between Nationalist China and the U.S.S.R., the Soong-Stalin agreements of August, 1945, was heralded by so pro-Nationalist a magazine as *Life* as a promise of "genuine peace" in the Far East.[42]

It was a weak China, unable to fill the power vacuum which the defeat of Japan would create, that the United States government dreaded. Stalin's recognition of the Nationalist government as the central authority in China was most reassuring, therefore, and subsequent Soviet statements were even more encouraging. Thus in June, 1945, the new President, Harry S. Truman, could inform his special representative in China, Patrick J. Hurley, that:

> 1. Stalin has made to us a categorical statement that he will do everything he can to promote unification under the leadership of Chiang Kai-shek.

[41] Levi, *Modern China's Foreign Policy*, 244.
[42] *Yalta Papers*, 352, 356; *Life*, XIX (September 10, 1945), 42.

2. That this leadership will continue after the war.

3. That he wants a unified stable China and wants China to control all of Manchuria as a part of a United China.

4. That he has no territorial claims against China, and that he will respect Chinese sovereignty in all areas his troops enter to fight Japanese.

5. That he will welcome representatives of the Generalissimo to be with his troops in Manchuria in order to facilitate the organization of Chinese administration in Manchuria.

6. That he agrees with America's "open door" policy in China.

7. That he agrees to a trusteeship for Korea under China, Great Britain, the Soviet Union, and the United States.[43]

Certainly this seemed to offer that promise of "a strong, stable, and united China" which was the objective set forth in the President's Briefing Book for the Yalta negotiations when it stated: "We regard Sino-Soviet cooperation as a *sine qua non* of peace and security in the Far East and seek to aid in removing the existing mistrust between China and the Soviet Union and in bringing about close and friendly relations between them."[44]

The same outlook underlay American-Soviet relations. "President Roosevelt and I saw alike with regard to Russia," wrote Cordell Hull. "We both realized that the path of our relations would not be a carpet of flowers, but we also felt that we could work with Russia. There was no difference of opinion between us that I can recall on the basic premise that we must and could get along with the Soviet Government."[45]

No one could have expected the Russians to enter the war against Japan for the sole purpose of saving American lives. It is understandable that some territorial agreement was reached. It is less understandable, however, that there was almost no discussion of Russian claims. It is by no means impossible that the Russians would have satisfied themselves with only the northern and central Kurile Islands. But nobody ever raised the question. Nor did anybody counter the other Russian demands. The Americans might have reminded

43 Truman, *Year of Decisions,* 269.

44 *Yalta Papers,* 356–57.

45 Hull, *Memoirs,* II, 1467.

Stalin that his demands violated not only Russia's treaty with Japan of 1925 but also her treaty with China of 1924. In the former she had declared that the treaty ending the Russo-Japanese War "remains in full force," and in the latter she had renounced "the special rights and privileges relating to all concessions in any part of China acquired by the Tsarist Government under various Conventions, Treaties, Agreements, etc." Probably Roosevelt felt that Stalin could not be swayed and that nothing would be gained by antagonizing him. But by agreeing that in 1904 Japan had been the aggressor, Churchill and Roosevelt put the finger on their own countries, for it was with English and American moral and financial support that Japan ventured to challenge Russia in apparent defense of the Open Door.

Roosevelt and Churchill missed a golden opportunity to remind Stalin of earlier Communist condemnations of the czarist government's role in the Russo-Japanese War and to accuse him, tongue in cheek, of "deviationism." But perhaps it was just as well, for when Churchill had reminded Stalin at Teheran in another connection of the old Communist slogan "no annexations and no indemnities," Stalin had only replied with a broad grin: "I have told you that I am becoming a Conservative." Stalin asserted at the end of the war that the Russian people had been looking forward to the defeat of Japan to liquidate the blemish cast upon their country in 1904, that "for forty years we the people of the older generation have waited for this day." This was contrary not only to the traditional party line but also to current Russian feelings. General Deane observed in Moscow that Russia's entry into the war against Japan evoked relatively little enthusiasm or interest.[46]

Yet, when all this has been said, it must be remembered that the United States did not "give away" at Yalta anything

[46] Harriet L. Moore, *Soviet Far Eastern Policy, 1931–1945* (New York, 1945), 159, 175; Iosif V. Stalin, "Obrashcheniia tovarishcha I. V. Stalina k narodu" [Speech of Comrade Joseph V. Stalin to the People], as cited by B. A. Romanov, *Ocherki diplomaticheskoi istorii russko-iaponskoi voiny 1895–1907* [Outlines of the Diplomatic History of the Russo-Japanese War, 1895–1907] (Moscow, 1947), 3; Winston S. Churchill, *Closing the Ring* (Boston, 1951), 398–99; Deane, *The Strange Alliance*, 311.

that it was within her power to withhold except by making war against her Russian ally. In the words of Secretary of War Henry L. Stimson, the concessions to Russia on Far Eastern matters which were made at Yalta were "generally matters which are within the military power of Russia to obtain regardless of U. S. military action short of war. The War Department believes that Russia is militarily capable of defeating the Japanese and occupying Karafuto [Sakhalin], Manchuria, Korea and Northern China before it would be possible for the U. S. military forces to occupy these areas. Only in the Kuriles is the United States in a position to circumvent Russian initiative. If the United States were to occupy these islands to forestall Russian designs, it would be at the direct expense of the campaign to defeat Japan and would involve an unacceptable cost in American lives."[47] Stimson's statement points to the essential meaning of Yalta, so far as American interests in the Far East were concerned. Yalta enabled the United States virtually to ignore the Japanese forces on the mainland of Asia and thus to concentrate upon the Japanese home islands. This was an asset which facilitated the exclusive postwar occupation by the United States of the real heart of Far Eastern industry—Japan.

It was not the Yalta agreement, but failure to live up to the agreement that furthered postwar conflict. Perhaps the breakdown in Russo-American co-operation was inherent in the amorality of Communism; perhaps it was due to the age-old inability of comrades-in-arms to remain comrades-in-peace. As Stalin said at Yalta: "It is not so difficult to keep unity in time of war since there is a joint aim to defeat the common enemy, which is clear to everyone. The difficult task will come after the war when diverse interests tend to divide the Allies."[48]

The Yalta agreements were not faultless, but their imperfections lay in the limitation of the human mind, in man's inability to gaze into the future. Churchill summed this up when, on the eve of Yalta, in one of his more humble

[47] Department of Defense, "The Entry of the Soviet Union into the War against Japan," 70. See also *ibid.*, 20.
[48] James F. Byrnes, *Speaking Frankly* (New York, 1947), 44.

From William Nelson (ed.), *Out of the Crocodile's Mouth, Russian Cartoons about the United States* (Washington, D. C., 1949).

"THE SHAVE"

Krokodil, the most famous humor magazine in the U.S.S.R., printed this cartoon in 1945 to commemorate the unity of the three Great Powers against Japan.

moments, he wrote to Foreign Secretary Eden concerning the difficulty of long-range planning for a postwar world: "Guidance in these mundane matters is granted to us only step by step, or at the utmost a step or two ahead."[49] The Far Eastern sequel to Yalta has borne out Churchill's statement, and additional verification has been provided by the appearance of flaws in the plans for world order which the Big Three drafted there.

[49] Churchill, *Triumph and Tragedy,* 351.

CHAPTER V

The Big Three and the United Nations

ONE OF THE MAJOR problems discussed at Yalta was the creation of a world organization to preserve the peace. Britain and Russia had been politely interested in the project, but it was chiefly at the initiative of the United States that proposals had been drafted and discussed in 1944 and that the creation of the United Nations received a major place on the agenda at Yalta. Roosevelt went to Yalta determined to win British and Soviet agreement to the establishment of the security organization before the end of the war, and to win agreement to the kind of organization which he and his advisers thought desirable. The organization, he was convinced, must be acceptable both to the American public and the smaller nations of the world. Roosevelt's sense of the importance of winning Soviet and British co-operation in founding such an organization may well have caused him to make concessions on regional matters, much as Wilson did in 1919.

The main questions which were delaying the creation of the U. N. were two: (1) How heavily were the Great Powers to be represented in the Assembly of the U. N.? Was the Soviet Union to be allowed to have the multiple seats (and votes) which Stalin had demanded? (2) How thoroughly were the Great Powers to dominate the world organization? Were they to have complete right of veto on all questions that might come before the all-important executive committee of the proposed U. N., the Security Council, as Stalin had proposed? On the first of these questions Roosevelt was to fight without the support of Churchill, and compromise; on the second, with British backing, he got what he and his Department of State wanted at Yalta.

THE AMERICANS DO THEIR HOMEWORK

Soon after the termination of the Dumbarton Oaks conference (see pp. 19–24), the State Department initiated detailed
studies of the voting formula for the U. N. Security Council
and the question of extra seats for the U.S.S.R. in the U. N.
Assembly.[1] A committee headed by Acting Secretary of State
Stettinius took up these problems in early October. In the
Department of State, Dr. Leo Pasvolsky supervised U. N.
studies as Director of the Office of Special Political Affairs.
Near the end of October Alger Hiss, special assistant to Pasvolsky, prepared for the President's use draft proposals on the
voting formula. The drafts proposed that parties to disputes,
including the Great Powers, should not be allowed to vote on
resolutions relating to "the pacific settlement of disputes between nations," but insisted that each permanent member be
able to prevent the Security Council from taking "diplomatic, economic or military measures to maintain peace and
security." "Under such a formula," the State Department
writers asserted, "judicial and quasi-judicial procedures would
be based on the traditional Anglo-American principle that a
party to a dispute should not be able to prevent consideration
of that dispute." However, this formula would also protect
the right of the United States to prevent the use of its armed
forces "without its specific consent." This position, it will be
seen, was the one maintained successfully by the United States
at Yalta.[2]

Meanwhile, Churchill had informed Roosevelt of his approaching visit to Moscow, and noted that the question of
the peace organization would probably come up. He frankly
informed the President that in his opinion "the only hope"
for the creation of a world organization lay in acceptance of

[1] The Dumbarton Oaks proposals and subsequent proposals of amendments
and counterproposals are available in volume three of the following major
source on the origins of the U. N.: United Nations Information Organization,
*Documents of the United Nations Conference on International Organization,
San Francisco, 1945* (20 vols., New York, 1945).

[2] United States, Department of State, *The Conferences at Malta and Yalta,
1945* (Washington, 1955), 46; (hereinafter cited as *Yalta Papers*); United States,
Department of State (Harley Notter, ed.), *Postwar Foreign Policy Preparation,
1939–1945* (Washington, 1949), 376–77.

Great Power veto rights on all questions before the Security Council. He added that it was with regret that he had come to this view, contrary to his first thought on the subject. The President, in answer to Churchill's request for his views on the matter, replied that he thought the Security Council voting question should not be raised until he could meet with Churchill and Stalin. But, in view of indications that the British had adopted the Soviet position on voting, some of the State Department planners attempted to adjust their position to the new prospects. They proposed that, if the British and Russians should insist categorically upon the unanimity rule, the United States should accept it as a temporary solution of the problem in order to get the U. N. organized. Opposition soon developed to this view within the State Department, however. James C. Dunn, Director of the Office of European Affairs, insisted that if the Russians demanded Great Power veto privilege in all Security Council questions, then the organizational meeting to create the United Nations should be postponed. Dunn did not believe that the United States should join Britain and the U.S.S.R. in presenting the Soviet proposal to the other nations which would be invited to participate in founding the U. N.[3]

Acting Secretary of State Stettinius, who would soon be formally named as Hull's successor, in mid-November presented Roosevelt with detailed outlines of proposed American policy on four of the questions left open at Dumbarton Oaks. On the question of voting, he recommended that the United States support the following principles: (1) parties to a dispute should refrain from voting on decisions of the Security Council relating to investigations of disputes, on appeals by the Security Council for peaceful settlement of disputes, and on recommendations by the Security Council pertaining to methods and procedures of settlement; (2) the unanimous vote of permanent members of the Security Council would be required whenever the Security Council voted on the existence of threats to the peace or actual breaches of the peace and U. N. action to suppress such threats or breaches

[3] *Yalta Papers*, 47–48; State Department, *Postwar Foreign Policy Preparation*, 377; Winston S. Churchill, *Triumph and Tragedy* (Boston, 1953), 219–20.

of the peace. Such a formula, Stettinius held, recognized fully the special position of the Great Powers and would mean that no one could proceed against any one of them without its consent.[4] The President accepted this compromise proposal in a meeting with Stettinius and his advisers on November 15, saying that it was unlikely, in the final analysis, that the United States would agree to "our not having a vote in any serious or acute situation in which we may be involved." In view of the uncertainty about the time of the next Big Three meeting, Roosevelt agreed that the voting proposal should be made clear at once to Churchill and Stalin.[5]

Roosevelt's message to the Russian Marshal on December 5 was drafted by Alger Hiss, whose chief assignment in the State Department in this period, as it was later at Yalta, concerned the development of the United Nations organization. In support of the American view on the rule of unanimity, the President reminded Stalin of the strengthened moral position the Great Powers would gain by declining to ask for undue concessions. Such self-denial would "certainly make the whole plan, which must necessarily assign a special position to the Great Powers in the enforcement of peace, far more acceptable to all nations." It would demonstrate that the leadership of the Great Powers was to be based not alone on size, strength, and resources "but on those enduring qualifications of moral leadership which can raise the whole level of international relations the world over."[6] But Roosevelt's appeal to Stalin on moral grounds was unfruitful. The Russian chief, when informed of the President's attitude, asked for time to study the questions which had been raised. More than ten days passed, to the President's displeasure, before Molotov informed W. Averell Harriman, the United States ambassador in Moscow, that unity among the Great Powers must be maintained from the beginning without exception, but agreed that the question of Security Council voting should be left open for the approaching conference of the Big Three. Marshal

---

[4] *Yalta Papers*, 51.
[5] *Ibid.*, 56.
[6] *Ibid.*, 58–60; State Department, *Postwar Foreign Policy Preparation*, 381–83.

Stalin a short time later cabled the President his regrets that Russia could not give way on its position relative to unanimity. And he warned that a split among the Great Powers, with fatal consequences, would ensue from any limitation upon unanimity.[7]

The Russian attitude on this matter was clarified somewhat by Harriman at the end of December. Attributing Stalin's reaction to a distrust of the outside world, the United States ambassador reported that the Soviet chief could not believe that non-Russian powers could be impartial in a dispute involving the Soviet Union. He also feared, Harriman suggested, that the other nations of the world would likely condemn the U.S.S.R. for some of its diplomatic objectives toward neighbor countries like Iran and Poland. The Russians seemed to look upon the security organization as a means of protection against an aggressor nation and to doubt that it could be useful in settling disputes between themselves and other countries by judicial or mediatory means. Harriman believed that the Soviet leaders had taken a final stand against the American voting formula and could be changed only by a threat on the part of Britain and the United States, backed by the smaller nations, to stay out of the peace organization if Russia refused to modify her policy. Indicating a need for firmness, Harriman concluded that "we should face realistically the far-reaching implications of the Soviet position and adjust our policies accordingly."[8]

THE RUSSIANS HOLD FIRM

At the beginning of 1945 no agreement had been reached with the Russians on U. N. voting procedures, and the State Department was uncertain of the British position on a possible compromise formula. The President, aware of these and other current causes of friction among the Allies, remarked in his annual message to Congress on January 6, 1945, that the nearer the Allies came to defeating the enemy "the more we inevitably become conscious of differences among the victors." He insisted, however, that the Allies must not let

[7] *Yalta Papers*, 62–64.
[8] *Ibid.*, 64–66.

the differences divide and blind them to their "more important common and continuing interests in winning the war
and building the peace." He spoke of his concern about the
Polish and Greek situations, but concluded that these and
other problems connected with the liberation of Europe must
not be allowed "to delay the establishment of permanent
machinery for the maintenance of the peace."[9]

Roosevelt on January 8 took up the major unsettled problems affecting the United Nations with Stettinius, Dunn,
Pasvolsky, and Charles Bohlen. Pasvolsky presented a list of
seven substantive decisions on which the vote of the Security
Council would be required. On the following Security Council decisions unanimity of the permanent members would be
necessary: (1) the admission, suspension, and expulsion of
members, (2) the determination of the existence of a threat
to the peace or a breach of the peace, (3) the use of force or
the application of other measures of enforcement, (4) the
approval of agreements for the provision of armed forces,
(5) the settlement of all matters relating to the regulation of
armaments, and (6) the determination whether a regional
arrangement is consistent with the purposes and principles of
the general organization.

Only in the seventh category of decisions, those which related to the peaceful settlement of disputes, must a permanent member of the Security Council, when party to a dispute, abstain from voting. The State Department believed
that without this provision there was danger of losing some
support among the small nations and of providing liberal
critics with an argument against the peace organization. The
State Department representatives made clear that in the case
of a hypothetical quarrel between the United States and
Mexico, mentioned by the President, the United States would
refrain from voting on measures of conciliation and peaceful
settlement, but that no final decision could be taken on
enforcement action without its affirmative vote. The President, who followed the discussion closely, said that he would
make every effort to convince the Russians of the need for a
compromise formula. "He said he thought he knew Molotov

[9] State Department, *Postwar Foreign Policy Preparation*, 383–84.

well enough to speak plainly to him, and was sure that he could work out with him a satisfactory solution to take care of our situation." It was this compromise voting formula which had been sent to Moscow on December 5, and which the American delegation subsequently would present at Yalta.[10]

Pasvolsky on January 11 discussed the voting procedure with Soviet Ambassador Andrei Gromyko. When Pasvolsky stressed the importance of the moral position of the Great Powers, Gromyko rejoined that the British and Americans were emphasizing too many "moral, juridical, and organizational issues, and paying too little attention to the political side of the question." The Russian ambassador's chief concession was to state that it might be possible to permit any matter to be *discussed* in the Security Council, while still requiring a unanimous vote by all permanent members on any proposed action.[11] The conversation next turned to the Soviet demand for sixteen votes in the world organization, and Pasvolsky asked if Gromyko really believed that the sixteen Soviet Republics were independent countries as that term was commonly understood. The ambassador, who had already said that they were more important than Guatemala or Liberia, assured Pasvolsky that they were to be given control of their foreign affairs. Pasvolsky replied that the Big Three would have to decide on the sixteen votes. The State Department, in assessing the significance of Gromyko's statements, concluded merely that his mind was not closed on the voting procedure question.[12] The President that same January 11 discussed the voting procedure and the proposed sixteen votes for the Soviet Union with seven members of the Senate Foreign Relations Committee. He declared that he was "unsure whether the Soviet position on unanimity was a bad position" and that we might have to yield to them on that point but that, in his view, the Soviet government would give up its demand for "votes" for the sixteen Soviet Republics.[13]

Two days later, on January 13, the State Department was

---

10 *Yalta Papers,* 66–68.
11 *Ibid.,* 68–71.
12 *Ibid.,* 72–73. For subsequent Russian comments, see *ibid.,* 76.
13 State Department, *Postwar Foreign Policy Preparation,* 384–85.

informed orally that the British had accepted the American voting formula. Formal acceptance followed on January 14. Neither Churchill's memoirs nor the State Department records explain the change from Churchill's position of October, 1944. But good news from the British was balanced by ominous intimations from the Russians. On January 13 Gromyko told Pasvolsky that the Soviet Union was much interested in the creation of a trusteeship system under the future world organization, and the Russian frankly indicated that the U.S.S.R. expected to assert its voice in the future management of the colonies of Italy and Japan. Comedy relief in this discussion was provided when Gromyko and Pasvolsky, in Pasvolsky's words, "jokingly" explored "the possibility of placing the [headquarters of the world] organization in the Caucasus."[14]

Meanwhile, detailed Briefing Book papers on the voting procedure and membership questions had been prepared by the State Department for the President's use during the Yalta conference. The President was advised that acceptance of the American formula on voting was more important than ever, because many Americans and many small nations would oppose the Russian proposal. It would be difficult, the State Department continued, for some of the small nations to get support of their people for entry into an organization "which would bear every earmark of a great-power alliance." The American experts warned: "Taken in conjunction with the fact that we may have to acquiesce in some unsatisfactory peace settlements, all this would inevitably impair both our moral prestige and our political leadership in the world and might come perilously close to defeating the great cause in which we are now exercising so vigorous a leadership."[15] The Briefing Book reminded the President of various types of questions on which permanent members should not have veto power, and the special categories on which their unanimous vote would be required.

Roosevelt was fully aware of the main points in the State Department papers before he went to Yalta. At Malta, where

14 *Yalta Papers*, 77.
15 *Ibid.*, 85–87.

the British and American staffs met to discuss common problems before proceeding to the Crimea conference, the American position was discussed in a foreign ministers meeting. The British representatives agreed that acceptance of this voting formula was virtually essential to the creation of the world organization.[16]

VOTES AND VETOES AT YALTA

The troublesome question of voting in the Security Council was first discussed informally by the Big Three at Yalta. During a dinner on the evening of February 4, Stalin indicated that some of the small countries seemed to feel that the Great Powers had been forced to shed their blood to free them, and were attacking the Big Three for failing to take their interests into consideration. Roosevelt agreed with Stalin that the three Great Powers represented at the table should write the peace. The Prime Minister agreed that the small powers should not be allowed to dictate to the greater ones, but reminded his colleagues that the Great Powers should exercise their power with moderation and respect the small countries. Later in the evening, when Roosevelt and Stalin had left the dinner, Churchill, Stettinius, and Eden remained behind to discuss the voting procedure in the Security Council. The Prime Minister admitted his inclination to support the Russian view on voting "because he felt that everything depended on the unity of the three Great Powers and that without that the world would be subjected to inestimable catastrophe." Eden objected vigorously to this view, saying that there would be no attraction to small countries to join the United Nations organization under the conditions the Russians proposed, and that he doubted that the British public would support it. Churchill brushed this aside by asserting that he didn't agree "in the slightest" inasmuch as "he was thinking of the realities of the international situation." The discussion ended with the two British leaders in obvious disagreement on this key issue.[17]

16 *Ibid.*, 89–90, 504.
17 *Ibid.*, 589–91.

Agreement to Restrict the Veto

The voting procedure issue was presented formally at the plenary session of the conference on February 6. Stettinius, at Roosevelt's request, outlined the voting formula which had been sent to Churchill and Stalin on December 5, 1944. The Russian Marshal asked if there had been any changes made since then and was told that there had been only minor drafting changes. Unfortunately the interpreters became confused in explaining this situation and, as Stettinius recalls, "there was an unpleasant moment when the Russians thought we were trying to slip something over on them." Gromyko, in the same spirit of helpfulness he had shown earlier in Washington, came to the rescue and explained the situation to Stalin and Molotov. Stettinius then continued his arguments, declaring that unless freedom of discussion were permitted in the Security Council, "the establishment of the World Organization which we all so earnestly desire in order to save the world from the tragedy of another war would be seriously jeopardized."[18]

Soviet strategy at Yalta on U. N. matters was, like Roosevelt's on Germany and Poland, one of postponement. When the Russians asked for time to consider the voting question, Churchill supported Roosevelt. He stated that he had not liked the initial proposals made on voting at Dumbarton Oaks, but that he now considered the American suggestions satisfactory. He added that it might otherwise appear to some that the Big Three were trying to rule the world, although they were actually trying to save it from the horrors of war. He felt that to eliminate suspicion and to preserve harmony the Big Three should make "a proud submission."

Arguing that the interests of the Great Powers would be protected by the American proposal, Churchill cited the example of a possible Chinese demand for the return of Hong Kong. In such a case, he noted, neither power would be able to vote in the Security Council in regard to the methods of settlement but each would have a veto on any decision

---

[18] Edward R. Stettinius, Jr. (Walter Johnson, ed.), *Roosevelt and the Russians: The Yalta Conference* (Garden City, 1949), 140–46.

adverse to its interests. Stalin broke in to ask about a possible demand by Egypt for return of the Suez Canal. Churchill, apparently nettled by what he took to be an affront to the British Empire, asked to be permitted to continue with the question of Hong Kong. Later, he replied that the procedure which applied to the Chinese question would apply to the Egyptian case as well. The President then reminded both Churchill and Stalin that at Teheran the Great Powers had recognized the supreme responsibility of the nations to make a peace which would "command good will from the over-whelming masses of the peoples of the world." [19]

Stalin, suspicious and fretful because of the apparent Anglo-American solidarity in this question of voting, reacted defensively to the Prime Minister's reference to possible fears that the Great Powers were trying to rule the world. He said that he was sure that neither the United States nor Great Britain had any such desire "and that that left only the U.S.S.R." He added ironically that it looked as if Britain and the United States had accepted a document which would avoid any such accusation, but that the third power had not agreed. Far more important than the voting procedure, Stalin said, was the need to create an organization which would keep the peace for at least fifty years. Stalin declared that "as long as the three of them lived none of them would involve their countries in aggressive actions, but after all, ten years from now none of them might be present." Therefore, continued the Marshal, the main problem was to work out a covenant which would prevent conflicts between the Big Three. [20]

Anxious to postpone action on the question of voting in the Security Council Stalin now stated that he had not had an opportunity to study the Dumbarton Oaks proposals be-cause he had been busy with other matters. Stettinius was quick to notice that this was apparently just an excuse, since the Russian leader seemed to be well aware of the proposals which had been drawn up the previous fall. Stalin revealed the source of some of his anxiety over voting when he declared that his colleagues in Moscow could not forget that during

[19] *Yalta Papers,* 660–65, 673–75; Stettinius, *Roosevelt and the Russians,* 144.
[20] *Yalta Papers,* 665–66.

the Russo-Finnish War of 1939–40, the Soviet Union was expelled from the League of Nations at the instigation of Britain and France. Churchill replied that at the time those countries were "very, very angry" with Russia, and that such expulsion would be impossible under the Dumbarton Oaks proposal. Stalin, after asking how the Prime Minister could guarantee that such action would not be taken again, went on to add that he was not talking so much about expulsion as he was about the organization of public opinion against one country. The British leader, in his rejoinder, expressed doubt that Roosevelt or Stalin would lead a savage verbal attack against Britain and he was sure that this applied to other countries as well. Roosevelt now intervened to say that his main interest lay in the unity of the Great Powers. He thought if they had differences, however, these would be known to the outside world, no matter what the voting procedures were. He declared that full and free discussions in the Security Council would promote unity and "would serve to demonstrate the confidence which the Great Powers had in each other and in the justice of their own policies."[21] After this exchange the Russians asked for a short intermission.

During the break, Stettinius took Churchill and Eden to his quarters, where they talked further about voting. The Prime Minister indicated that he now understood the American draft proposal on voting in the Security Council for the first time, and he thought the same thing was true of Stalin. Both Churchill and his Foreign Secretary declared that they now had high hopes that there would be a world organization after all.[22]

Just after breakfast on February 7, Harry Hopkins and James F. Byrnes met with the State Department staff members and told them that the voting formula was more important than anything else at the moment, and that they should subordinate everything else to this point in the foreign ministers meeting at noon. But Molotov persisted in his postponement tactics. When Stettinius raised the voting issue in the conference, the Russian Foreign Commissar replied that it

21 *Ibid.*, 666–67; Stettinius, *Roosevelt and the Russians*, 148.
22 *Yalta Papers*, 677; Stettinius, *Roosevelt and the Russians*, 150.

had not been referred to the meeting by the plenary session, and that while he had some questions, he was not prepared to discuss them at the foreign ministers conference.

It is not clear whether Churchill or members of his staff discussed the question further with the Russians or whether they had a change of heart on their own, but later that afternoon, just before the plenary session, the Prime Minister confidently informed Roosevelt: "Uncle Joe will take Dumbarton Oaks."[23] The Russians proved Churchill a wise prophet by approving the United States proposal on voting procedure at the four o'clock meeting of the Big Three on February 7. In one of the important concessions of the conference, made before Roosevelt conceded to any Soviet demands, Molotov simply announced that in the light of Stettinius' report and Churchill's explanations of the previous day, the U.S.S.R. felt that the new formula guaranteed the unity of the Great Powers in questions concerning the preservation of the peace. Since this has been "the main Soviet purpose at Dumbarton Oaks," said Molotov, and the Russians believed that the new proposals "fully safeguarded this principle," he could state that the American proposals were acceptable and that his delegation "had no comments to offer." The final protocol of the conference failed to spell out the details of the American pre-conference proposals, but specifically ruled against the exercise of veto privilege by a Great Power in a case involving the peaceful settlement of a dispute to which it might be a party. No member of the Security Council which was a party to a dispute was to vote on resolutions for the pacific settlement of that dispute. It remained for the "Cold War" to prove how insubstantial the Soviet concession would be in practice. At Yalta it seemed a significant victory for the Americans and for international co-operation.[24]

Three Seats for the Soviets

Before the western Allies could congratulate themselves

[23] Stettinius, *Roosevelt and the Russians,* 161–62, 172.

[24] *Yalta Papers,* 711–12; Churchill, *Triumph and Tragedy,* 357–58; James F. Byrnes, *Speaking Frankly* (New York, 1947), 38; Stettinius, *Roosevelt and the Russians,* 173–76.

upon the firm Russian "yes," Molotov made the proposal which must have been behind his gracious acceptance of the American voting suggestion. Without pausing after the initial announcement, he reminded his listeners of Gromyko's demand at Dumbarton Oaks for extra votes for the individual sixteen republics of the U.S.S.R. Anticipating Allied opposition, he added that he had no desire to repeat the request for sixteen votes, but would be satisfied with the admission of two or three republics as original members. Roosevelt saw at once that he had been maneuvered into a position from which it was difficult to oppose the Soviet demand and passed to Stettinius a note saying: "This is not so good." Molotov sought to justify his proposal by reference to the full-fledged membership of the British dominions in the international organization. He asserted that White Russia (Byelorussia), the Ukraine, and Lithuania had won their right to a place in the United Nations by their sacrifices in the war.[25]

The President, while thanking Molotov for Russian agreement to the American voting formula, hedged on the request for extra votes for the Soviet Republics. He feared that the grant of such representation would destroy the principle of one vote for each sovereign power. Stalin, who may have thought that his gesture of conciliation was being poorly rewarded, began to show signs of irritation. Hopkins, who had been watching proceedings, suggested to Roosevelt that he "should try to get this referred to Foreign Ministers before there is trouble."[26] The President quickly adopted this suggestion and proposed it to Churchill and Stalin.

But on this issue Roosevelt was to get no help from Churchill. Because of his desire to keep separate representation for the British dominions, and perhaps because he wished to win agreements from Stalin in return for the concession to the Soviet Republics, the Prime Minister supported the Russian Marshal. Paying tribute to the work of the British dominions during the war, he added that he would not wish them excluded from participation in the international organization

---

[25] *Yalta Papers,* 711; Stettinius, *Roosevelt and the Russians,* 174.

[26] *Yalta Papers,* 713–14; Robert Sherwood, *Roosevelt and Hopkins, An Intimate History* (New York, 1948), 856.

and that, therefore, he had great sympathy with the Russian desire to do something for the Soviet Republics. Besides, he added, his heart went out to mighty Russia (the Byrnes notes state that Churchill said "White Russia") which "though bleeding was beating down the tyrants in her path." He could understand the Russian view, he continued, because the U.S.S.R. was faced with the prospect of having only one vote in the U. N. General Assembly, where six seats would be filled by the British bloc. He was glad that the President had not made a negative response to the Russians. Apparently trying to win several points at once, the Prime Minister adopted Stalin's postponement tactics in the U. N. problem; he doubted, he said, that an organizational meeting could be held before the end of the war. The President, anxious to have a conference as soon as possible, pressed for prompt examination by the foreign ministers of the Soviet member- ship proposal, the date and place of the United Nations Conference on World Organization, and the list of nations to be invited. The Big Three decided that the foreign min- isters would be asked merely to report their reactions to the various proposals to the heads of government of the three powers.[27]

That evening the Prime Minister, in a letter to Deputy Prime Minister Clement Attlee, further clarified his motives. "For us to have four or five members, six if India is included, when Russia has only one is asking a great deal of an Assembly of this kind." He thought that in view of "other important concessions by them which are achieved or pending" he should like to be able to make a friendly gesture toward the Russians. He felt that three votes were not excessive, and indicated that he would like War Cabinet approval of the Russian proposal at Yalta or at a later meeting. Churchill, like Roosevelt, looked upon the day's agreement as a good sign, and his message to Attlee noted that despite "our gloomy warning and forebodings Yalta has turned out very well so far."[28]

That evening the President, in reviewing with Stettinius

[27] *Yalta Papers,* 714–15; Byrnes, *Speaking Frankly,* 39.
[28] Churchill, *Triumph and Tragedy,* 359–60.

the happenings of February 7, mentioned that Stalin was concerned about Ukrainian nationalism and felt that a vote for that republic was essential in the interest of Soviet unity. He also thought that the three votes were needed if Stalin was to win the approval of his Moscow colleagues for Russian participation in the world organization. Roosevelt indicated his indignation at the idea of sixteen votes for the Soviet Union, but saw nothing preposterous in two extra votes. He was also aware that the British were embarrassed by the fact that even India, though not a sovereign state, would have a vote, and that as a result they could not oppose three votes for Russia. The main things of importance, the President stressed, were to defeat the Germans, to maintain Big Three unity, and to get them around a table to work out world organization. There would be approximately fifty seats in the Assembly, he said, and he wondered what difference two extra votes for the U.S.S.R. would make. After all, he concluded, the actual power would reside in the Security Council and each country would have only one vote there.[29] It was thus clear that neither the Prime Minister nor the President would seriously oppose the Russian request.

One of the President's experts (presumably Hiss), unaware of Roosevelt's reaction, drafted for Stettinius a list of arguments against including any of the individual Soviet Republics among the initial members of the peace organization. When the foreign ministers met at noon on February 8, Eden expressed British sympathy for two or three extra votes for the Soviet Union. Molotov anticipated the arguments in the Hiss memorandum by declaring that while Australia and Canada were members of the British Empire, they still would have a vote. He insisted that amendments to the Soviet constitution in 1944 had given the Soviet Republics freedom to make their own contacts with foreign governments. Stettinius and Eden suggested that instead of settling the matter at once they present it to the forthcoming conference of the United Nations. Molotov persisted, however, and requested the foreign ministers to sign a public statement asking that two or three votes in the Assembly be given to the Soviet Union, but

29 Stettinius, *Roosevelt and the Russians*, 186–87.

Stettinius answered that he would have to reserve his answer until he could see the President. He added, however, that he hoped to give a favorable reply before the end of the day.[30]

A subcommittee consisting of Hiss, Gromyko, and Gladwyn Jebb, the British representative, was appointed to draw up the foreign ministers' report. After they had prepared a draft, the British representative agreed to have it typed. Sometime between the adjournment of the subcommittee and the four o'clock meeting of the Big Three, Foreign Secretary Eden apparently talked to Roosevelt and got some sign of approval from the President for two extra votes for the Russians. When Hiss at the plenary session first looked at the newly typed copy of the report, he protested to Eden that it contained a statement of American support for the Russian proposal, and that this had not been agreed. Eden replied: "You don't know what has taken place." Roosevelt had not mentioned to Stettinius any discussion he had had with the British, and Stettinius had just heard the President state that somehow the United States delegation would have to accept the proposal, when Stalin came into the room. When the American Secretary of State began to tell of the foreign ministers meeting, the President broke in to say that they had approved the agenda. When Stalin asked if this included extra votes for Russia, Roosevelt answered that it did. These developments, which both Stettinius and Hiss have emphasized, did not indicate that there was anything underhanded about the agreement. It did reflect the way in which Roosevelt often acted as his own Secretary of State and it is, in retrospect, a significant commentary on Hiss's lack of influence over the proceedings at Yalta.[31]

The subcommittee's recommendations, read to the conference by Eden, who had presided over the foreign ministers meeting that day, were: (1) the United Nations Conference on World Organization was to be summoned to meet on April 25, 1945, (2) the meeting would be held in the United States, and (3) the states to be invited would be those which, at the end of the Yalta conference, should have signed the United

[30] *Ibid.*, 192–95; *Yalta Papers*, 736–37, 746–47.
[31] *Yalta Papers*, 991–92; Stettinius, *Roosevelt and the Russians*, 195–97.

Nations Declaration. The United Nations conference should decide upon the list of original members, and at that time the delegates of the United Kingdom and the United States would support membership for two Soviet Republics in addition to the membership of the U.S.S.R. as a whole.

Molotov then asked whether the Ukrainian and White Russian republics, the two he had mentioned for the extra seats, could participate in the approaching United Nation's conference if they were to sign the United Nations Declaration by March 1. The President pointedly talked of other matters, and the Prime Minister announced that he preferred to hold to the present signers of the United Nations Declaration for the first meeting, but that if other states were added, he would favor including the Soviet Republics. Stalin, aware that Roosevelt was strongly opposed to the idea, stated that he did not want to embarrass the President and if he would explain his difficulties, they would see what could be done. Roosevelt declared that his objection was technical, but he thought the matter of giving three votes to one country should be put before the founding conference. He agreed that all three Allied powers would support the Soviet request then. Stalin then repeated Molotov's suggestion of the possibility that the two republics sign the United Nations Declaration in order to obtain representation at the organizing conference. When the President replied that he did not think this would "overcome the difficulty," Stalin withdrew his request.[32]

On the last day of the meeting, however, when the communiqué was being drawn up, Molotov suggested that a statement be added that the Yalta conferees had recommended that the U. N. conference—which was to meet in San Francisco—should invite the two Soviet Republics to be original members of the organization. Roosevelt said that such a statement would be embarrassing to him, and Churchill added that if it appeared without an explanation of the American position it would cause trouble. He also added that three members of the British War Cabinet had objected to the arrangements. He put an end to Molotov's pressure by saying that before he could agree to the suggestion it would be necessary to ask for an adjournment of several days so that he could consult the dominions. Stettinius has noted that the President wanted to have a chance to explain the concession to Congressional leaders in the United States before the proposal got any publicity. He also added that the American delegation was in disagreement over the proposal and that some members hoped it might be possible to persuade the Soviet Union to withdraw its request. But no such opportunity ever arose.[33] Thus, the final protocol, approved on February 11, omitted the Soviet Republics from the list of nations to be invited to the conference at San Francisco, but stated that when the meeting was held, the United Kingdom and the United States would support a proposal to admit the Ukraine and White Russia to original membership in the United Nations.[34]

Three Votes for the United States?

After the conclusion of the plenary session of February 8, James F. Byrnes, who had been surprised by the President's concessions on extra votes for the Soviet Republics, reminded Roosevelt of the effective use opponents of the League of Nations had made in 1919 of the "Five votes for Britain" issue. He felt that Americans now realized that the British dominions were independent, but would know that the Soviet Republics were not. He urged the President to ask for two additional votes for the United States in order to forestall trouble. He was seconded in this by Edward J. Flynn, Democratic leader from New York who had come along with the Roosevelt party to Yalta, and apparently by Hopkins. At their urging the President wrote Churchill and Stalin on February 10. He spoke of political troubles which might be raised in the Senate over the award of three seats to the U.S.S.R. and asked if they would agree to an equal number of seats for the United States. Churchill assented, declaring that the United States should "propose the form in which their undisputed equality with every other Member State should be expressed."

[33] *Yalta Papers,* 926–28; Stettinius, *Roosevelt and the Russians,* 281–82.
[34] *Yalta Papers,* 976.

Marshal Stalin replied that he, too, was prepared to support officially such a proposal. It was to be through American choice that the United States came to have one vote in the Assembly, notwithstanding the Soviet and British concession.[35]

AFTER YALTA

In listening to Byrnes and Flynn, Roosevelt saddened many liberal supporters, who felt that he had weakened his moral position vis-à-vis the Soviet Union. A few weeks after the conference, in explaining his position to the American delegation to the San Francisco conference, the President stressed the fact that he had talked the Russians into taking fewer votes than they had demanded and into agreeing to an equal number of votes for the United States. He said that American delegates to the United Nations conference were free to vote as they pleased on the issue, but that he had told Stalin that if he were a delegate he would vote for the extra seats for the U.S.S.R. Senator Vandenberg, the leading Republican on the delegation, commented: "This will *raise hell.*"[36] (Italics in the original.)

But, in the final analysis, Roosevelt's U. N. policy at Yalta must be praised or damned in terms of the desirability of obtaining British and Russian co-operation in the world organization. Without their support no U. N. could be founded or could work effectively; to get their support, compromise was essential. Therein lay the essential meaning of Yalta in the history of man's search for world order. Furthermore, it should be remembered that the Russians and British had accepted the American voting procedure, and that Roosevelt's strong stand against sixteen votes for the Soviet Republics held the Russians to the minimum number they would settle for. While the concession was something Roosevelt did not care to defend, it was not a serious blow to the U. N. Charter and it gave the Russians no great increase in power

[35] *Ibid.,* 966–68; Byrnes, *Speaking Frankly,* 40–41; Stettinius, *Roosevelt and the Russians,* 282–83.

[36] Arthur H. Vandenberg, Jr. (ed.), with the collaboration of Joe Alex Morris, *Private Papers of Senator Vandenberg* (Boston, 1952), 159–60.

in the Assembly, as events have fully shown. Moreover, Roosevelt at Yalta won approval of pre-April negotiations regarding the troublesome question of territorial trusteeships for the U. N. (The exact terms appear in the Appendix to this volume.)

Most important of all, Roosevelt won from Churchill and Stalin an agreement to call the United Nations Conference on World Organization before the war's end. At Yalta the President demanded that agreement be reached on details of the organization before the territorial concessions were made. He may have hoped, like Wilson, that such peace machinery might help remove injustices of the peace settlement. Had he lived to hear Vandenberg's defense of the U. N. Charter in June, 1945, just before the United States Senate overwhelmingly accepted membership in the United Nations, Roosevelt might have felt that the Republican senator from Michigan was speaking for him. Vandenberg declared that the United Nations organization served the intelligent self-interest of the United States; that it offered "our only chance to keep faith with those who have borne the heat of battle." And he added:

I have signed the Charter with no illusions regarding its imperfections and with no pretensions that it guarantees its own benign aims; but with no doubts that it proposes an experiment which must be bravely undertaken in behalf of peace with justice in a better, happier, and safer world.

. . . .

Within the framework of the Charter, through its refinement in the light of experience, the future can overtake our errors. But there will be no future for it unless we can make this start. . . .[37]

Critics of the U. N. compromises at Yalta must ask whether the postwar world has been better or worse for having had the United Nations to help keep a semblance of East-West order in the midst of the "Cold War." After ten years of U. N. contributions to world peace, the answer can hardly remain in doubt.

[37] United States House of Representatives, 79th Congress, 1st Session, *Congressional Record*, XCI; 6981–82.

CHAPTER VI

Yalta in Retrospect

THE YALTA conference ended on February 11 on notes of friendship and good will. At the final banquet the evening before, Churchill declared hopefully in his toast to Stalin that the "fire of war had burnt up the misunderstandings of the past." But he more accurately summarized the general meaning of Yalta later when, in writing of the agreements reached at the meeting, he concluded: "All now depended upon the spirit in which they were carried out."[1]

PRAISE AND HOPE

Roosevelt and Churchill returned home by easy stages while communiqués summarizing some of their agreements were circulated throughout the world. The Far Eastern agreements could not be made known, of course, until after Russia actually entered the war against Japan. Similarly, the agreements to consider the dismemberment of Germany and the detailed statement on reparations for the Soviet Union could not be published, lest they give Nazi propagandists ammunition and thereby prolong the war in Europe. But the communiqué did make known all the Yalta agreements concerning Poland and summarized the essence of the Yalta agreements concerning the United Nations. (Agreements which were not made public immediately after the conference appear in italics in the Protocol of Proceedings, which is published in the Appendix to this volume.)

In the United States and Great Britain, the political leaders, press and public, on the basis of the Yalta communiqué, gave high praise to the work of the Crimea conference. *Time*, largest news magazine of the United States, spoke for many segments of public opinion in reporting that Yalta might

[1] Winston S. Churchill, *Triumph and Tragedy* (Boston, 1953), 392–94.

turn out to be the most important conference of the century. It praised the special recognition by the conferees of the principle of free and unfettered elections in liberated territories and the reaffirmation of the Dumbarton Oaks principles, which would "reassure many a citizen that World War II was not being fought in vain." The magazine reported that Congress, in its first, informal reaction, "overwhelmingly" approved the results of the conference. *Time* drew attention to the special statement of the former isolationist leader, Senator Arthur H. Vandenberg, that Yalta reaffirmed "basic principles of justice to which we are deeply attached, and it undertakes for the first time to implement these principles by direct action." Herbert Hoover was quoted as saying that the conference offered "a great hope to the world," and Senator Alben W. Barkley, the majority leader of the Senate, declared that he regarded it "as one of the most important steps ever taken to promote peace and happiness in the world." These opinions, delivered before some of the Yalta agreements were known, emphasized those achievements which Roosevelt had put first at the Crimea conference, the effort to make effective the organization of the U. N. in accordance with the principles outlined at Dumbarton Oaks.[2]

At first most of the western world rejoiced at Big Three agreement on the important issues of war and peace. Germany and Japan were to be defeated, peace to be restored, and Good was to reign in the world. The first protests were raised by the Polish leaders abroad. The Polish government in exile received the Yalta communiqué on the evening of February 12 and denounced it next morning as a violation of the principles of the Atlantic Charter and the right of every nation to protect itself. And when Prime Minister Churchill asked the House of Commons on February 27 to approve his actions at Yalta, he was attacked because of his concessions to the Russians on the Polish question. To his critics he spoke of Stalin's solemn pledges and declined "absolutely" to embark on a discussion of Russian good faith. He admitted that

[2] *Time*, XLV (February 19, 1945), 15; Robert Sherwood, *Roosevelt and Hopkins, An Intimate History* (New York, 1948), 870.

many imponderables lay ahead, but cautioned that it was a mistake to look too far into the future. "Only one link in the chain of destiny," he added, "can be handled at a time." A great majority in the House of Commons approved the Yalta decisions, but twenty-five members, most of them Conservatives, voted against Churchill, and eleven members of the government abstained.[3]

Roosevelt on March 2 made his report on Yalta to a joint session of Congress. Sitting to avoid the use of heavy braces on his legs, he showed the exhaustion of his long trip and the exertions of twelve years in the Presidency in his haggard face, his almost unique reference to his infirmity, and in the thickness of his speech. He asked the support of Congress and the American people in carrying out the Yalta decisions, saying that without their backing the meeting would have produced no lasting results.

THE ONSET OF DISILLUSIONMENT

The initial praise for those Yalta agreements which were known in February, 1945, soon gave way to criticism of Russia in the American press. In the United Nations Conference for World Organization at San Francisco in April, 1945, and in pre-armistice negotiations in March and April, the U.S.S.R. began to empty the reservoir of good will which it had built up in the West in the last years of the war. At San Francisco in April, 1945, Molotov began the tactics of negation which were to make *nyet* a dirty word in Western lexicons. Before the war ended in Europe in May, Soviet activities in the Baltic states, Rumania, Hungary, and Poland caused uneasiness among the western Allies. By the end of 1945 it was apparent that Red Army occupation forces intended to despoil their area of Germany, reform its society in the Soviet image, and integrate it into the Soviet orbit. But for a time American soldiers who had seen their friends killed by German arms and who regretted their years spent in a war they had not wanted actually welcomed Russian occupation of Germany on the grounds that the Red forces would punish the Nazis as they deserved. Despite some alarm over Soviet

[3] Churchill, *Triumph and Tragedy*, 400–402.

activities in eastern and central Europe, the American people in the latter half of 1945 and the early part of 1946 were intent on getting the troops home as soon as possible.

Expansion of Russian Influence in Europe

Even before the German surrender was signed at Reims in May, 1945, the Soviet Union began the policy of creating satellite states on its borners. Old-time Communist agitators, deserters, expatriates, exiles, escaped prisoners, and apprentice conspirators began to find their way to power. Some emerged from resistance ranks, where they had served courageously during part of the war years, or were sent back from the Soviet Union to their former homes to organize or strengthen Communist cadres in key government ministries. In some cases they reached power directly; often they infiltrated labor or agrarian regimes and ultimately eliminated or won over those who initially opposed them. Some of the Communist-controlled countries invited Soviet military missions, which virtually ran the armed forces of the countries concerned and gave backing to the police forces of such states. In Hungary, Rumania, Yugoslavia, and the Russian zone of Austria, the Russians gained a strong foothold.

The China Deal Falls Through

The treaty agreements of August, 1945, between Nationalist China and the U.S.S.R. soon proved disappointing. Part of the troubles arose, however, because of the weakness and unfavorable location of Nationalist Chinese troops. At the war's end Chiang Kai-shek's troops were concentrated in southwest China, pushed there by the Japanese or sent there for possible use in Burma. Forces of Red China were in a better position to co-operate with the Soviet forces in the north and northeast.

The Soviet Union declared war on Japan on August 8, almost exactly three months to an hour after the end of the war in Germany, and launched attacks against the Japanese in Manchuria. On August 12 the Japanese asked for an armistice, and on August 15 General Douglas MacArthur, Supreme Commander for the Allied powers, issued an order, approved by the President, directing Japanese commanders within China (excluding Manchuria), Formosa, and French Indochina north of the sixteenth parallel to surrender to Nationalist Chinese forces. Enemy forces in Manchuria, Korea north of the thirty-eighth parallel, and Karafuto (southern Sakhalin) were to surrender to the Red Army. President Truman on August 16 refused Stalin's demand that the northern half of the Japanese island of Hokkaido be added to the list of areas to be handed over by the enemy to the Russians. Meanwhile, General Albert C. Wedemeyer, who commanded United States forces in China, had been directed by the Joint Chiefs of Staff to support Nationalist Chinese efforts to reoccupy areas in China held by Japanese troops, to help Chiang Kai-shek transport his troops to key areas in China, but to avoid becoming involved "in any major campaign in any part of the China Theater." Americans on both sides of the Pacific soon became worried over Chinese Communist activities. General Marshall on August 17 cabled MacArthur that there was great anxiety in Washington over the possibility that Japanese surrender to the Chinese Communists might deepen the schism in China. The State Department, he added, had suggested that MacArthur make clear to the Japanese that the clause in the Potsdam declaration of July dealing with the return of Japanese armed forces to their peaceful occupations applied only to those who surrendered to Chiang Kai-shek.[4]

American pressure on the Chinese Communists helped pave the way for conversations between Mao Tse-tung, the Red Chinese leader, and Chiang Kai-shek. But while they talked during the last half of August and the first half of September, Chinese Communist troops extended their control across a great part of northern China and the lines of communications to Manchuria. In September the United States began transporting by air three Chinese armies from southwest China to key sectors in the east and north. Nearly 50,000 American Marines were landed in the September-

[4] For general information on this period see the following: United States, Department of Defense, "The Entry of the Soviet Union into the War against Japan: Military Plans, 1941–1945" (mimeographed report released on October 19, 1955), 89–107; Herbert Feis, *The China Tangle* (Princeton, 1953), 339–42.

October period in the area of Tsingtao, Tientsin, Peiping, and Chinwangtao. Toward the Manchurian border, Chinese Communists refused to co-operate with Nationalist Chinese who had been sent to take over former Japanese-occupied territory. In some places commanders of American transports undertaking to land Nationalist troops were warned by the Chinese Reds that, since no Japanese were in the area, any effort by the Americans to land the Nationalists would likely be looked upon as an American attempt to interfere in internal politics.

In view of these and other incidents, General Wedemeyer declared in November that if the Marines were retained in northern China they would become involved in fighting. He recommended that either all American forces in the Chinese theater of operations, including the Marines, be withdrawn or his directive changed to justify their retention and use. A few days earlier General Wedemeyer had cautioned that although Soviet forces were making a show of co-operating with the Nationalists, they seemed to be creating conditions which favored the efforts of the Chinese Communists to acquire areas in northern China and Manchuria and prevent the government of Chiang Kai-shek from retaking them. In his report of November 20, 1945, General Wedemeyer made clear the extent to which the Chinese-Soviet deal had fallen through. Outlining the grave difficulties which would face Chiang Kai-shek unless he entered on a policy of reform in northern China, and predicting the unlikelihood of his occupying Manchuria unless he reached agreements with the Chinese Communists and the U.S.S.R., Wedemeyer concluded: "It appears remote that a satisfactory understanding will be reached between Chinese Communists and the National Government."[5] Nothing more was needed to show that the Yalta concessions, ratified by China in August, 1945, had been for naught.

SUSPICION BEGINS AT HOME

In the five years between the end of World War II and the beginning of war in Korea, American distrust and fear of

[5] Feis, *The China Tangle,* 355–67, 396–404.

Soviet Russia increased as the Chinese Communists mastered all of continental China, Communist parties made election gains in France and Italy, and the U.S.S.R. imposed an "Iron Curtain" over most of central and eastern Europe.[6] Greece, Turkey, and Iran were threatened and the western sector of Berlin was menaced with starvation by a Soviet blockade. Russian benediction was given to the North Korean attack in 1950 and to the later Chinese entry into the battle against the United Nations forces. The calling up of American troops for service in Korea intensified the sense of betrayal and frustration which had been created by the earlier aggression. To all Americans it was a forcible and sickening reminder that the war against totalitarianism had merely reached the intermission period in 1945, not the final curtain. Realization that years of war had brought only the briefest of respites from conflict created a mass anger which reached the point of hysteria when it was found that the Russians had the secret of that monstrous invention and "ultimate" weapon, the A-bomb.

Suspicion grew rapidly in the atmosphere of fear and anger and defeat, generated in the years 1945–50. When Whittaker Chambers, self-confessed, former Russian agent, produced papers allegedly given him by Alger Hiss, a respected State Department official who had been at Dumbarton Oaks, at Yalta, and at San Francisco, it seemed that the Soviet plot ran everywhere. Political maneuvers for partisan advantage became intertwined with security measures. Liberals, who suspected that the Hiss case was a contemporary parallel of the "Dreyfus affair" intended to destroy the remaining architects of the New Deal and Fair Deal as well as to catch Communists, undertook to defend Hiss on the assumption that he could not be guilty because he *must* not be. When he was convicted of perjury, they were rendered speechless and virtually powerless for a season. The indictment or conviction of other officials increased the fear of the American public. When it was found that a number of atomic scientists, as Communists, or in the name of world

6 A valuable outline of Soviet aims and tactics may be found in Hugh Seton-Watson, *From Lenin to Malenkov: The History of World Communism* (New York, 1953), especially, for this period, 210–27, 248–329.

science, or with a cosmic naïveté about the best means to keep the peace of the world, had handed over secrets to the Russians, it seemed that no one could be trusted.

It was in this period of unbridled suspicion that the Yalta conference commitments, known by 1946 to be more numerous than originally supposed, were wrenched out of historical perspective and blamed for most of the evils in world politics since February, 1945. As a result, Yalta's historical significance has been confused, its decisions exaggerated, and its effect on the course of subsequent events distorted. Above all, the historical context in which Yalta occurred was overlooked. Forgotten was the fact that the Soviet Union had borne the main brunt of the German attack in 1941 and 1942, while Britain and the United States were trying to hold on in the Pacific and were gathering their forces for a return to Europe. Forgotten were wartime fears in the West that Russia might succumb or that she might decide to let the western Allies and Germany fight a costly war of attrition. Forgotten also was the fact that in the years 1942–45 co-ordination of Anglo-American and Russian pressure against Germany had brought victory in Europe. As a result of this forgetfulness, all Soviet gains at Yalta seemed uncalled for or part of a conspiracy to aid Russia. Yalta became a symbol for betrayal and a shibboleth for the opponents of Roosevelt and of international co-operation.

Each year after 1945 thus brought increased demands for "the whole truth" about Yalta. The defeat of Chiang Kai-shek focused attention on the part the Yalta Far Eastern concessions supposedly played in his downfall. The beginning of the war in Korea raised the question of whether or not Yalta had been responsible for Communist influence in that country. The recall of MacArthur led his supporters to assert that his advice, had it been sought in 1945, would have prevented concessions to the Russians. The year 1955 saw the publication by the State Department of documents on the Crimea conference. These were followed by Department of Defense releases. Neither set of documents backed the thesis of "betrayal and sellout" presented so often in the halls of Congress and during the political campaigns of 1952.

NO BETRAYAL AT YALTA

The State Department and military advisers who drew up the briefing papers and memoranda for President Roosevelt's use at Yalta and the officials who accompanied him to the conference did not mislead him into making wrongful concessions to the Russians. On nearly every concession made at the Crimea conference State Department advisers were more anti-Russian than Roosevelt or Churchill. Secretary of State Stettinius and his staff stood firmly against the exaggerated Soviet demands and no one did more than Ambassador Harriman to warn the President against them. Papers written by Hiss before and during the Yalta conference opposed the Russian demand for unlimited veto power in the Security Council of the proposed U. N. and contested the Soviet claim to special representation in the U. N. It is clear from the Hiss notes on the conference and from Charles Bohlen's testimony before the Senate Foreign Relations Committee in 1953 that Hiss's role was confined almost exclusively to United Nations questions. The published record of everything that Hiss wrote and said on the subject fully reflects a concern for safeguarding American interests. Roosevelt's final approval of the extra seats for the Russians took Hiss by surprise and found him saying a few minutes before the President's approval that the Americans had not agreed to the Russian request. It is an extreme and unfounded application of the principle of guilt by association to argue that Hiss's presence at Yalta and San Francisco in some way tainted those conferences with perjury and subversion.

Yet, concessions were made to the Russians at Yalta, and the most significant thus far have been those concerning the Far East. For a variety of reasons these Far East concessions have given rise to the most pronounced denunciations of the Yalta conference. Among these reasons are the following: (1) attacks against Yalta by a coalition of proponents of Chiang Kai-shek, opponents of Roosevelt and Marshall, and the champions of MacArthur, (2) an uninformed assumption that it was Yalta that caused the downfall of Chiang Kai-shek, (3) a general prejudice against "secret diplomacy" among the American people and the fact that the agreements were reached privately by Roosevelt and Stalin, (4) the weakening of American and Japanese defenses which the concessions represented, and (5) a conviction that Roosevelt had no moral right to grant Chinese territory to the Russians.

Bohlen's arguments that Churchill was not present at the discussions on the Far East because the United States was largely responsible for that theater of the war and that China was excluded because Russia was then unwilling to be connected openly with arrangements dealing with the Far East are cogent but not conclusive. The fact that the agreement was quickly reached regarding territory belonging to neither of the conferees is hard to reconcile with Wilsonian ideals of "open covenants openly arrived at" and with the spirit of the Atlantic Charter and the Cairo Declaration.

But the suggestion that Roosevelt's promise to seek Chiang Kai-shek's agreement to concessions in the Far East brought the downfall of Nationalist China has been effectively denied by Harriman and Bohlen, and is not borne out by the facts of twentieth-century Chinese development. The willingness of Chiang to carry out these concessions in return for Russian recognition of his government has already been noted. Arguments that the United States did not properly back Chiang Kai-shek against Mao Tse-tung and that Marshall and his advisers weakened the Nationalists in insisting on compromises with the Chinese Communists should not be charged against the negotiators at Yalta, whatever their foundation in fact. Actually, in 1945 the Generalissimo thought he had a good arrangement with Stalin and for a time after the war his armies seemed to be strongly situated in parts of northern China. Overextension of supply lines, failure to get firm possession of the liberated territory, overconfidence, poor leadership, inflation, refusal to reform Kuomintang corruption, failure to satisfy the land hunger of the Chinese peasant, and, above all, the failure of Stalin to keep his promises to Chiang Kai-shek are the chief explanations for the Nationalist debacle of 1946–50. Strategically, the grant of the Kuriles and southern Sakhalin to a potential enemy of the United States was unsound. In case of a future war between the United States and the U.S.S.R. the American position would be definitely weakened. But few Americans thought of such a war in 1945.

The moral aspects of the concessions have worried liberal supporters of Roosevelt and angered his opponents. To those who had observed the spread of late nineteenth- and early twentieth-century imperialism, concessions to the Soviet Union at the expense of China smelled of an ancient evil. The names Dairen, Port Arthur, and the South Manchurian Railway reminded the West of the Treaty of Shimonoseki, the Russo-Japanese struggle for power in Korea and Manchuria in 1904–1905, and the steady march of Japan toward control of the Far East. The 1945 grant of concessions which the czar's representatives had once won from a defenseless China smacked of a return to the breakup of China. In the disillusionment which came after 1946 many people forgot that the territory Russia gained in 1945 had not been in China's control since 1905. Within a few weeks after the war ended, the Russians held the various ports and possessions which had been promised them, without the Nationalists ever being in contact with the territory involved. Later, Stalin returned part of these areas to the technical control of the Chinese Communists, who in turn made concessions to the Russians.

Despite these extenuating arguments, and the explanations presented earlier, there is no real defense on *moral* grounds of the Far Eastern concessions to the Soviet Union. It is the one point at which Roosevelt openly went back to the type of arrangement which he and other western leaders had previously condemned. Morality and reality were in conflict; reality won. Defenders of the Far Eastern concessions can only justify them in terms of (1) the need of Russian aid against Japan to shorten the war in the Far East and save American lives, or (2) the need to prolong wartime co-operation with the U.S.S.R. into the postwar era.

WAS RUSSIAN AID NEEDED IN THE FAR EAST?

Many critics of the Yalta conference have insisted that Russian participation was not needed. One group points to possession of the A-bomb and overwhelming naval and air superiority in the Pacific to prove that the United States at the beginning of February, 1945, needed no assistance to defeat Japan.

Knowledge of the A-bomb at Yalta

Major General Leslie R. Groves, military head of the atomic bomb project, at the end of December, 1944, notified General Marshall, Secretary Stimson, and President Roosevelt that one atomic bomb, possessing enormous destructive power, would be ready for use about the first of August, 1945, that one more would be ready toward the end of 1945, and that others would follow, apparently at shortened intervals thereafter. Colonel William S. Considine, who was assigned to the Manhattan atomic project in 1944–45, testified in 1951 that he informed Secretary Stettinius at Yalta that a successful bomb would in fact be constructed, that it would be ready about the first of August, and that such a bomb would wreck a large-sized city. These facts might well have made the military and political advisers of the President far more sanguine about their prospects of an early victory than they were. However, in the absence of an actual explosion of a bomb, there was some ground for military advisers, who had to fight until the end of the year with one bomb, to proceed on the basis that the bomb would be a bonus and not the weapon which would bring early victory.

Furthermore, the military advisers of the President were less positive concerning the value of the A-bomb than was the head of the Manhattan project. Of these the least hopeful was Admiral Leahy, Chief of Staff to the President. Leahy has frankly admitted that although General Groves in September, 1944, had made the most convincing report on the possibilities of the atomic bomb he had heard up until that time, he still did not have "much confidence in the practicability of the project." Less than a week before the actual dropping of the bomb on Hiroshima, Leahy told King George VI that he did not think it would be as effective as expected. "It sounds," he added, "like a professor's dream to me." President Truman in his memoirs has confirmed the admiral's skepticism on the subject. So far as Leahy was concerned, the development of the bomb did not affect the question of Russian aid one way or the other. His faith in 1944 and in 1945 lay in the navy; he was convinced that the fleet could defeat the Japanese without ground force help.[7]

The Navy Argument

Fleet Admiral Ernest J. King has written that he, Leahy, Fleet Admiral Chester W. Nimitz, and other naval officers felt that the defeat of Japan could have been accomplished by sea and air power alone, without the necessity of the actual invasion of the Japanese home islands by ground forces. According to King, he and Leahy reluctantly acquiesced in the decision to attack the home islands, feeling "that in the end sea power would accomplish the defeat of Japan." Yet, on June 21, 1951, Admiral King wrote Senator William Knowland that at the time of the Yalta conference he was "agreeable" to the entry of the U.S.S.R. into the war against Japan. "Our contention," he continued, "was that blockade and bombardment could bring about Japanese capitulation, and that in connection with this course of action, engagement of the Japanese armies in Manchuria would hasten that capitulation."[8] This throws great light on the Far Eastern concessions. No one doubted at Yalta that the Japanese would be ultimately defeated, nor that a blockade might gradually starve the Japanese islands into submission. But Americans in the spring of 1945 had no desire to leave millions of soldiers, sailors, and airmen under arms, waiting for the ultimate surrender of the Japanese, eighteen months or more in the future.

The Air Force Story

Some critics have declared that air intelligence experts knew that Japan was finished and that if General Henry H. Arnold had been well enough to attend the Yalta conference, he could have made the President aware of this fact and thus have prevented concessions to Stalin. Such a statement ap-

[7] United States, Department of State, *The Conferences at Malta and Yalta, 1945* (Washington, 1955), 383–84; William D. Leahy, *I Was There* (New York, 1950), 269, 318, 431.

[8] Ernest J. King and Walter Muir Whitehill, *Fleet Admiral King, A Naval Record* (New York, 1952), 591, 598.

parently assumes that the air force was then engaged in massive operations of such a type that air bombardment could have ended the war in the Pacific quickly without ground action. This hopeful thesis has been refuted by the arguments of General Laurence S. Kuter, who represented General Arnold at Yalta:

> By March 9, 1945, only 22 small-scale B-29 strikes had been flown against Japan from the Marianas. Although the size of these strikes was steadily growing, the average number of airplanes to reach Japan from the Marianas at the time of the Yalta conference was eighty. The Yalta conference ended exactly one month before the first of the effective medium-altitude fire-bomb strikes on Japanese cities had been delivered. . . . It was sixty-five days before the first five-hundred-airplane strike could be delivered. . . .[9]

The bad reputation now attached to Yalta, Kuter concluded in 1955, has arisen from subsequent political experience with Russia, and "to some extent from misinformation generated by partisan oratory and nourished by shaky memories."

The Army Wanted Help

While it was believed that American naval and air forces had gained superiority in the Pacific by February, 1945, military planners forecast that the war against Japan would likely last eighteen months after the defeat of Germany, with possible casualties, according to Secretary of War Stimson, of at least 500,000 and possibly as many as a million men.[10] The first months of the 1945 campaigns had produced constantly mounting totals of dead and wounded. As has been noted (Chapter I), casualties at Iwo Jima and Okinawa confirmed the trend. In the spring General MacArthur himself favored Russian action in support of his offensives against the Japanese home islands. This notwithstanding, in October, 1955, General MacArthur declared that he was not consulted about concessions to the Russians and that he considered them fan-

[9] Laurence S. Kuter, *Airman at Yalta* (New York, 1955), 4, 9.

[10] Henry L. Stimson and McGeorge Bundy, *On Active Service in Peace and War* (New York, 1947), 617-19. See also Harry S. Truman, *Year of Decisions* (Garden City, 1955), 265.

tastic.[11] This argument is irrelevant. It is not the responsibility of the soldier to make political arrangements; rather it is to state what is necessary to accomplish his mission. MacArthur had only to notify Marshall of his needs, and the Chief of Staff had only to inform Roosevelt of army requirements in the Pacific. After that it was the President's duty to provide that aid on the best terms he could obtain. Had he refused to seek Soviet aid against Japan, he would almost certainly have been criticized by military commanders in 1945 instead of after his death.

It is interesting to note two contemporary reactions of Pacific veterans to the August, 1945, entry of the Russians into the war. General Robert L. Eichelberger, commander of the Eighth Army, declared: "Whether Japan surrenders in the near future or decides to fight on in a suicide finish, the entrance of Russia into the Pacific War has hastened the end of World War II." And the way the common soldier felt was revealed by the comment of Sergeant Hubert Eldridge of Kentucky, who told reporters: "I've been in the army four and a half years. Maybe those bombs and those Russians will help me get out now." The hope of getting home alive and quickly, clearly expressed in this statement, was the collective wish of the American soldiers in the Pacific; and that wish was one of the political realities that shaped the Yalta agreements.[12]

What Would the Russians Have Done Without Concessions?

But the western Allies need not have promised the Russians anything, say the critics; Stalin would have fought Japan without concessions. Without Russian documents, one can not say positively what the Soviet Union would have done. Stalin had made a deal with an enemy in 1939; in 1945, he might conceivably have remained true to his 1941 treaty of neutrality with Japan, or even have converted it into a pact of alliance, if the Japanese had offered him concessions which he could not obtain from China with American help. Various

[11] The above statement of MacArthur's desires should be compared with the newly published assertions by Courtney Whitney, *MacArthur: His Rendezvous with History* (New York, 1956). See Chapter I, n.32, *supra*.

[12] New York *Times*, August 10, 1945.

roads were open to Stalin in the spring and summer of 1945. He might have made a deal with Japan in return for concessions in Manchuria and Korea; he might have remained neutral in the Far East until the United States suffered heavy casualties and then entered at peak strength into the Pacific war. Either of these policies would have enabled the Red Army to dominate Europe, while the United States and Britain withdrew their forces from Germany and Italy to the Pacific. Finally, Stalin might have attacked Japan without any agreement regarding the future terms of peace.

In view of the Russian ability to take what they wanted in 1945 without Allied agreement, in view of the additional aid the Allies needed in Europe and the Pacific, and in view of what Chiang Kai-shek was willing to give in August, 1945, for what he thought to be recognition by the Soviet government, one must conclude that the Far Eastern concessions at Yalta did not seem excessive in February, 1945. Even today it is difficult to avoid the conclusion that if Stalin had not received them from Roosevelt and Churchill he would have sought them—or even greater gains—from someone else or have taken them without Allied or Chinese consent. The terms of the Yalta agreements concerning the Far East were in the nature of a Roosevelt-Stalin contract and constituted not only concessions to Stalin but also restraining limitations. It was not Roosevelt's fault that Stalin later broke the contract.

THE MEANING OF YALTA

"It is a mistake," wrote Winston Churchill to Foreign Secretary Eden one month before the Yalta conference, "to try to write out on little pieces of paper what the vast emotions of an outraged and quivering world will be either immediately after the struggle is over or when the inevitable cold fit follows the hot." "These awe-inspiring tides of feeling," he added, "dominate most people's minds, and independent figures tend to become not only lonely but futile."[13] The Prime Minister, with the prescience he so often showed, in these words pointed clearly to the problems which faced the Allies

[13] Churchill, *Triumph and Tragedy*, 351.

when they came to talk of the final victory and the beginnings of peace. The thirst for vengeance, the rapidly shifting desires of the public, and the unique difficulties of the democratic leader were thus graphically stated.

Churchill was aware that a responsible leader cannot escape the consequences of his acts. To mobilize the full support of the British and American people for war against Germany and Japan, he and Roosevelt had encouraged strong feelings against the aggressors. In order to maximize the war effort against the Axis states, Roosevelt and Churchill had often followed the rule of expediency in their dealings with the Soviet Union and other associated powers. Both leaders, perhaps mindful of the sneers of critics in the twenties at Wilson's World War I idealism, had tended to make their pleas at the level of self-preservation. Public demands for stern justice had been both acknowledged and spurred by the 1943 demand, which was never withdrawn, for unconditional surrender. At Yalta the free world still wanted punishment and reparation for Lidice, Rotterdam, Coventry, Nanking, Shanghai, Bataan, and Pearl Harbor. The story of the Malmedy massacre was still being circulated to troops in the field in Europe at the time of the Crimea conference. The full horrors of Buchenwald and Dachau were not yet known, but their stench was abroad.

Criticism of the actions of the Big Three at Yalta thus becomes in part an indictment of long-established Western assumptions about popular democracy. Roosevelt and Churchill were restricted in their actions at Yalta by the patterns of thought and action which their people demanded and which they themselves had laid down. As practical political leaders, they dared not go too far beyond what their followers would accept. One finds both a partial criticism and a partial explanation of the Yalta negotiations in one of the main theses of Walter Lippmann's thoughtful book, *Essays in the Public Philosophy*. "When the world wars came," Lippmann has written, "the people of the liberal democracies could not be aroused to the exertions and sacrifices of the struggle until they had been frightened by the opening disasters, had been incited to passionate hatred, and had become intoxicated with unlimited hope." The enemy had to be portrayed as evil incarnate, and the people told that when this particular opponent had been forced to unconditional surrender, "they would re-enter the golden age." Lippmann contends that the people of the western democracies have shown a compulsion to error which arises out of a time lag in democratic opinion and have compelled their governments "to be too late with too little, or too long with too much, too pacifist in peace and too bellicose in war, too neutralist or appeasing in negotiation or too intransigent."[14]

The meaning of Yalta cannot be grasped unless the conditions under which the conference leaders worked are remembered. In February, 1945, the Allied peoples generally agreed that Germany and Japan must be severely punished and cured of aggressive tendencies. Agreement was widespread that Germany and Japan must be effectively disarmed and their heavy industries restricted in order to prevent them from making war in the future. The western powers generally acknowledged that the U.S.S.R. had suffered terribly in the war and should receive compensation from the common enemies. Thoughts of the postwar era were pervaded by a desire to counterbalance the power of Germany and Japan by the force of the "world policemen" who had co-operated to win the war. Roosevelt certainly hoped, and probably believed until the last weeks before his death, that he could sit down at a table with Stalin and Churchill and work out solutions to the problems of the world. The Big Three tended, as a result, to give smaller states little opportunity to shape their own futures. The President strongly believed that Soviet expansive tendencies would be allayed when the U.S.S.R. won security on its European and Asian frontiers.

Other assumptions likewise encouraged Roosevelt to overestimate the possibilities of postwar co-operation with the Soviet Union. Knowledge that Russia had been severely damaged in the early years of the war with Germany led him to surmise that the U.S.S.R. might require a generation to recover. Some Washington officials believed that the Soviet Union would be dependent upon postwar economic aid for

[14] Walter Lippmann, *Essays in the Public Philosophy* (Boston, 1955), 19–21.

her recovery, and that for this reason Stalin could be counted upon to maintain good relations with the United States. In short, one must remember both the war-born opportunism and the hopes and fears of 1945: concessions which would shorten the war and save lives would be acceptable to the people of the West; the formation of a workable United Nations organization held hope for the correction of any basic errors which might have been made in the various peace arrangements; and, more realistically, it was feared that the Soviet Union might become the center of opposition to the West unless bound as closely as possible to its wartime allies.

All these factors powerfully asserted themselves when the Big Three met in the Crimean palace of the czar in February, 1945. But yet another factor loomed large in the conference at Yalta. The disintegration of Germany meant that the force which had dominated central Europe since 1938 was gone and that its place in central-eastern Europe would be taken by the Soviet Union. A disarmed Italy and a weakened France could not be expected to balance the enormous power of the Red Army. Britain, seriously drained of her capital wealth by the heavy exactions of the war and lacking the manpower reserves to challenge a potential enemy of Russia's strength, could not hope to redress the balance of Europe as she had for two centuries. The people of the United States viewed their exertions in Europe as temporary and hoped for their early termination; they were in no state of psychological readiness to take up Britain's traditional role. The approaching defeat of Japan threatened to create a power vacuum in the Far East like that which Hitler's defeat would leave in Europe. Thus concessions at Yalta inevitably reflected the powerful position of the Soviet Union in Europe and its potential power in the Far East. Personal diplomacy at Yalta came to grips with the basic realities of a new balance of power in the world at large, and the freedom of action of the individual statesman was greatly restricted by these impersonal forces. Therein lies the overriding fact about the conference; without its comprehension, the meaning of Yalta is sure to be missed.

Several courses were open to the western leaders at Yalta

in dealing with the new set of power relationships. It was possible to make minimum concessions to Stalin and hope for Russian co-operation and goodwill; it was possible to break off discussions at the first sign of demands which would ratify the new power relationships or create a greater imbalance in world politics than already existed; and it was possible to state certain moral positions in indignant and ringing Wilsonian phrases. Roosevelt and Churchill selected the first course, believing and hoping that it would bring victory and at the same time save the peace. They gained something by forcing the Russians to put their promises on record; but they could not make Stalin keep his word. The United States and Great Britain have at least the moral right and, technically, the legal right to use Soviet violations as the basis for repudiation of Allied concessions at Yalta, for it was the Soviet breach of contract that started the "Cold War."

After 1952 Eisenhower and Dulles faced the same alternatives which confronted Roosevelt and Stettinius in 1945: the Russians must be lived with, or they must be fought. There were elements of kinship between Roosevelt's belief that he could achieve real peace by sitting down with Churchill and Stalin and Eisenhower's attempt in 1955 to settle world problems in conferences at "the summit." And there were even clearer similarities between the "spirit of Geneva" of 1955 and the spirit of Yalta a decade earlier. Both were predicated upon the necessity of co-existence and both assumed a mutual desire for co-operation. In 1955, as in 1945, American efforts to co-operate "bumped, very hard indeed, against the great stone face of Communism."[15] Thus the Geneva conferences of 1955 may in another day be as violently and as generally attacked as Yalta was assailed after 1946. If so, the result will be neither sound history nor wise politics.

The vitality of a democratic society certainly demands constant and well-informed criticism of leadership. But neither the free world nor the United States can be made strong by irrational denunciations of its leaders and cries of treason which grow out of frustration and fear. It was from these manifestations of national immaturity that the myth of the

[15] *Life*, XXXIX (November 21, 1955), 46.

Yalta "betrayal" arose. The western world justifiably looks today to the United States for rational leadership and an infusion of confidence, not for mass hysteria and symptoms of a national inferiority complex. The country which constantly tears at its vitals and heedlessly destroys the reputations of its loyal public servants cannot give the sane and courageous guidance so desperately needed to calm the fears and solve the problems of a troubled world. In its reflections on Yalta, as in its conduct in world affairs, the United States can scarcely do better than adopt for its guidance the words of Washington: "Let us raise a standard to which the wise and honest can repair."

Appendix

PROTOCOL OF THE PROCEEDINGS OF THE CRIMEA CONFERENCE[1]

The Crimea Conference of the Heads of the Governments of the United States of America, the United Kingdom, and the Union of Soviet Socialist Republics which took place from February 4th to 11th came to the following conclusions.

I. *World Organisation*

It was decided:

(1) that a United Nations Conference on the proposed world organisation should be summoned for Wednesday, 25th April, 1945, and should be held in the United States of America.

(2) *the Nations to be invited to this Conference should be:*

(a) *the United Nations as they existed on the 8th February, 1945; and*

(b) *such of the Associated Nations as have declared war on the common enemy by 1st March, 1945. (For this purpose by the term "Associated Nation" was meant the eight Associated Nations and Turkey). When the Conference on World Organization is held, the delegates of the United Kingdom and United States of America will support a proposal to admit to original membership two Soviet Socialist Republics, i.e. the Ukraine and White Russia.*

(3) that the United States Government on behalf of the Three Powers should consult the Government of China and the French Provisional Government in regard to the decisions taken at the present Conference concerning the proposed World Organisation.

(4) that the text of the invitation to be issued to all the nations

---

[1] The "Protocol of Proceedings" expressed the major agreements concerning Europe which were made at Yalta. It was published two years later by the Department of State (March 24, 1947). It is reprinted here from the *Yalta Papers*, 975–82. *Significant* agreements which were not made public immediately in the communiqué are presented here in italics.

which would take part in the United Nations Conference should be as follows:

Invitation

"The Government of the United States of America, on behalf of itself and of the Governments of the United Kingdom, the Union of Soviet Socialist Republics, and the Republic of China and of the Provisional Government of the French Republic, invite the Government of _____ to send representatives to a Conference of the United Nations to be held on 25th April, 1945, or soon thereafter, at San Francisco in the United States of America to prepare a Charter for a General International Organisation for the maintenance of international peace and security.

"The above named governments suggest that the Conference consider as affording a basis for such a Charter the Proposals for the Establishment of a General International Organisation, which were made public last October as a result of the Dumbarton Oaks Conference, and which have now been supplemented by the following provisions for Section C of Chapter VI:

" 'C. *Voting*

'1. *Each member of the Security Council should have one vote.*

'2. *Decisions of the Security Council on procedural matters should be made by an affirmative vote of seven members.*

'3. *Decisions of the Security Council on all other matters should be made by an affirmative vote of seven members including the concurring votes of the permanent members; provided that, in decisions under Chapter VIII, Section A and under the second sentence of paragraph 1 of Chapter VIII, Section C, a party to a dispute should abstain from voting.'*

"Further information as to arrangements will be transmitted subsequently.

"In the event that the Government of _____ desires in advance of the Conference to present views or comments concerning the proposals, the Government of the United States of America will be pleased to transmit such views and comments to the other participating Governments."

Territorial Trusteeship

It was agreed that the five Nations which will have permanent seats on the Security Council should consult each other prior to the United Nations Conference on the question of territorial trusteeship.

The acceptance of this recommendation is subject to its being made clear that territorial trusteeship will only apply to (a) existing mandates of the League of Nations; (b) territories detached from the enemy as a result of the present war; (c) any other territory which might voluntarily be placed under trusteeship; and (d) no discussion of actual territories is contemplated at the forthcoming United Nations Conference or in the preliminary consultations,[2] and it will be a matter for subsequent agreement which territories within the above categories wll be placed under trusteeship.

II. *Declaration on Liberated Europe*

The following declaration has been approved:

"The Premier of the Union of Soviet Socialist Republics, the Prime Minister of the United Kingdom and the President of the United States of America have consulted with each other in the common interests of the peoples of their countries and those of liberated Europe. They jointly declare their mutual agreement to concert during the temporary period of instability in liberated Europe the policies of their three governments in assisting the peoples liberated from the domination of Nazi Germany and the peoples of the former Axis satellite states of Europe to solve by democratic means their pressing political and economic problems.

"The establishment of order in Europe and the re-building of national economic life must be achieved by processes which will enable the liberated peoples to destroy the last vestiges of Nazism and Fascism and to create democratic institutions of their own choice. This is a principle of the Atlantic Charter—the right of all peoples to choose the form of government under which they will live—the restoration of sovereign rights and self-government to those peoples who have been forcibly deprived of them by the aggressor nations.

"To foster the conditions in which the liberated peoples may exercise these rights, the three governments will jointly assist the people in any European liberated state or former Axis satellite state in Europe where in their judgment conditions require (a) to establish conditions of internal peace; (b) to carry out emergency measures for the relief of distressed peoples; (c) to form interim governmental authorities broadly representative of all democratic elements in the population and pledged to the earliest possible establishment through free elections of govern-

[2] The final "s" of "consultations" was added with pen and ink. The change is not initialed in the margin.

ments responsive to the will of the people; and (d) to facilitate where necessary the holding of such elections.

"The three governments will consult the other United Nations and provisional authorities or other governments in Europe when matters of direct interest to them are under consideration.

"When, in the opinion of the three governments, conditions in any European liberated state or any former Axis satellite state in Europe make such action necessary, they will immediately consult together on the measures necessary to discharge the joint responsibilities set forth in this declaration.

"By this declaration we reaffirm our faith in the principles of the Atlantic Charter, our pledge in the Declaration by the United Nations, and our determination to build in co-operation with other peace-loving nations world order under law, dedicated to peace, security, freedom and general well-being of all mankind.

"In issuing this declaration, the Three Powers express the hope that the Provisional Government of the French Republic may be associated with them in the procedure suggested."

III. *Dismemberment of Germany*

It was agreed that Article 12 (a) of the Surrender Terms for Germany should be amended to read as follows:

"*The United Kingdom, the United States of America and the Union of Soviet Socialist Republics shall possess supreme authority with respect to Germany. In the exercise of such authority they will take such steps, including the complete disarmament, demilitarisation and the dismemberment of Germany as they deem requisite for future peace and security.*"

The study of the procedure for the dismemberment of Germany was referred to a Committee, consisting of Mr. Eden (Chairman), Mr. Winant and Mr. Gousev. This body would consider the desirability of associating with it a French representative.

IV. *Zone of Occupation for the French and Control Council[3] for Germany.*

It was agreed that a zone in Germany, to be occupied by the French Forces, should be allocated to France. *This zone would be formed out of the British and American zones and its extent would be settled by the British and Americans in consultation with the French Provisional Government.*

[3] The word "Council" is a substitution in pen and ink for "Commission" as typed. In the margin opposite the change is a small question mark. The change is not initialed.

It was also agreed that the French Provisional Government should be invited to become a member of the Allied Control Council[3] for Germany.

V. *Reparation*

The following protocol has been approved:[4]

1. Germany must pay in kind for the losses caused by her to the Allied nations in the course of the war. Reparations are to be received in the first instance by those countries which have borne the main burden of the war, have suffered the heaviest losses and have organised victory over the enemy.

2. *Reparation in kind is[5] to be exacted from Germany in three following forms:*

a) *Removals within 2 years from the surrender of Germany or the cessation of organised resistance from the national wealth of Germany located on the territory of Germany herself as well as outside her territory (equipment, machine-tools, ships, rolling stock, German investments abroad, shares of industrial, transport and other enterprises in Germany etc.), these removals to be carried out chiefly for purpose of destroying the war potential of Germany.*

b) *Annual deliveries of goods from current production for a period to be fixed.*

c) *Use of German labour.*

3. For the working out on the above principles of a detailed plan for exaction of reparation from Germany an Allied Reparation Commission will be set up in Moscow. It will consist of three representatives—one from the Union of Soviet Socialist Republics, one from the United Kingdom and one from the United States of America.

4. *With regard to the fixing of the total sum of the reparation as well as the distribution of it among the countries which suffered from the German aggression the Soviet and American delegations agreed as follows:*

"The Moscow Reparation Commission should take in its initial studies as a basis for discussion the suggestion of the Soviet Government that the total sum of the reparation in accordance with the points (a) and (b) of the paragraph 2 should be 20 billion

---

[4] The original bears the notation in handwriting at this point: "Title to be added as in protocol." The title was not added, but the following was inserted in handwriting: "The Heads of the three Governments have agreed as follows:" The change is not initialed in the margin.

[5] The word "is" is handwritten, replacing "are" as typed. The change is not initialed in the margin.

dollars and that 50% of it should go to the Union of Soviet Socialist Republics."

The British delegation was of the opinion that pending consideration of the reparation question by the Moscow Reparation Commission no figures of reparation should be mentioned.

The above Soviet-American proposal has been passed to the Moscow Reparation Commission as one of the proposals to be considered by the Commission.

VI. Major War Criminals

The Conference agreed that the question of the major war criminals should be the subject of enquiry by the three Foreign Secretaries for report in due course after the close of the Conference.

VII. Poland

The following Declaration on Poland was agreed by the Conference:

"A new situation has been created in Poland as a result of her complete liberation by the Red Army. This calls for the establishment of a Polish Provisional Government which can be more broadly based than was possible before the recent liberation of the Western part of Poland.[6] The Provisional Government which is now functioning in Poland should therefore be reorganised on a broader democratic basis with the inclusion of democratic leaders from Poland itself and from Poles abroad. This new Government should then be called the Polish Provisional Government of National Unity.

"M. Molotov, Mr. Harriman and Sir A. Clark Kerr are authorised as a commission to consult in the first instance in Moscow with members of the present Provisional Government and with other Polish democratic leaders from within Poland and from abroad, with a view to the reorganisation of the present Government along the above lines. This Polish Provisional Government of National Unity shall be pledged to the holding of free and unfettered elections as soon as possible on the basis of universal suffrage and secret ballot. In these elections all democratic and anti-Nazi parties shall have the right to take part and to put forward candidates.

"When a Polish Provisional Government of National Unity

[6] The phrase "of the Western part of Poland" read "of Western Poland" as typed, but was revised by hand on the original, with no initials in the margin.

has been properly formed in conformity with the above, the Government of the U.S.S.R., which now maintains diplomatic relations with the present Provisional Government of Poland, and the Government of the United Kingdom and the Government of the U.S.A. will establish diplomatic relations with the new Polish Provisional Government of National Unity, and will exchange Ambassadors by whose reports the respective Governments will be kept informed about the situation in Poland.

"The three Heads of Government consider that the Eastern frontier of Poland should follow the Curzon Line with digressions from it in some regions of five to eight kilometres in favour of Poland. They recognise that Poland must receive substantial accessions of territory in the North and West. They feel that the opinion of the new Polish Provisional Government of National Unity should be sought in due course on the extent of these accessions and that the final delimitation of the Western frontier of Poland should thereafter await the Peace Conference."

VIII. *Yugoslavia*

It was agreed to recommend to Marshal Tito and to Dr. Subasic:

(a) that the Tito-Subasic Agreement should immediately be put into effect and a new government formed on the basis of the Agreement.

(b) that as soon as the new Government has been formed it should declare:

(i) that the Anti-Fascist Assembly of National Liberation (AUNOJ) will be extended to include members of the last Yugoslav Skupstina who have not compromised themselves by collaboration with the enemy thus forming a body to be known as a temporary Parliament and[7]

(ii) that legislative acts passed by the Anti-Fascist Assemb[l]y of National Liberation (AUNOJ) will be subject to subsequent ratification by a Constituent Assembly;[8] and that this statement should be published in the communiqué of the Conference.

[7] As typed, this subparagraph began "that the National Liberation Committee . . ." The changes were made in handwriting, with the initials of Charles E. Bohlen in the margin.

[8] As typed, this subparagraph began "that legislative acts passed by the National Liberation Committee . . ." The changes were made in handwriting, with the initials of Charles E. Bohlen in the margin.

IX. *Italo-Yugoslav Frontier*
  Italo-Austria Frontier[9]
Notes on these subjects were put in by the British delegation
and the American and Soviet delegations agreed to consider them
and give their views later.

X. *Yugoslav-Bulgarian Relations*
There was an exchange of views between the Foreign Secretaries on the question of the desirability of a Yugoslav-Bulgarian
pact of alliance. The question at issue was whether a state still
under an armistice regime could be allowed to enter into a
treaty with another state. Mr. Eden suggested that the Bulgarian
and Yugoslav Governments should be informed that this could
not be approved. Mr. Stettinius suggested that the British and
American Ambassadors should discuss the matter further with
M. Molotov in Moscow. M. Molotov agreed with the proposal of
Mr. Stettinius.

XI. *South Eastern Europe*
The British Delegation put in notes for the consideration of
their colleagues on the following subjects:
  (a) the Control Commission in Bulgaria
  (b) Greek claims upon Bulgaria, more particularly with reference to reparations.
  (c) Oil equipment in Roumania.

XII. *Iran.*[10]
Mr. Eden, Mr. Stettinius and M. Molotov exchanged views on
the situation in Iran.[10] It was agreed that this matter should be
pursued through the diplomatic channel.

XIII. *Meetings of the Three Foreign Secretaries*
The Conference agreed that permanent machinery should be
set up for consultation between the three Foreign Secretaries;
they should meet as often as necessary, probably about every three
or four months.
  These meetings will be held in rotation in the three capitals,
the first meeting being held in London.

  [9] No paper on the Italian-Austrian frontier has been found. Examination
of the minutes of the meeting of the Foreign Ministers on February 10, of the
British proposals attached thereto, and of the British note of February 11 suggests that the heading "Italo-Austria Frontier" should read "Austro-Yugoslav
Frontier."
  [10] Changed by hand from "Persia" as typed in the original. No initials in
the margin.

XIV. *The Montreux Convention and the Straits*

It was agreed that at the next meeting of the three Foreign Secretaries to be held in London, they should consider proposals which it was understood the Soviet Government would put forward in relation to the Montreux Convention and report to their Governments.[11] *The Turkish Government should be informed at the appropriate moment.*

The foregoing Protocol was approved and signed by the three Foreign Secretaries at the Crimean Conference, February 11, 1945.

E R Stettinius, Jr
V. Molotov.
Anthony Eden

[11] In the original as typed the phrase at the end of this sentence read "to the three Governments." The change was made by hand, with no initials in the margin.

Bibliographical Essay

The footnotes for this volume are designed to provide an extended guide to the sources upon which each chapter is based. The most important source for all chapters on the actual discussions at Yalta is: United States, Department of State, *The Conferences at Malta and Yalta, 1945* (Washington, 1955), hereinafter cited as *Yalta Papers*.

At least as early as 1948 congressmen demanded the publication of the "secret" story of Yalta. The Republican party platform of 1952, whose foreign policy plans were purportedly written by John Foster Dulles, declared: "The Government of the United States under Republican leadership will repudiate all commitments contained in secret understandings such as those at Yalta which aid Communist enslavement." This interest in the Yalta conference may have prompted the 1953 enthusiasm for the State Department's publication program. The State Department tends to confirm this in its Foreword statement that the *Yalta Papers* are "part of a special *Foreign Relations* publication program prepared by the Department of State in response to expressions of interest by several Senators and the Senate Committee on Appropriations in its report for the fiscal year 1954."

Certain general statements can be made about the publication of the *Yalta Papers*. First, it is unusual to have such emphasis on the early publication of conference minutes. The volumes on the Paris Peace Conference did not appear for many years after World War I. Secondly, while it has been the policy of the State Department for many decades to publish foreign-policy documents, special care was always taken to clear their contents with the governments concerned. In the case of the *Yalta Papers*, the final assent of the British government was apparently gained at almost the moment the papers were released. Thirdly, the papers which have been published in the past have been edited to remove indiscreet "asides" which might embarrass individuals still in office. This was not done in the case of remarks made at Yalta by Prime Minister Churchill and others. Some elisions were made, which served no useful purpose and, when "leaked" to the press, merely cast doubt on the completeness of the printed papers. This procedure created a certain degree of confusion which was capitalized on some months later by a discharged historian of the State Department. Although released by a Republican-controlled State Department through the action of a former administrative assistant to Senator Knowland, he declared that he was being "fired" because "holdover Democrats" in the State Department did not want him to print the truth about Roosevelt and the Yalta concessions. Fourthly, the State Department documents have normally been released without fanfare and certainly not through one newspaper. The procedure followed in this instance has stirred up criticism by historians as well as by politicians.

The belief, encouraged by a number of political speeches promising that the State Department files, when opened, would expose "gross incompetence" and possible "subversion" at Yalta, apparently was responsible for shrill charges of "suppressed information" when the *Yalta Papers* revealed little that was startlingly new and nothing that was criminal about the conference. A great part of the material in the *Yalta Papers* has been available to official historians and, through the Hopkins and Stettinius papers, to other historians for several years. On the other hand, publication of the *Yalta Papers* opens up some files not used before, especially those on pre-conference preparations, and makes available for the first time the main body of documents on the Yalta conference. By removing all restrictions from the papers, publication permits historians for the first time to discuss fully the "behind-the-scenes" negotiations at Yalta.

The first part of the *Yalta Papers* is devoted to pre-conference documents. It includes correspondence between the chief political leaders of the U.S.S.R., Great Britain, and the United States relative to a place of meeting and the main issues to be discussed. The background of the chief topics and the State Department Briefing Papers presented to the President are set forth in the collection. Documents are included from the files of the State, Treasury, and Defense Departments, and the Franklin D. Roosevelt Library. An effort was made to include material from private collections, but the State Department editors did not have access to private papers of former Secretary of State James F. Byrnes, former Secretary of State Edward R. Stettinius, and former Ambassador W. Averell Harriman.

The second part of the *Yalta Papers* includes minutes of the Anglo-American conference at Malta, on the way to Yalta, and minutes of the Yalta conference. The record includes minutes of the plenary sessions of Roosevelt, Churchill, Stalin, and their staffs, minutes of the military staff meetings, minutes of the foreign ministers meetings, and notes on private conversations between the heads of government. There was no single set of official minutes of the Yalta conference, and the *Yalta Papers* include, therefore, notes kept by the following: Charles E. Bohlen, assistant to the Secretary of State and interpreter to the President; Alger Hiss, Deputy Director of the Office of Special Political Affairs; and H. Freeman Matthews, Director of the Office of European Affairs. Bohlen's notes are usually the most adequate, and he is the chief authority for the discussions between the President and Stalin. Both his notes and those of Matthews are well written and apparently complete; although they differ occasionally, they agree on most points, as do the notes taken by Hiss, which are, however, fragmentary and appear in the abbreviated form in which they were taken. Sometimes they have a colorful phrase which is lacking in the other two accounts.

The *Yalta Papers* by no means contain all the material available on the Yalta conference, and the editors of the State Department volumes have made an effort to call attention to much of the other material and to show where it fits into the minutes of the conference. Byrnes kept his own shorthand notes, some of which are reprinted in his *Speaking Frankly;* memoranda of Hopkins and Stettinius, not found in the *Yalta Papers,* were published in *Roosevelt and Hopkins* and *Roosevelt and the Russians.* Churchill said soon after the publication of the *Yalta Papers* that the minutes did not always agree with the British records. It is possible that future British publications, as American and Russian sources, may raise questions on some points discussed at Yalta and make clearer some dubious points. In the light of the additional information revealed by the Department of Defense in October, 1955, there seems to be no good reason for disagreeing with the State Department's statement in the introduction to the *Yalta Papers* that it "may be doubted . . . that any of these would change significantly the basic record of United States policy here presented." The Department of Defense account of military problems and plans connected with the Crimea conference ("The Entry of the Soviet Union into the War against Japan: Military Plans, 1941–1945," mimeographed report released to the press on October 19, 1955) contains material of considerable value, but it cannot be compared with the State Department publication in completeness.

The most comprehensive historical treatment of the relations between the wartime allies of 1941–45 is a Royal Institute of International Affairs publication: William Hardy McNeill, *American, Britain & Russia: Their Cooperation and Conflict, 1941–1946* (London, 1953). The specific problems of planning for peace are most fully treated in Redvers Opie and Associates, *The Search for Peace Settlements* (Washington, 1951), a Brookings Institution publication. See also the briefer and earlier account by William L. Neumann, *Making the Peace, 1941–1945: The Diplomacy of the Wartime Conferences* (Washington, 1950).

CHAPTER I

THE STRUGGLE FOR A NEW ORDER

OFFICIAL DOCUMENTS AND PRIVATE PAPERS: The chief sources are: United States, Department of State, *The Conferences at Malta and Yalta, 1945* (Washington, 1955); Walter Millis (ed.), with the collaboration of E. S. Duffield, *The Forrestal Diaries* (New York, 1951); Joseph C. Grew (Walter Johnson, ed.), *Turbulent Era, a Diplomatic Record of Forty Years, 1904–1945* (2 vols., Boston, 1952); Arthur H. Vandenberg, Jr. (ed.), with the collaboration of Joe Alex Morris, *The Private Papers of Senator Vandenberg* (Boston, 1952).

MEMOIRS: Winston S. Churchill, *The Second World War* (6 vols., Boston, 1948–53); John R. Deane, *The Strange Alliance: The Story of Our Efforts at Wartime Co-operation with Russia* (New York, 1947); Cordell Hull, *Memoirs of Cordell Hull* (2 vols., New York, 1948); Ernest J. King and Walter Muir Whitehill, *Fleet Admiral King, A Naval Record* (New York, 1952); William D. Leahy, *I Was There* (New York, 1950); Robert E. Sherwood, *Roosevelt and Hopkins, An Intimate History* (New York, 1948); Edward R. Stettinius, Jr. (Walter Johnson, ed.), *Roosevelt and the Russians: The Yalta Conference* (Garden City, 1949); Henry L. Stimson and McGeorge Bundy, *On Active Service in Peace and War* (New York, 1947).

GENERAL ACCOUNTS AND INTERPRETATIONS: Herbert Feis, *The Road to Pearl Harbor* (Princeton, 1950), presents an excellent summary of American dealings with Japan on the eve of the war. It is pro-Roosevelt. William L. Langer and S. Everett

Gleason, *The Challenge to Isolation, 1937–1940* (New York, 1952) and *The Undeclared War, 1940–1941* (New York, 1953), provide detailed summaries of American diplomacy in the prewar period. They are based on State Department documents and are considered "official" accounts. Dwight E. Lee, *Ten Years: The World on the Way to War* (Boston, 1942). This volume, which appeared just at the entry of the United States into war, is still valuable as a reminder of contemporary opinion. C. C. Tansill, *Back Door to War, 1933–1941* (Chicago, 1952), is based upon some of the State Department records used by Langer and Gleason, but this volume reaches wholly different conclusions about American policy in the prewar years. Gerhard L. Weinberg, *Germany and the Soviet Union, 1939–1941* (Leiden, 1954), provides a scholarly account of the origins of the Nazi-Soviet Pact of 1939, the growth of friction between Germany and Russia, and German preparations for the invasion of the U.S.S.R. in June, 1941. This study is based upon primary sources and its bibliography (183–208) offers a remarkably full guide to available documentation, memoirs, and other secondary studies. Mark S. Watson, *Chief of Staff: Prewar Plans and Preparations* (Washington, 1950), a volume of the official history, *The United States Army in World War II,* contains valuable material on American planning in 1940–41. Sumner Welles, *Where Are We Heading?* (New York, 1946) and *Seven Decisions that Shaped History* (New York, 1950), are valuable accounts by the former Undersecretary of State of the framing of the Atlantic Charter and the drafting of the Charter of the United Nations organization.

Chapter II

WHAT TO DO WITH GERMANY?

The basic account upon which this chapter is founded is a manuscript of some two hundred pages by the author of this chapter: *Dilemma in Europe:The German Problem in Great Power Diplomacy, 1941–1945.* A very brief but accurate and perceptive review of pre-1945 planning for peace with Germany may be found in United States, Department of State, *The United States and Germany, 1945–1955* (Washington, 1955). The following longer studies were completed as doctoral dissertations in European universities, were based chiefly upon source materials available in English, and appeared before the Department of State began to publish minutes and other records of the wartime conferences: Harold Strauss, *The Division and Dismemberment of Germany* (Ambilly, 1952), the best of the three studies mentioned here; Heinz Günther Sasse, "Die ostdeutsche Frage auf den Konferenzen von Teheran bis Potsdam," *Jahrbuch für die Geschichte Mittel-und Ostdeutschlands* (Tübingen), II (1953), 211–82; Wolfgang Wagner, *Die Entstehung der Oder-Neisse-Linie* (Stuttgart, 1953).

THE EVOLUTION OF UNITED STATES POLICY FOR POSTWAR GERMANY: The most valuable brief contributions on the development of planning by civilian officials and experts are those by two participants: E. F. Penrose, *Economic Planning for the Peace* (Princeton, 1953), 216–92; and Philip E. Mosely, "Dismemberment of Germany: The Allied Negotiations from Yalta to Potsdam," *Foreign Affairs*, XXVIII (April, 1950), 487–98; and, also by Mosely, "The Occupation of Germany: New Light on How the Zones were Drawn," *Foreign Affairs*, XXVIII (July, 1950), 580–604. German readers may wish to consult an article which reflects Mosely's revelations: Wolfgang Wagner, "Besatzungszonen und Spaltung Deutschlands," *Aussenpolitik* (Stuttgart), V (August, 1954), 496–508. Some of the key documents and a very critical discussion are presented by James P. Warburg, *Germany—Bridge or Battleground* (New York, 1946). The mechanics of State Department policy formulation, and some of the substance of German policy, may be gleaned from a publication which is basic to any research on this subject: United States, Department of State (Harley Notter, ed.), *Postwar Foreign Policy Preparation, 1939–1945* (Washington, 1949). Public statements, and some not published until after the war, are available in the Department of State, *The Axis in Defeat: A Collection of Documents on American Policy toward Germany and Japan* (Washington, n.d.).

ANGLO-AMERICAN MILITARY PLANNING FOR THE OCCUPATION OF GERMANY: Plans for Germany as evolved at SHAEF or conveyed to General Dwight D. Eisenhower from Washington are discussed in Forrest C. Pogue, *The Supreme Command* (Washington, 1954), 339–58, and *passim*. United States Army planning has been discussed by several scholars who participated in the events they describe. See especially the accounts by Merle Fainsod and Dale Clark in Carl J. Friedrich and Associates, *American Experiences in Military Government in World War II* (New York, 1948); Hajo Holborn, *American Military Government, Its Organization and Policies* (Washington, 1947), 1–53; and Harold Zink, *American Military Government in Germany* (New York, 1947). But by far the most exhaustive study of the evolution of American military planning known to the author of this chapter, and one which shows the impact of American and Allied civilian policy on military planning, has not yet been published: Paul Y. Hammond, "JCS 1067 Policy for Germany" (scheduled to appear as part of the Twentieth Century Fund's Study of Civil-Military Relations, Harold Stein, Research Director, Princeton University). Professor Stein was kind enough to make a draft of this study (dated June 20, 1955) available to the author for comment and criticism. Credit is given in the footnotes to Chapter II for the specific contributions which the Hammond study has made to the development of this chapter.

THE GERMAN PROBLEM AT THE YALTA CONFERENCE: The essential facts and a persuasive apology for the Yalta commitments are most readily available in Edward R. Stettinius, Jr. (Walter Johnson, ed.), *Roosevelt and the Russians: The Yalta Conference* (Garden City, 1949). Other memoirs by participants are cited in the footnotes for this chapter. An excellent but highly critical brief survey of the conference is presented by Chester Wilmot, *The Struggle for Europe* (New York, 1952), 628–59, the best one-volume history of the war in Europe, 1939–45, though one which offers a highly pro-British and sometimes unrealistic interpretation. Significant new material has appeared on the Yalta conference in *The Conferences at Malta and Yalta, 1945* (Washington, 1955). A fuller statement of the sources for Chapter II appears among the footnotes for this study.

CHAPTER III

RUSSIAN POWER IN CENTRAL-EASTERN EUROPE

ACCOUNTS BY PARTICIPANTS: The most important source of information on the central-eastern European problems at Yalta is also provided by *The Conferences at Malta and Yalta, 1945*. Indispensable are the memoirs of such participants in the conference as Winston S. Churchill, *The Second World War* (6 vols., Boston, 1948–53); Edward R. Stettinius, Jr. (Walter Johnson, ed.), *Roosevelt and the Russians: The Yalta Conference* (New York, 1949); Robert E. Sherwood, *Roosevelt and Hopkins, An Intimate History* (rev. ed.; New York, 1950); James F. Byrnes, *Speaking Frankly* (New York, 1947); William D. Leahy, *I Was There* (New York, 1950); Charles E. Bohlen's testimony on the Polish discussions before the United States Senate, 83rd Congress, 1st Session,

Hearings before the Committee on Foreign Relations: Nomination of Charles E. Bohlen, March 2, and 18, 1953 (Washington, 1953).

OTHER MEMOIRS: Memoirs of other Americans who played important roles in the discussions preceding or immediately following Yalta include Cordell Hull, *Memoirs of Cordell Hull* (2 vols., New York, 1948); William H. Standley and Arthur A. Ageton, *Admiral Ambassador to Russia* (Chicago, 1955); Arthur Bliss Lane, *I Saw Poland Betrayed* (Indianapolis, 1948); and Harry S. Truman, *Year of Decisions* (Garden City, 1955). Several key Polish diplomats and leaders have written memoirs. Indispensable are the Polish government in exile's ambassador to the United States, Jan Ciechanowski, *Defeat in Victory* (New York, 1947); Stanislaw Mikolajczyk, *The Rape of Poland* (New York, 1948), by the Polish Peasant party leader and member of the post-Yalta fusion government; General Wladyslaw W. Anders, *An Army in Exile* (London, 1949); and General T. Bor-Komorowski, *The Secret Army* (London, 1950).

SECONDARY ACCOUNTS: It is impossible here to present more than a few references to the vast specialized literature on the Polish and central-eastern European wartime problems. Among the most useful English-language scholarly studies are two volumes in the Royal Institute of International Affairs series: William Hardy McNeill, *America, Britain, & Russia: Their Cooperation and Conflict, 1941–1946* (London, 1953); and the sections by Sidney Lowery and Hugh Seton-Watson in Arnold and Veronica M. Toynbee (eds.), *The Realignment of Europe* (London, 1955). The article by Wladyslaw W. Kulski, a wartime minister in the Polish embassy in London, "The Lost Opportunity for Russian-Polish Friendship," *Foreign Affairs,* XXV (July, 1947), 667–84, is written with considerable "inside" knowledge. The monograph on the German-Polish frontier problem by Wolfgang Wagner, *Die Entstehung der Oder-Neisse-Linie* (Stuttgart, 1953), contains a useful bibliography of German- and Polish-language references, as does Hans Günther Sasse, "Die ostdeutsche Frage auf den Konferenzen von Teheran bis Potsdam," *Jahrbuch für die Geschichte Mittel-und Ostdeutschlands* (Tübingen), II (1953), 211–82.

Every discussion of the highly controversial Polish problem betrays some measure of bias and emotionalism. Very critical of Soviet and American wartime diplomacy, but to a much lesser degree of British action, are John A. Lukacs, *The Great Powers and Eastern Europe* (New York, 1953); Chester A. Wilmot, *The*

Struggle for Europe (London, 1952); and R. Umiastowski, *Poland, Russia, and Great Britain, 1941–1945: A Study of the Evidence* (London, 1946). Considerably more restrained in judgment is Hugh Seton-Watson, *The East European Revolution* (London, 1950). The studies by Samuel L. Sharp, *Poland: White Eagle on a Red Field* (Cambridge, Massachusetts, 1953); James T. Shotwell and Max Laserson, *Poland and Russia, 1919–1945* (New York, 1945); and I. Deutscher, *Stalin, A Political Biography* (New York, 1949), will not please Russians and Poles in equal measure, but all merit attention.

Somewhat broader in their background scope are the important studies by Bernadotte E. Schmitt (ed.), *Poland* (Berkeley, 1945); Raymond Leslie Buell, *Poland: Key to Europe* (New York, 1939); Hugh Seton-Watson, *Eastern Europe between the Wars, 1918–1941* (Cambridge, 1946); R. R. Betts (ed.), *Central and South East Europe, 1945–1948* (London, 1950); S. Konovalov (ed.), *Russo-Polish Relations: An Historical Survey* (Princeton, 1945); and Joseph S. Roucek (ed.), *Central-Eastern Europe: Crucible of World Wars* (2nd rev. ed.; New York, 1948).

Listed in the footnotes are a few more specialized references to certain Polish problems, as well as to some of the principal books on the Yugoslav and Greek political problems during the later years of the war. There is an unpublished Ph.D. dissertation by Stanley P. Wagner, "The Diplomacy of the Polish Government-in-Exile, September, 1939, to June, 1945," University of Pittsburgh, 1952–53, which the author of Chapter III was unable to consult before this volume went to press.

CHAPTER IV

YALTA AND THE FAR EAST

RUSSIAN INTERESTS IN THE FAR EAST: Gaston Cahen (transl. by W. Sheldon Ridge), *Some Early Russo-Chinese Relations* (Shanghai, 1914); John A. Harrison, *Japan's Northern Frontier* (Gainesville, 1953); Maurice Hindus, *Russia and Japan* (Garden City, 1942); Prince A. Lobanov-Rostovsky, *Russia and Asia* (New York, 1933); Harriet L. Moore, *Soviet Far Eastern Policy, 1931–1945* (New York, 1945); G. I. Nevel'skoi, *Podvigi Russkikh Morskikh Ofitserov na Krainem Vostoke Rossii 1849–1855* [Exploits of Russian Naval Officers in the Russian Far East, 1849–1855] (St. Petersburg, 1878); Harold M. Vinacke, *A History of the Far East in Modern Times* (5th ed.; New York, 1950); Ken Shen Weigh, *Russo-Chinese Diplomacy* (Shanghai, 1928); George Alexander

Lensen, "Early Russo-Japanese Relations," *The Far Eastern Quarterly*, X (November, 1950), 2–37; Lensen, "The Russo-Japanese Frontier," in *Florida State University Studies*, XIV (1954), 23–40; Lensen, *Report from Hokkaido: The Remains of Russian Culture in Northern Japan* (Hakodate, 1954); Lensen, *Russia's Japan Expedition of 1852 to 1855* (Gainesville, 1955).

AMERICAN INTERESTS IN THE FAR EAST: Paul Hibbert Clyde, *The Far East* (2nd ed.; New York, 1953); Tyler Dennett, *Americans in Eastern Asia* (New York, 1941); Payson J. Treat, *Diplomatic Relations between the United States and Japan, 1853–1895* (2 vols., Stanford, 1932); United States, Department of State, *United States Relations with China* (Washington, 1949); United States Senate, 79th Congress, *Investigation of the Pearl Harbor Attack: Report of the Joint Committee on the Investigation of the Pearl Harbor Attack* (Washington, 1946); William Appleman Williams, *American-Russian Relations, 1781–1947* (New York, 1952).

JAPAN'S DECISION TO EXPAND SOUTHWARD: Hugh Borton, *Japan since 1931* (New York, 1940); Robert J. C. Butow, *Japan's Decision to Surrender* (Stanford, 1954); Hugh Byas, *The Japanese Enemy* (New York, 1942); Toshikazu Kase (David Nelson Rowe, ed.), *Journey to the Missouri* (New Haven, 1950); Paul Schmidt, *Statist auf diplomatischer Bühne 1923–1945: Erlebnisse des Chefdolmetschers im Auswärtigen Amt mit den Staatsmännern Europas* (Bonn, 1950).

MAJOR SOURCES ON THE FAR EASTERN QUESTION AT YALTA: The fullest records of the discussions of Far Eastern problems at Yalta are presented in *The Conferences at Malta and Yalta, 1945*. The most detailed account of Russo-American negotiations concerning the Far East before and after Yalta is in John R. Deane, *The Strange Alliance: The Story of Our Efforts at Wartime Cooperation with Russia* (New York, 1947). Supplementary sources, though limited in data because of the secrecy of the Far Eastern deliberations, are: James F. Byrnes, *Speaking Frankly* (New York, 1947); Winston S. Churchill, *Triumph and Tragedy* (Boston, 1953); Cordell Hull, *The Memoirs of Cordell Hull* (2 vols., New York, 1948); Ernest J. King and Walter Muir Whitehill, *Fleet Admiral King, A Naval Record* (New York, 1952); William D. Leahy, *I Was There* (New York, 1950); Walter Millis (ed.), with the collaboration of E. S. Duffield, *The Forrestal Diaries* (New York, 1951); Robert E. Sherwood, *Roosevelt and Hopkins, An Intimate History* (New York, 1948); Edward R. Stettinius, Jr. (Walter Johnson, ed.), *Roosevelt and the Russians: The Yalta Conference*

(Garden City, 1949); Henry L. Stimson and McGeorge Bundy, *On Active Service in Peace and War* (New York, 1947). Critical commentary is to be found in the following works: Max Beloff, *Soviet Policy in the Far East, 1944–1951* (London, 1953); Claude A. Buss, *The Far East* (New York, 1955); David J. Dallin, *Soviet Russia and the Far East* (New Haven, 1948); Foster Rhea Dulles, *America's Rise to World Power, 1898–1954* (New York, 1955); Herbert Feis, *The China Tangle* (Princeton, 1953); Gerald M. Friters, *Outer Mongolia and Its International Position* (Baltimore, 1949); Werner Levi, *Modern China's Foreign Policy* (Minneapolis, 1953); Sumner Welles, *Seven Decisions that Shaped History* (New York, 1951); Felix Wittmer, *The Yalta Betrayal: Data on the Decline and Fall of Franklin Delano Roosevelt* (Caldwell, 1953), an example of the most extreme and intemperate criticism; Aitchen K. Wu, *China and the Soviet Union* (New York, 1950).

CHAPTER V

THE BIG THREE AND THE UNITED NATIONS

The chief sources for this chapter in addition to memoirs and general histories cited for earlier chapters are: United States, Department of State, *The Conferences at Malta and Yalta, 1945;* United States, Department of State (Harley Notter, ed.), *Postwar Foreign Policy Preparation, 1939–1945* (Washington, 1949). Fullest documentation on the origins of the U. N. is to be found in United Nations Information Organization, *Documents of the United Nations Conference on International Organization, San Francisco, 1945* (20 vols., New York, 1945), especially in volume three. See also Redvers Opie and Associates, *The Search for Peace Settlements* (Washington, 1951); William Hardy McNeill, *America, Britain & Russia: Their Cooperation and Conflict, 1941–1946* (London, 1953); World Peace Foundation, *The United Nations in the Making: Basic Documents* (Boston, 1945), 7–98; Leland Matthew Goodrich and Edvard Hambro, *Charter of the United Nations, Commentary and Documents* (2nd ed.; Boston, 1949), 6–19; and Amry Vandenbosch and Willard N. Hogan, *The United Nations: Background, Organization, Functions, Activities* (1st ed., New York, 1952).

The following doctoral dissertation, in progress at Stanford University in 1955, may be expected to throw much additional light on the problems treated in Chapter V of this volume: Brownlee S. Corrin, "The United Nations, the United States and the U.S.S.R. from Dumbarton Oaks to Korea: A Study in Controversy and Cooperation."

CHAPTER VI

YALTA IN RETROSPECT

GENERAL WORKS: Laurence S. Kuter, *Airman at Yalta* (New York and Boston, 1955), is the first volume to appear which gives an airman's point of view of the Yalta conference. Louis Morton, "The Military Background of the Yalta Agreements," *The Reporter*, XII (April 7, 1955), contains interesting background information by the chief of the Pacific Section of the Office of the Chief of Military History, Department of Defense. Walter Lippmann, *Essays in the Public Philosophy* (Boston, 1955), while not directed specifically to the problems involved in the Yalta conference, has many thought-provoking pages about the difficulties of democratic leaders in dealing with problems of peace and war. Oscar J. Hammen, "The 'Ashes' of Yalta," *South Atlantic Quarterly*, LIII, (October, 1954), suggests that Roosevelt miscalculated in assuming that the Russians were willing to co-operate and that they were so weak they would have to follow the lead of the West. Raymond J. Sontag, "Reflections on the Yalta Papers," *Foreign Affairs*, XXXIII (July, 1955), holds that the policy of the western powers at Yalta, while in part a failure, laid the moral basis for the postwar American stand against the Soviet Union; our willingness in 1945 to seek a workable solution to world problems has emphasized the broken pledges of the Russians. Rudolph A. Winnacker, "Yalta—Another Munich?" *Virginia Quarterly Review*, XXIV (Autumn, 1948), one of the early articles on Yalta, stated a number of basic truths which are still valid. For an examination of the questionable standing of the Yalta commitments in international law, see Stephen C. Y. Pan, "Legal Aspects of the Yalta Agreement," *American Journal of International Law*, XLVI (January, 1952), 40–59.

Index